THE END-USER REVOLUTION

CD-ROM, Internet and the changing role of the information professional

Edited by
Richard Biddiscombe

*Arts and Humanities Team Leader, Information Services,
University of Birmingham*

LIBRARY ASSOCIATION PUBLISHING
LONDON

Published by
Library Association Publishing
7 Ridgmount Street
London WC1E 7AE

First published 1996
Reprinted 1997

British Library Cataloguing in Publication Data
A catalogue record for this book is available from the British Library

ISBN 1-85604-173-5

For Louis

Typeset in 10/12pt Classical Garamond and 18/20pt Avant Garde by Library Association Publishing
Printed and made in Great Britain by Bookcraft (Bath) Ltd, Midsomer Norton, Avon.

Contents

List of contributors v

Introduction: the end-user revolution and the information
   professional 1
Richard Biddiscombe

1   CD-ROM publishing and the needs of the user 6
   Duncan Christelow

2   The third undertow 20
   C. J. Armstrong

3   Meeting the demand for CD-ROM databases 35

   Case study 1: Academic libraries 35
   Will Wakeling

   Case study 2: Public libraries 43
   Heather Kirby

   Case study 3: Special libraries 53
   Peter Bysouth and Maureen Sullivan

4   Improving user access to CD-ROM databases:
   technical issues 64
   Morag Watson

5   The changing role of the reference librarian 79
   Richard Biddiscombe

6   Training the end-user 96

   Case study 1: Academic libraries 96
   Aileen Wade

   Case study 2: Public libraries 110
   Colette Batterbee

7   CD-ROM and document delivery 119
   Andrew Cameron

8   Developing in-house CD-ROM databases 135

   Case study 1: The RAM database at Nottingham Trent
   University 135
   Jim Corlett

Case study 2: *Glagow on disc* 148
David Buri and Robert Anderson

9 **Networking and the end-user revolution 155**
Richard Biddiscombe

10 **The changing role of professional education for information professionals 173**
Bruce Reid and Pauline Rafferty Brown

11 **The continuing end-user revolution 187**
Ray Lester

Index 197

List of contributors

Robert Anderson

Robert Anderson is the Information Technology Librarian at Glasgow School of Art. He previously held a similar position at Edinburgh's Napier University.

Chris Armstrong

Chris Armstrong worked as a research officer at the College of Librarianship Wales before starting his own research and consultancy company, Information Automation Limited (IAL), which runs the Centre for Information Quality Management on behalf of The Library Association and the UK Online User Group. Chris is a member of the UKOLUG Management Committee.

Collette Batterbee

Colette Batterbee is currently a research student at the City University's Department of Information Science. Her PhD is concerned with the factors affecting the use and non-use of open access CD-ROMs in UK public libraries.

Richard Biddiscombe

Richard Biddiscombe is Arts and Humanities Team Leader, Information Services, at the University of Birmingham. He has been a member of The Library Association Council, and Hon Secretary of the University, College and Research Group. He is The Library Association's contact with CD-ROM SPAG.

Pauline Rafferty Brown

Pauline Rafferty Brown is a senior lecturer in the School of Information Studies at the University of Central England (UCE) in Birmingham where she teaches information retrieval, information and media, and popular fiction.

David Buri

David Buri is Architecture Librarian at Glasgow School of Art, Scotland. He was previously Deputy Librarian at the Institution of Civil Engineers.

Peter Bysouth

Peter Bysouth is International Contracts Manager for information products and services utilized within the new Glaxo Wellcome Research and Development organization, and is a specialist in the provision of published information.

Andrew Cameron

Andrew Cameron is the Information Specialist for Life Sciences at Aston University's Library and Information Services. He has much experience of biomedical information, and has a special interest in library publicity and public relations matters.

Duncan Christelow

Duncan Christelow was a member of the UK sales department at Pergamon Press, before joining the electronic publishing industry with Chadwyck-Healey in 1989. He is now UK Sales Manager with specific interest in the academic library market.

Jim Corlett

Jim Corlett joined Nottingham Trent University from the Lyon Playfair Library at Imperial College in 1979. He at present holds the post of Faculty Liaison Officer for Engineering and Computing. Jim is a member of the Development Team for the Edinburgh Engineering Virtual Library (EEVL) and of the Project Liaison Group for the Focused Investigation of Document Delivery (FIDDO) Electronic Library projects.

Heather Kirby

Heather Kirby is Head of Reference and Information Services at Croydon Libraries, where she has taken a lead in developing the first CD-ROM network in a British public library. She is currently involved in the management and implementation of Croydon Libraries Internet Project, to explore the use of the Internet in public libraries.

Ray Lester

Ray Lester is Librarian at the London Business School. His long academic library career follows experience as an information scientist and systems analyst.

Bruce Reid

Bruce Reid is Course Director of the BA(Hons) Information Studies Programme at the University of Central England (UCE) in Birmingham. He is an academic adviser to TAPin, one of the eLib projects.

Maureen Sullivan

Maureen Sullivan has spent ten years working in the Information Services Department of Glaxco (now Glaxo Wellcome), where she has specialized in providing information support to its research scientists.

Aileen Wade

Aileen Wade is Campus Librarian at Sheffield Hallam University. She is a member of: the Edulib Steering Group (an eLib project) which is establishing a national network of electronic library accredited trainers; the National Datasets Steering Group; the GANNET National User Group; the BUBL Steering Group and the JANET User Group for Libraries, of which she is Chair. She was a member of the Study Team on the SUPERJANET Project on Information Services.

Will Wakeling

Will Wakeling is Assistant Director of Information Services, Collection Management, at the University of Birmingham. Will serves on the UK National Preservation Office's Working Party of Preservation Administrators. He has been an active member of the UK Serials Group, latterly as Chairman.

Morag Watson

Morag Watson is Head of Networked Information Services at the University of Edinburgh. She was previously Systems Librarian at the University of Birmingham.

Introduction: the end-user revolution and the information professional

Richard Biddiscombe

Users have been empowered by their ability to connect directly to electronic information sources. The consequent challenges made to the traditional methods, values and work practices of library staff are evident across the profession and reflected in the pages of this book.

Increasing numbers of users, having been liberated into a post-modern world of information provision, are finding that as a consequence, they are in less need of some traditional library services. Those professionals who seek to organize knowledge and control access to it may seem of little relevance to these people. End-users can, after all, search the sources themselves, create their own information sources – on the Web – for others to access, and communicate with each other to get help and advice.

Libraries are therefore being forced to change because increasing numbers of users are no longer solely dependent on a static storehouse to satisfy their information needs. Nor do they rely on the intermediary skills of a librarian to answer an enquiry or search for information. New services are consequently being demanded of libraries, and new skills are expected from the staff within them.

Such changes are not, of course, limited to the information professions – the end-user revolution will soon bring profound changes to the wider community. Education and government, economic and social organizations, all are having to begin a reassessment of their traditional concepts and time-honoured practices.

The changes that are taking place are not evenly spread; some of the more traditional aspects of work and its organization remain largely unaffected, at least for the present. However, the division between those who perform these traditional roles and those who are having to adjust to new ones is becoming more pronounced. In publishing, for example, there is a growing division between those who are concerned mainly with the printed word and those who are developing new products for the information age. In librarianship there is a widening division between those who manage lending and technical services and those who are information specialists and managers.

In many ways the value placed upon library functions has been turned on its head. What were regarded as essential aspects of the profession, such as cataloguing, acquisitions and even library management, are less important than they were. In contrast those long-time Cinderella aspects such as user education, liaison work, publications and publicity are now regarded as essential elements.

In this brave new information environment many individual librarians may feel threatened and insecure. This will be inevitable, especially for those whose training and background never prepared them for such profound change. If many end-users can now gain access to information for themselves, search full text publications online and seek help directly from a specialized user group, then what future long-term role exists for the librarian?

What is emerging, and what this book is intending to show, is that there is a new role for what we must increasingly refer to as the information professional. It is also very evident that many of the new skills need not be practised in a traditional library setting. Teaching, help and advice on databases, the exploitation of information sources and the development of publishing programmes can all be performed away from the library – in the user community itself if necessary.

Many of the new library information skills will overlap with those in the other, related, information professions such as publishing and the wider media industry. Whether such convergence will eventually bring the common elements together in a realignment of the information professions remains to be seen. Certainly this convergence should bring a broader consensus about information issues, from all information professionals. Common interest and values should unite them on issues such as database quality and freedom of information, giving them a wider role in protecting and promoting the interests of their client groups.

Such developments bring into question the content of the present curriculums at schools of librarianship and information science. The search for greater relevance in the courses which are presently offered is essential if those leaving universities are to meet the needs of prospective employers. A number of such departments of information science have closed in the USA, presumably because they failed to attract enough students. In Chapter 10 Bruce Reid and Pauline Rafferty Brown describe the results of their survey of potential employers and discuss the type of skills which the market place is now demanding.

That market place is broader than it was and reflects the changing nature of an information professional's work. Libraries are still, however, the main employer of the graduate from library and information studies departments. Consequently the majority of this book's chapters are concerned with libraries and although academic libraries figure largely they are not its sole concern. Case studies from both public and special libraries are also included, but those from the academic sector are in the majority. This is because it is in this sector that the empowerment of the end-user is most evident, so far. The lessons being learned in higher education are presented here as a sort of pilot study for the problems which public libraries are set to encounter as the Internet begins to transform their services.

Between the utopian promise of a fully liberated and self-sufficient end-user, and the prospects for the library of the future, there lies the present reality. Librarians have always prided themselves on the services they provide to information seekers, and held themselves up as impartial intermediaries, organizing and disseminating information on behalf of their users. As the survey carried out for this book (and reported in Chapter 9) shows, the supportive role played by librarians is still highly regarded by library patrons. It is now the need for education and guidance through print and Web publications which points the way to the sort of function that will be increasingly in demand for the foreseeable future.

This book presents, through reports on present practice, case studies, and background articles, some of the problems encountered in this new environment. It outlines the progress made in adapting traditional skills and practices to the new information environment. Its scope is wider than just librarianship and offers a broader picture of the wider world of the information professional.

In the first chapter Duncan Christelow discusses some of the ways in which publishers have sought to cope with the end-user revolution. In the UK the CD-ROM SPAG (Standards and Practice Action Group) was, uniquely, set up as a working group between competing publishers. Its purpose has been to improve cooperation and share experience in order to ensure better access for users. It illustrates how publishers are having to adapt and interact with their users in a new way.

This blurring of boundaries is illustrated in Chapter 8 by means of two case studies describing the development and publishing of CD-ROM databases by library staff. These projects help to illustrate two ways in which it is possible to take on a new, pro-active role in developing database provision. In the first, Jim Corlett illustrates the way in which an important in-house information source, already produced on paper, can be transferred to an electronic format; while in the second, David Buri and Robert Anderson show how librarians can exploit existing collections or adapt library resources and produce a value-added commercial database.

Producing databases is one thing, but ensuring their quality is another. For some years now, there has been an increasing concern amongst librarians about this issue. Librarians have drawn up sets of criteria and brought pressure to bear on database producers. The process illustrates the wider responsibility that information professionals have for protecting the interests of their users. In Chapter 2, Chris Armstrong, the Director of the UK Centre for Information Quality Management, argues that database providers have a responsibility to the researcher for detailed and accurate information about the content and scope of the databases they offer, but that equally, information professionals have a vital role to play in monitoring the process.

The issue of database quality is debated by Andrew Cameron in Chapter 7. Here, not only are the qualities of the ADONIS and the Business Periodicals Ondisc databases discussed, but their potential, and relative merits, as vehicles for document delivery are compared. The discussion is very much based on the problems which need to be considered by librarians when trying to provide better end-user services. It illustrates the need for librarians to consult closely with their clientele before replacing print-based material with electronic formats.

Consultation with the client group over adding electronic databases, and the need to change traditional library procedures when doing so is covered in the three case studies in Chapter 3. Will Wakeling describes the new procedures in place at the University of Birmingham, where a devolved budgeting arrangement makes consultation an essential element of the process. Heather Kirby describes the changes that have been made necessary in Croydon Public Libraries, where the involvement of local user groups has led to important changes in the library service as a whole. The introduction of end-user searching in the special library context is described in the third case study. Here Peter Bysouth and Maureen Sullivan show how the role of industrial librarians has been changed, but has not been rendered unnecessary, through the provision of direct database access to company personnel.

The same conclusion is drawn in Chapter 5 in the discussion on the changing role of the reference librarian. In a rapidly developing end-user environment, the traditional intermediary function is in less demand, for end-users can search networked CD-ROM databases or the Internet for themselves. However, the skills gained by reference librarians over the years can be adapted to the new environment and used in different ways. The role of intermediary can still thrive, but through the provision of training, advice, software packages and Internet signposting.

Training is one of the most pressing needs for end-users at the present time. The provision of information skills training programmes is a growing aspect of university teaching. The need for them is illustrated by the responses to the survey questionnaire reported in Chapter 9.

Further aspects of training are covered in Chapter 6. In the first case study Aileen Wade outlines the comprehensive nature of a formalized programme at a British university. Elements of this, if not the whole course, will be recognized by many librarians in this field. What may be more unusual is the provision of training in public libraries, and in the second case study Colette Batterbee surveys the extent of provision in the British public library sector. This is augmented by the specific example of public library training described by Heather Kirby in Chapter 3.

Much of the impetus for end-user searching has depended on robust and adequate networks. The catalyst has been the rapid development of local area networks on university campuses, and of wide area networks for data transmission. In Chapter 9 the discussion centres around the history and organization of these, describing some of the services which are being offered by librarians for the benefit of all end-users. It reports the findings of an international survey of end-users whilst making suggestions on how librarians can continue to influence information provision.

A sound and reliable local network infrastructure must underlie the provision of an end-user service. Making available networked databases is not a simple task, yet users demand a seemless and continuous service. Morag Watson in Chapter 4 outlines some of the problems with which systems librarians have to cope. She also describes some new developments which will do much to satisfy some of the demands for a single search interface. In commenting on the quality of the technical support offered by some database publishers she brings the discussion back to Chapter 1 and the role of the publisher.

In the final chapter Ray Lester poses the question as to whether we should be planning for the end of libraries as we know them. It is one which is asked, either explicitly or implicitly, throughout the book. Numerous questions about the future of the information professional are also to be found. It is clear that there are a number of opportunities and options available.

One certainty is that there is no option other than to accept that change is inevitable. It is not possible to remain as we are; it will be necessary for everyone to re-examine traditional methods and systems in the light of end-user needs and demands. If this book helps to provide background material for the continuing discussion surrounding these issues it, will have achieved what it set out to do.

1

CD-ROM publishing and the needs of the user

Duncan Christelow

Introduction

To assert that I am a publisher in the traditional sense of the word would be to stretch the truth, though as UK Sales Manager of one of Europe's largest electronic publishers I am indeed my company's public face to many librarians and users in the UK. There is an important distinction to be made here, because the simple aim of the publishing company is to sell as many units of published material as possible, whereas my role also includes representing the end user within his or her company. This dichotomy is really the crux of this chapter, as I will examine the ways in which electronic publishing companies have reviewed their operating practices in the light of user needs. Many readers may be wondering already whether cold economic influences have a greater influence upon a publisher than the users' needs, and of course all publishers will wish to be seen as responsive to the needs of their user community. So, what is the truth?

My argument is that electronic publishing has brought with it an increased need for cooperation and interaction between publisher and end-user. Publishers have realized that, without an informed and sympathetic end-user, their product will not satisfy within the library, and alternatives will be sought. I will show that this has been noted, with a range of evidence including: the formation of the CD-ROM Standards and Practices Action Group (CD-ROM SPAG); changes in structure within publishing companies; publishing policy changes; and changing roles for those employed by publishers. I shall begin by giving a brief account of the birth and life of CD-ROM SPAG, looking at some of the most important issues covered by the group in greater depth, before examining the ways in which publishers have developed their working practices since the advent of CD-ROM.

CD-ROM Standards and Practices Action Group

CD-ROM SPAG was set up in 1990, when a group of like-minded publishers came together to form the Group. At the inaugural meeting, held at the Department of Trade and Industry in April of that year, the membership set a course to collaborate in those areas of greatest concern to the user community. It was agreed that it would be in the best interests of the overall health and prosperity of the market to adopt common standards wherever possible, and thus to avoid the danger that users might fail to derive the maximum advantage from the technology. Three Task Forces were set up to provide centres of expertise in the areas of Technology, User Interests and Public Affairs, whilst a Steering Committee had responsibility for guiding and monitoring the priorities and achievements of the Group.

The first objectives of CD-ROM SPAG were summarized as follows:

> To identify and promote International Standards, to devise and recommend codes of practice and pro tem standards as necessary, applicable to the use of CD-ROM based systems for information handling for the benefit of the user community. Further to reach a point in this endeavour to render the group's continued existence unnecessary.

In mid 1991 CD-ROM SPAG produced a document proposing a transformation to a paid membership organization. Until then membership had been free and success had been the result of voluntary effort from a relatively small number of active contributors. With the rapid growth of the CD-ROM industry, it became clear that more resources were needed and this in turn led to the membership fee. The aim of the group continued to be to make CD-ROMs easier to use, with a view to promoting wider use. The interests of the user remained the most important factor, whilst involving all those concerned with using CD-ROM as a vehicle for information handling.

The introduction of a membership fee paid for proper administration, which in turn expanded the opportunities for mounting seminars and commissioning consultancy reports. The first seminar arranged by CD-ROM SPAG was an introduction to the medium, which took place in December 1990. This was followed in July 1991 by a second, entitled 'CD-ROM in Practice' which provided an opportunity for those with no previous experience to find out about the basic technology.

This type of seminar has also helped the publisher to formulate effective policies, as it is an ideal forum for a user to raise important issues for discussion by the group. Joint seminars have been run with the cooperation of The Library Association, leading to the further involvement of end-users. CD-ROM SPAG has become an important player in the information world and acts as a crucial channel for the spread of information both between individual publishers and between the publishers and users themselves. CD-ROM SPAG was not set up to create standards, but rather to identify codes of practice to which its full members might reasonably be asked to adhere. Great strides have been made towards this goal since CD-ROM SPAG's inception, as the following case studies will illustrate.

The help desk

Initially, CD-ROM SPAG's efforts were concentrated on those issues that had been raised by the pioneering users. Most early CD-ROM publishers were working with limited experience and resources, and most members of CD-ROM SPAG in 1990 had been involved in creating the very first discs. All had encountered the obvious teething troubles, whilst the biggest problems for both publishers and end-users concerned installation and technical difficulties. It was decided to address this issue, so the first job for the Technology Task Force was to design and produce a diagnostics diskette.

The belief was that the help desk is the most important service offered by the publisher as far as the user is concerned. It is the area that will create the most stress in the relationship between publisher and user, and because the user is likely to be suffering inconvenience when calling for help, it is crucial for the publisher that problems are dealt with promptly and efficiently. To this end, the development of a diagnostics diskette was an enlightened idea. CD-ROM SPAG members were able to hold a stock of this diskette and send it to users with difficulties. Inserting the diskette in the drive and running the programme gave essential details on the user's system, which could be read over the phone or faxed to the publisher's help desk staff. This approach may seem a little old-fashioned now in the age of e-mail and computer viruses, but it was a boon to the early help desk staff as well as to beginners in the library.

CD-ROM SPAG has also spent time on the procedures of running a help desk. This essential aspect of a publisher's customer service support caused many problems on account of staff inexperience in the necessary administrative practices. With CD-ROM SPAG guidance, each publisher soon built up a huge database of common problems. The mounting of CD-ROMs on networks brought with it a completely new generation of difficulties, and publishers and users alike have benefited greatly from the cooperative atmosphere generated between publishers through the activities of CD-ROM SPAG. A Help Desk Code of Practice was produced for members, offering advice regarding the availability, experience and role of the help desk. The responsibilities of the publisher, data provider and software provider were clarified, as well as the levels of knowledge expected from help desk staff. CD-ROM SPAG proposed that one responsibility of the help desk was to represent the voice of the user within an organization, and when possible to offer sensible and impartial advice on general hardware and networking issues. The end-user has undoubtedly benefited from CD-ROM SPAG's involvement in this area, and standards of support from publishers have risen with the growth in cooperation between help desk staff in different companies.

Consistent interfacing

Another of CD-ROM SPAG's early projects was a study into the possibilities for standardizing interfaces. Of all early topics of discussion between publishers and users, this issue was the most often discussed. The general feeling amongst publishers was that it was impossible to provide the extent of conformity that most librarians were looking for, and it was argued that nobody could seriously expect databases of very different types to be interrogated in the same way. CD-ROM SPAG members were producing bibliographic, full-text, abstract and cartographic discs, all of which required special interfaces. Furthermore, who could expect competitors to ignore their commercial instincts and settle for an interface that could not be further developed without committee agreement?

Nevertheless, the CD-ROM SPAG User Interests Task Force carried out an extensive survey of the differing interfaces in use by its members. This served to alert members that there may be some common ground and the result was that some changes were made in the functions of certain keys. The vast majority of interfaces were DOS based at this time, so it was possible to make sure, for example, that everybody's help was to be found by hitting F1! Today's interfaces reflect agreements made in the early 1990s, and the growth of Windows interfaces now gives the user a certain level of uniformity under that environment.

Similar work was progressing in the USA, where the CD-ROM Consistent INterface Committee (CD-CINC) was formed by the Special Interest Group on CD-ROM Applications Technology (SIGCAT). CD-CINC's aim was to search for consistency in both the description and method of carrying out standard functions in typical CD-ROM software. CD-ROM SPAG made an official statement on the subject, but felt that the limited agreement that had been achieved by its members represented the greatest likely extent of conformity. This is still a live issue, as illustrated by the latest client-server solutions, markup standards such as SGML and HTML, and the Z39.50 Protocol, all of which will give users greater control over the look and feel of their own interface.

Software installation standards

CD-ROM SPAG's User Task Force set out to produce codes of practice on software installation in August 1991. The resulting document was a blueprint for all CD-ROM publishers and the following summary shows that pertinent factors at that time still apply today. We may now take for granted some of the issues listed, but at the time many publishers had not considered the five basic areas covered by the document: installation, default settings, file copying, configuration and warning messages.

Installation

The installation programme should be simple enough to be carried out by a novice user within ten minutes, excluding file copying time. No action should be carried out on the user's hard disk without a clear explanation of what is going to be done, or without the option of aborting the installation.

Default settings

No assumption should be made concerning the drive letters of floppy, hard or CD-ROM drive. Thus if default settings are included, the user will be able to make alterations with ease. If a sub-directory is required into which files are to be copied, the user should be able to alter the default name with ease. The installation programme should identify any name clashes with existing directories or files.

File copying

The user should be given some indication that installation is progressing. Preference would be for a progress bar, but at least some form of indicator should be given. Before copying begins, the installation programme should check available space on the hard drive, whilst the ability to abort should be available at all times.

Configuration

Installation should never make alterations in the computer's configuration without informing the user, and then options for editing or aborting should be given.

Warning messages

Installation programmes should be capable of warning the user of potential difficulties concerning their own system settings. For example, memory requirements should be compared with those available, and the user should be informed of any potential problems. Finally, the installation software should always display its version number so as to facilitate easy technical support.

Product description and sales literature standards

Members of CD-ROM SPAG contributed to the current standards for the level of technical information found in promotional literature. These basic rules are now regarded as absolute standards and it is a reflection of the efforts of members that technical information found in promotional material is now of a very high quality. It is vital that users are informed of minimum hardware and software requirements, particularly with the current rapid advancements in the technical specifications of new computers. Network capability and printer requirements are now equally important.

Furthermore, a joint working party was set up between CD-ROM SPAG and BIC to identify those elements necessary to describe a CD-ROM when information on CD-ROM publications is being transmitted. Minimum levels of information were specified to facilitate consistency in publishers' databases, as well as enabling other parties (libraries, agents, resellers) to receive and process information in this format. It was envisaged that the identified data elements would be mapped into UKMARC format in due course. Six categories of information were identified, covering bibliographic detail, contents, description, hardware, software and networking. It is also recommended that where appropriate the publisher should apply ISBN or ISSN.

This exercise led to a concrete development for all users of CD-ROM that is widely applied today.

Who's who?

The benefits of CD-ROM SPAG membership to a publisher are greatly enhanced by attendance at the regular meetings, which are now held every two months. Discussions tend to spill over the official end time of most meetings and there is ample opportunity for non-technical networking to take place. In order to facilitate communication channels between members, a 'Who's who?' document is now available. This lists, entirely at the discretion of each member, areas of personal expertise which might be called upon by other members. Of course this improves the level of technical support which can be granted by any individual publisher to their users.

Data quality

CD-ROM SPAG addressed this issue through a joint seminar with The Library Association, held at LibTech '93, University of Hertfordshire. An article which reviews the seminar appears in *Online and CD-ROM review*, 17 (5), October 1993, 310–12. The following chapter to this will examine the issues of data quality in depth, but it is worth commenting here briefly on the importance of quality in the context of electronic data. Besides the basic question of data quality, few software interfaces make extensive use of fuzzy logic when making searches, so it is clear that any full-text material must be accurate in order to be found electronically by the end-user. Publishers have become much more mindful of this issue since the advent of CD-ROM and their concern is entirely justified.

Licensing, pricing and networking policies

Throughout the entire life of CD-ROM SPAG, the related issues of licensing, pricing and networking policies have always remained at the head of the list of most frequently discussed topics. From the very first CD-ROM databases, publishers have adopted a variety of different approaches towards methods of charging and these differences were often magnified by networking policies which used different criteria for calculating premiums. There have also been meetings touching on matters such as the requirement to return expired discs and the ownership of leased data. CD-ROM SPAG's work in these areas has benefited the entire information community.

As a group, CD-ROM SPAG began to address these issues with a view to gaining feedback from their users and attempting the best possible standardization. Early meetings were able to agree that publishers could never hope to conform on the details of policy, but that the Group might issue guidelines to its members and furthermore could take the opportunity to act as a clearing

house for policy, comment and discussion. It was agreed that the group needed to convey collectively the message that the publishers are entitled to a fair
return when mounting databases on networks which give wider access, but
that the pricing levels and licensing details should be left to the publishers.

CD-ROM SPAG has now conducted two seminars on the subject of pricing
and networking and, with part of the income generated, reports have been
commissioned into CD-ROM network monitoring, metering and control systems and, most recently, CD-ROM licensing issues. A further seminar, based
upon the findings of the report into CD-ROM licensing issues, took place at
the LibTech Exhibition at Hatfield on 6 September 1995.

The most recent CD-ROM SPAG report examined the wording of a sample of standard licence agreements, making recommendations for future agreements. The report, which was carried out by EPS, a London based consultancy specializing in electronic publishing (and a CD-ROM SPAG member), in
cooperation with London solicitors Bird & Bird, is now published and available for purchase, but it is worth examining in some depth here in order to
illustrate the benefits of this type of work to end-user and publisher alike. The
most tangible benefit for all is the inclusion of a recommended form of licence
with a legal commentary.

The report found that there was a huge degree of variation between the
licences studied, though there was an encouraging conformity in many clauses. Nevertheless, in one case a repossession clause was included which was
unlikely to be enforceable; in 40% of agreements there was no mechanism to
ensure that the user was committed to the agreement; and in 15% of agreements it was not clear whether the transaction constituted a sale or a lease.

Andrew White, who was with Bird & Bird at the time of the writing of the
report, drew upon the common clauses to prepare the recommended form
after deriving a checklist of terms to include. A European Database Directive
has already been published, which is due to be implemented in 1997. This will
have major implications for the existing law, which is increasingly influenced
by Europe. Generally, the level of protection granted to publishers by the new
law is likely to be reduced, so it is increasingly important that the agreements
are drawn up with specialist advice. The introduction of the EC directive
Unfair Contract Terms Directive will also mean that publishers will need to be
very careful of the terms and conditions of their agreements. It has also been
suggested that attention should be paid to networking within the licence agreement, both on a local and wide area basis.

Apart from the benefits to publishers in the preparation of licence agreements in the future, this report also highlights the areas which users should
examine when purchasing or leasing electronic information.

CD-ROM SPAG's other published report in this field is entitled *CD-ROM
network monitoring, metering and control systems*, from research carried out
by the Library Information Technology Centre at South Bank University. The
reasoning behind the commissioning of the report was that members of CD-

ROM SPAG were becoming increasingly concerned about the network licensing problems associated with the growing number of institutions running local and wide area networks. Those publishers wishing to make charges by concurrent users were interested to hear of software developments which might assist in licence definitions, whilst at the same time CD-ROM SPAG felt that the report would be attractive to libraries considering a network monitoring system. The objective of the project was to survey the existing systems, both software and hardware, for measuring, metering and otherwise controlling the use of CD-ROM publications installed on networks. Furthermore, an analysis of these systems was made with a view to measuring how well the needs of CD-ROM publishers and users were met. In some cases, the programmes only offer reports on use; whilst in others it is possible to place a restriction on the number of concurrent users for each database. Other attractive features include the availability of virus protection and password protection features. Over 30 systems were evaluated, giving a very good overview of the current situation in this field. Publishers and users alike were able to make informed decisions as a result of CD-ROM SPAG's coordinating skills, and publishers gained information which then enabled them to improve their networking policies.

Meanwhile, two CD-ROM SPAG seminars were arranged in March 1993 and September 1994, in cooperation with TFPL and The Library Association respectively. The importance of the issue is illustrated by the desire to repeat the original seminar theme, and it is likely that further seminars on the subject will take place in the future, especially in the current climate of change!

The first seminar, *CD-ROM network pricing policy*, held at The Barbican on 17 March 1993, was reviewed in *Information world review*. Publishers were represented by speakers from Context (Michele Green), Oxford University Press (Ruth Glynn), CD-ROM Systems (Robin Fitton), Chadwyck-Healey (Duncan Christelow) and Whitaker (David Whitaker), whilst the end-user was represented by Sarah Ward of Sheffield Hallam University and Iain Skelly of Wirral Metropolitan College. Of the delegates, over one quarter were librarians, so the objective of providing a forum for discussion between publishers and end-users was achieved.

The second seminar took place at the LibTech Exhibition and Conference on 8 September 1994. This was an even more specific meeting, concentrating on the published report on CD-ROM network monitoring and control, with contributions from Robin Fitton and Duncan Christelow, as well as Sue Robertson from Kingston University, who was able to give delegates first hand information from her experiences in implementing such a system at her university. Again, the achievement was to promote debate between publisher and end-user, and delegates found the feedback invaluable. CD-ROM SPAG's achievements in the area of network pricing have been considerable, and though the arguments are well rehearsed, they are worthy of inclusion here.

First, let us consider the justification for a networking charge. Depending upon the size of the network, users will feel varying degrees of satisfaction with the different policies adopted by publishers. There is a world of difference between having a few PCs linked together in a single room in a library and a wide-area network covering different sites of a single institution, or even different institutions. This final scenario describes JANET, as well as networks such as METTNET, which is based at Wirral Metropolitan College and links with other colleges in the north west and midlands, so in itself covers a wide variety of situations.

When considering the justification for this charge, let us think of the printed book. One book can be read only by a single individual at any one time, which is equivalent in CD-ROM terminology to one concurrent user, or one simultaneous access. Libraries tend to purchase multiple copies of the books that are most regularly in demand, and they would not normally expect to receive discounts for these multiple purchases. Similarly, institutions with multiple sites would not expect to receive discounts when purchasing multiple copies of printed matter, nor could they reasonably expect to do so. CD-ROM was originally intended to behave as a single workstation database, with the outstanding benefit being that a huge amount of data (many times greater than the capacity of a hard disk at that time) can be stored on a portable disc that can then be used with any compatible computer, anywhere. If networking had never become a possibility, it is unlikely that there would be any debate over the issue of paying for additional users and sites, because in order to have more than one simultaneous access, it would be necessary to have multiple copies of the disc. The advent of networking has certainly led to a very much superior service to the end-user, but the historical development of the system gives a very strong justification for the introduction of some form of additional charge for the networking benefits.

Every argument has a counter-argument, though, and the end-user does have some ammunition in the basic network-charge justification debate. Many CD-ROM databases are created from multiple-volume printed works, and many others draw together a wide variety of sources. The equivalent databases in printed form could be consulted by a number of people at the same time. One could point to two databases from Chadwyck-Healey's portfolio to illustrate this point. The British Library *General catalogue of printed books* comprises 360 volumes but only one set of CD-ROMs, or 360 theoretical concurrent users for the printed form as against only one for the CD-ROM. *The English poetry full-text database* contains the full text of the works of over 1,300 different poets, taken from a total of 4,500 printed sources. Of course few libraries in the world (if any) would have each of these texts, and it is something of an exaggeration to propose that the paper version of this database could accommodate 4,500 concurrent users, but this type of comparison should be made by publishers when considering their own policies.

Furthermore, the use of printed matter tends not to be controlled by a licence agreement in the same way that a CD-ROM database may be.

Specifically, books can be moved from one library or site to another quite legitimately, and interlibrary loans are readily available for rarer or more expensive materials. CD-ROMs tend not to be available for use in this way, and licences often restrict access to a specific site or building, and almost always to a member of the purchasing institution. This leads to a justified belief amongst many librarians that they do have a right to a reasonable amount of widespread access to a CD-ROM without paying a vastly inflated licence fee. They may also point to the publisher's ethics, which would traditionally dictate that the information should be disseminated as widely as possible, and that restrictive practices such as network restrictions should be against the publisher's principles. Easy access and wide distribution are beneficial to the publisher because they promote the medium and the product.

On the basis of the comparison with the printed book, the evidence is even, without a clear-cut argument either way. But a CD-ROM is not a book, and a publisher such as myself would wince at the thought that the two could be compared directly, especially in terms of price. Publishers add value to data by producing them in electronic form, even when the CD-ROM is simply an electronic version of an existing work. In cases where a much larger collection of printed books is brought together to produce a much larger database, the value of the entirety of the publication is created by the publisher, through identifying the right combination of data and investing in the CD-ROM's development.

To this value-added publication, the ability to network does add further to the value of the original single-workstation purchase. Any librarian would expect to pay for a network version of computer softwares such as spreadsheets and word-processors, and very often these charges would be applied to each workstation, rather than for simultaneous users. However, CD-ROM databases may not be the primary reason for the implementation of the network, and there may be cases where the librarian may be required to make databases available over the network for the practical operation of library services, rather than because of any widespread demand or CD-ROM usage. Whatever the reasons for networking, and however justified the increased charges are on the grounds of increased access, it cannot be denied that the costs of publishers have increased as a result of CD-ROM networking. Additional investment has been made to accommodate new networking softwares as they have been developed, and increased training has been necessary for help desk staff. The majority of publishers have embraced the concept of networking and feel that some sort of return on this investment is justified. At the same time users must remember that their immediate supplier may not have complete control over the charging mechanism applied to any one specific database. There may be impositions made by the software developer or data provider which lead to charges other than those chosen by the publisher. In these cases, there may be competing sources such as online databases which affect the marketing strategy employed. In some cases of significant commercial sensitivity, for example, a data provider may wish to control the very use of the data supplied on the disc, which can be achieved by means of physical control keys attached to the hardware. In effect the end-user is then paying by access, as with an online database.

On the assumption that the network charge is now generally accepted as reasonable, CD-ROM publishers have developed their policies with the needs of the end-users in mind. There are four main options for the method of net-work charging: by site, by user population, by nodes or workstations, and by concurrent users. Site-based networking charges have proved very popular with one sector of the user market, namely those with one single large site. It has also been cheap and easy for publishers to administer, which is an impor-tant factor in small to medium-sized companies. However, it is regarded as unjust by small multisite institutions, who may end up paying vastly more than much larger, more wealthy institutions. With the increase in wide-area net-works, site-based charging is beginning to look outdated.

Many observers would see user population as the fairest charging medium. Effectively each institution would then pay a different amount based upon the potential number of users. Unfortunately this would be an administrative nightmare, because each and every case would have to be examined and nego-tiated. It is impossible to say which departments would use each database, and neither publishers nor libraries could cope with the implications and added workload.

The concept of charging for each network node justifies inclusion only as a point of history. Few would argue today that such a method could be imple-mented fairly, and with thousands of terminals in many institutions, any charges generated this way would relate only very remotely to levels of usage.

In my view the only practical method of implementing networking charges today is by charging for concurrent accesses. Network control and metering can now assist librarians and publishers in setting effective licence levels, and the publisher still has flexibility in the amounts charged. The main drawback of this system is that libraries often have significant peaks of usage levels which may not normally be covered by the existing licence. Publishers must allow certain levels of tolerance in the system so that their users can have access to their data when they need it most, for example at examination time. Licences can include allowances to exceed the agreed level of users with special per-mission at busy times, potentially subject to an additional charge. Publishers must be careful not to deny access to their most important users, as today's stu-dents are tomorrow's information professionals.

Pricing is a crucial element of successful publishing, and whilst it is quite clear that there are many situations where users find it hard to understand pricing policy, the matter is one which is under constant review within pub-lishing companies. One possible future development may be for publishers to start considering price cuts for single-workstation CD-ROMs, whilst main-taining higher rates for network versions. This may enable a wider market place to develop for specialized CD-ROM databases which have until now been purchased in the main by institution or company libraries. The growth in home computers must logically lead to more academics and information professionals wishing to access data at home or on the move.

Of course each of these scenarios assumes that the data in question is mounted locally, on a CD-ROM basis. Many argued from the early days of the medium that it was a transient format, and whilst this is not pertinent to the overall discussion, many networks are now based upon copying CD-ROMs to hard disk, which effectively alters nothing except the speed of retrieval; also more and more data is likely to be supplied to the academic sector on a national basis, via systems such as BIDS and EDINA.

Access to the Internet is becoming more and more widely available, and this in turn is affecting the general attitude to information. 'Surfers' log on to the World Wide Web from companies, universities, colleges, schools and the home, obtaining information of varying quality with varying ease! For many there is no appreciation of quality, and quantity is king. This wide availability of the Internet as a medium could lead to a more significant change in publishers' views and policies than CD-ROM has, especially since so much information is readily available free of charge. The tendency to concentrate on quantity rather than quality may devalue information, and as end-users request access to existing CD-ROM databases through simple Web browsers like Netscape, the distinction between public-domain data and structured commercial databases will be blurred. Publishers will need to add value by providing more sophisticated client interfaces with data mounted on powerful servers, in an attempt to reproduce the CD-ROM's software more faithfully. They may also wish to provide their users with direct links to other sources, or access to multiple datasets through the same interface. It remains to be seen how these developments affect policy, but they will surely fuel the debate on charging methods and network licences.

Publishing companies and structural changes

It is clear that developments have moved the centre of attention away from the medium of CD-ROM. Publishers of CD-ROMs have often avoided calling themselves 'CD-ROM publishers', and this reflects the maturity of the medium, which has lost its original mystique. Whilst I would now avoid being 'medium-specific' whilst discussing electronic publications, I am in no doubt that it was the advent of the CD-ROM which brought about the major change in publishers' organization and working practices. The medium heralded new requirements for the librarian, and publishing companies reacted to and handled these in differing ways.

To begin with, the publishing companies were selling the idea as much as any data, because much of their market had yet to embrace the technology itself. Of course publishers are still doing this, but in different markets, both in the UK and overseas. Whilst the UK academic market is well advanced, there is still work to be done in the public library sector, which is several years behind the academic sector in hardware terms. Even so, equipment availability is still a major brake to sales in many (even very large) UK academic institutions. Many publishers became hardware providers, which proved to be rather an unhappy solution for traditional publishers, who found that they were unable to offer very competitive terms in an already competitive hardware market, and were daunted by technical issues.

Meanwhile other publishers and information providers found that providing a total solution, with hardware, CD-ROM players or juke boxes, was the only practical means to ensure compatibility. These companies quickly employed more staff in technical roles, and many of these early employees became very important players in the field of CD-ROM development and later networking. Of course many have been active and important in organizations such as CD-ROM SPAG!

Even in companies which decided not to become involved with hardware provision, it was quickly apparent that some level of technical support to customers was necessary. Sales and customer services staff gamely addressed troubleshooting issues, which was often an enlightening and productive development for the individuals involved. Meanwhile library staff went through the parallel sequence. CD-ROM SPAG was used as a discussion group for differently qualified support staff, and although technical difficulties with early CD-ROMs were very real, there was far less complexity attached to the resolution of problems on standalone workstations (as was the norm) than to today's network conflicts and memory-hungry programmes. Nevertheless, sales people found that more time was taken up solving problems than selling, and the vast majority of publishers chose to employ customer technical support officers to fulfil this role. It was usually necessary to employ these personnel within the sales environment, rather than as part of the software development team, because customer service was the main function of the role, and it was clear that a close liaison between sales and customer support teams would be required. Many publishers were contracting their software development out to other companies, so the technical support officer would provide the link between the end-user and this development, and the first line of support. Where software development was taking place in-house, the role could be expanded to include beta-testing at customers' sites, and the gathering of feedback from the end-user.

So a competely new and important person was brought into the relationship between publisher and library. The reputation of many electronic publishers and suppliers would stand or fall depending on this person's abilities, and this marks a fundamental change in the way these companies operate.

The arrival of a dedicated customer technical support team is not the only alteration in the structure of publishing companies brought about by the advent of electronic media. The new medium has led to an increased investment in time for sales people working with libraries, demonstrating interfaces and presenting exhibitions. Such presentations are time-consuming and require preparation, and office support roles have expanded with the administration of demonstration CD-ROMs. Complex subscription and networking structures have meant more work for accounts departments, and of course there has been a huge investment by publishers in the development of new product and software. Overall, the advent of CD-ROM and the development of electronic databases has led to a huge growth in staff costs for publishers.

Aside from the new positions that have been created, individual staff members have found themselves performing rather different roles than they were used to. Whilst many sales departments have expanded to cope with the complexity and value of the data which has become available, their members have also learnt to adjust their roles. They must absorb the views of users and relay those views to the management of their company, whilst at the same time presenting the policy decisions of their company to their users, effectively becoming the pivotal interface between publisher and library. In the electronic information world, the librarian is faced with a plethora of choices and sources, and a reliable representative will reap dividends by presenting facts fairly and consistently.

Publishers of electronic information are now more responsive to their users' needs. New electronic databases have required significant input from academics and librarians, and it has been my personal experience that this increased cooperation has become more influential in recent times. Electronic databases offer so much more to researchers and information professionals alike that it is crucial that developments are coordinated and appropriate to the target markets. The advent of CD-ROM has certainly brought about a change in publishers' working practices, but we are really only at the beginning of that electronic revolution. Whilst CD-ROM SPAG's original objectives may have been satisfied, the job is far from over. The increased availability of data through national networks, client-server systems and Internet means there are new issues to address, but the foundations which have been built by its members must be built upon into the 21st century. I hope and expect to see continued and increased cooperation between publisher and user with the joint aim of developing and providing more and better electronic resources for this and future generations.

2

The third undertow

C. J. Armstrong

Knowledge is of two kinds. We know a subject ourselves, or we know where we can find information upon it. (Dr Johnson, 1775)

Introduction

As one of the foremost lexicographers of his day, Dr Johnson was certainly in a position to make such a statement; it probably represented a view forced upon him over many hours of diligent research. In the two centuries since he penned those words, the volume of knowledge available to us has increased beyond measure. Few amongst us can even boast that they 'know a subject' comprehensively, and while the modern segmentation of society, community, work and knowledge means that it is both reasonable and normal to pass through life ignorant of work in many spheres of human endeavour, it has to be remembered that the totality of human knowledge grows and is enriched by the work in these alien spheres.

In other words, while all human knowledge continues to grow, the capacity of the human brain cannot keep pace. Consequently, as the years pass it becomes increasingly necessary to place more reliance on Johnson's second kind of knowledge.

We are in Daniel Bell's 'post-industrial society' but it is all too easy to call it a space age, a computer age or an information age; as Toffler suggested in *The Third Wave*, such labels are inadequate, narrowing our focus rather than expanding our understanding.[1-2] Indeed, the thesis of *The Third Wave* is that humanity faces change – colliding waves of change – in every field of endeavour, and that many such clashes are revolutionary in their outcome. If the 'Third Wave' is categorized by anything, it is clearly change, and as society struggles to manage change – be it technological or philosophical – the need for information increases. This may be limiting, but today's society lives in an age that is dominated by information and communication.

Whatever the medium of the message – and it may be print, television, the Internet, electro-optical publishing, conventional online or real-time systems – the content relays information to the reader. The communication of information is the sole reason for the existence of such media. Information may be thought of as a tool of the workplace, but it is also increasingly targeted at schools or home users. Increasingly services such as CompuServe, America Online, Prodigy, Lotus Notes: Newsstand, Microsoft Network Online and Europe Online – consumer information utilities – are offering information directly to the user. No matter where the service is targeted, in every case the central purpose is to deliver an answer to a user need or query.

Workers in any domain – researchers in education, business analysts, market researchers, physicists, doctors or chemists – have frequent needs for information. They need to discover related research, other companies' products, chemical substances, product availability and any number of items of information which cannot be obtained locally. Outside the professional areas, school children are daily being taught the practical applications of Dr Johnson's theory, while interactive television – not to mention the Internet and the myriad CD-ROM-based products – will bring a virtual library into the home. Every day the potential market for information increases.

If the acquisition of personal knowledge relies on the availability of a universal repository of knowledge, then access to that knowledge – and the means of access – become paramount in importance. As Needham noted, 'All societies depend for their very existence on the communication of knowledge. The more complex the society and the more complex its knowledge, the more complex does this matter of communication become'.[3] As the means of communication improve and speed up, the organization of knowledge in order to facilitate and simplify access becomes increasingly important.

In a society founded on information – a society of information users – there must clearly be a corresponding group of information providers. This is no new concept: information has been provided or published in printed form since Gutenberg, and in China since 932AD – but the electronic information age described in *The Third Wave* brings a new immediacy to the dissemination of information. It also brings many new players into the arena, for no longer is publishing the sole domain of book and journal publishers. New publications may be advanced by members of the computer industry: system providers, system integrators, software developers, and so on. The point is made succinctly in a 1995 report from Ovum: 'Publishing companies are facing stiff competition from IT companies of all sizes who are entering the market'.[4] Publishers and librarians have always been in privileged positions at the gateways to knowledge, and being aware of this have made efforts to provide suitable material. With the new speed, reach, immediacy and power of electronic publishing, a special responsibility now rests on the shoulders of the publishers.

Never before has so much material been made available so readily to so many! Every aspect of information technology conspires to facilitate and speed up the creation and transmission of documents. Society has come a long way since the messenger with a cleft stick, or even since the days of the penny-black stamp; and while the oft-forecast paperless office or paperless society is as far away today as it ever was, the technology of the nineties does allow a message typed in a UK office to be received in an Australian university only seconds later. The same technology allows electronic journals – 'e-zines' – to be circulated with equal ease. Some are simply the electronic counterpart of a print original, but others have never, and will never, see paper. They exist only as network phantasms to be viewed, saved or forwarded at a reader's whim. It is the work of seconds to disseminate an article or report to millions of Internet users, and anyone can become his or her own publisher at the press of a key.

But this ease of delivery should not imply a casual approach – there is an enormous gulf between delivering and publishing, and practitioners of the former should not imagine that they are experts in the latter. The 'third wave' may have been precipitated by technology, but in today's high-tech age technology has a tendency to lead by the nose. Douglas Adams once quipped that multimedia was an invention looking for a necessity to mother it; and while this is no longer true, tasks if not necessities have long since justified the cleverness of multimedia, and the elemental candour behind the statement points to a near-universal tendency that characterizes much technology. 'We can do it so now let's find a job for it.' It may seem cynical or even Luddite to say so, but often products arrive on an unsuspecting market with little in the way of market research to demonstrate a need. Does the average parent of today really want to invest in a microcomputer so that the toddler can colour in pictures on the screen or learn to read with a simulacrum book? And yet there are hundreds of CD-ROMs targeted at just that market. Is anyone ever going to lie in bed with a laptop computer on the next pillow in order to read the latest Terry Pratchett novel? And yet there are electronic books aplenty. Indeed, is there any evidence that home users want access to the hundreds of newspapers and reference works offered by some consumer-oriented services?

Never mind the questionable morality of allowing ourselves to be led by the marketing vision of technological wizards. Should we – can we safely – accept everything that is offered?

If technology has enabled this huge advance in information delivery mechanisms, it has also empowered the man and woman in the street. In the workplace, the old reliance on a library or information unit often gives way to a do-it-yourself mentality, while hitherto inaccessible information becomes accessible in the home. The term 'end-user' or 'end-user searcher' has been bandied around the literature of information science for some time and is generally taken to imply that databases are to be searched by the person who ultimately needs the information, rather than by an intermediary skilled only in information science and search techniques. In many organizations, end-user searching has become sufficiently established to allow end-users themselves to become experts in information handling, knowledgeable about the variety of databases available to them, skilled in searching and aware of the need to assess the results. However, this is not always the case. One end-user went into print with the comment that 'As the facilities available expand, so expectations are raised. . . . Database providers themselves may not realize the degree of ignorance that potential customers like myself still have'.[5] With information so readily available outside the traditional library/information unit, many more end-users can have access to these information sources – indeed, in many cases they may make purchasing decisions without reference to such an information unit. In the home, the average children's PC is equipped with a CD-ROM reader and, while it is unlikely that these users will acquire MEDLINE or Compendex*Plus, they are among the foremost users of encyclopaedia and similar reference works. The day of the 'bedroom Bodleian' is here!

End-users in the home or the workplace have been recognized by both the computer and the information industry, with the result that many new information products are directly targeted away from the library. One, often unrecognized, corollary of this switch is the consequential lack of control exercised over their use. In cutting out this particular 'middle man', society has removed the one person who – in the old days – could point out deficiencies in the source, highlight the need for further investigation, warn about the lack of authority, suggest alternative sources of information, monitor coverage and control access to reference sources. As Stoker and Cooke recently noted, since the earliest days of librarianship it has been recognized that qualitative judgements about library materials and sources of information are an integral part of the job.[6] In 1876 Melvil Dewey suggested that it was no longer enough for a librarian to be merely a keeper and protector of books, because he or she also had to see that the library contained, 'the best books on the best subjects, regarding carefully the special wants of his [or her] community.' Over a hundred years later, the proliferation of reference books means that librarians still need to evaluate material, viewing the evaluation, whether in terms of an initial decision to acquire them or a subsequent decision as to their utility, as an important element of their professional work. Not only are the principles and practices of the evaluation and selection of materials a long-understood, core activity of librarianship, but the original concept and ideas on how this should be undertaken are now extended to material supplied on non-paper media.

In an electronic age, this evaluative activity is arguably of greater importance. As has already been noted, publishers share with librarians the privilege and responsibility of broadcasting information. Information is nebulous – it gains substance and power only in its representation – and in capturing and structuring knowledge, in publishing a database, the information provider or publisher faces an onerous task. A task which, because of its far-reaching effects, must not be undertaken lightly.

This is a special responsibility which must be honoured – never mind litigation or liability. Publishers, especially publishers of databases, have a moral obligation to create only products upon which users can rely. Disinformation, misinformation and part-information must not be allowed! There is a vulnerability factor to be taken into account. Electronic information means that users 'become in a way much more vulnerable, even though [they] appear to have far greater powers of decision-making' because of its availability.[7] In the same talk in late 1994, the Rt Hon. Tony Benn drew attention to the democratic control of information, asking, 'Who controls the information we receive with such pleasure on our screens?' Publishers have the job of acquiring, validating, structuring, making accessible, and selling the database, and any emphasis on selling should not eclipse a concern for the other tasks. Cynically, Gerhard Mantwill has suggested that as long as the number of active passwords is increasing, information providers are bound to take little notice of requests for quality improvement: attracting new users is cheaper than investing in the quality mechanisms which could bring about a perfect database.[8] But if any aspect of their task is less than perfect, these users are at risk.

And what is 'perfect'? The same electronic age which makes widespread publication so easy is responsible for both the huge volume of information available to the publishers and the apparent requirement of publishing speed. With so much data to process, 'perfect' – 100% right – is an impossibility. As David Minkoff of Datastream said, 'We all believe in zero defects . . . We don't set ourselves a target other than zero'. But if Datastream were to set itself a target of 1% of defects among 720 million data items, there could still be seven million complaints per month – 0.0001% still gives 700 complaints.[9] Users must also remember that there is a price to pay even for attempting perfection. Quality management costs in both money and time, and this is a price that users in some circumstances are not willing to pay. Yesterday's news is not only not news, it is worthless news! This poses two questions. How much are we, as users, prepared to pay for quality over and above what we already pay for access to information? And does quality have a sliding scale whereby the less urgent the publication of data, the higher the quality obtainable?

We can only answer these questions with another: how are the users to know?

Database quality

Conventionally – at least in manufacturing industry – quality is defined as a level which satisfies the requirements of a customer at a reasonable or economical cost which is acceptable to both the customer and the supplier.[10] The setting of such an agreed level implies a description or specification of the product against which it can be tested for conformance. In this model, an expectation of quality implies an agreed norm against which products can be evaluated. If the norm is generic, it may become a standard. Coming late to the concept of quality, the database industry has no such structure: specifications are largely internal to the database producer and any agreed levels of charging are based solely on the product as delivered at a given point in time. No levels of performance are established or published and no consequential standard has arisen.

Certainly, database producers publish database descriptions in their publicity material and in vendor catalogues, as well as information sheets such as those produced by KR DIALOG and KR Data-Star, but these do not amount to a specification. They have a very different purpose: they are either marketing tools or mini-manuals. As Alkula noted in 1989, there are no commonly acknowledged guidelines for database descriptions and so each producer presents such documents in its own way.[11] Often, this includes a degree of hyperbole or exaggeration intended to sell the database to potential users. Equally certain is the fact that each producer or information provider must have internal documentation which describes the scope and coverage of the database as well as the criteria for inclusion, field structure and so on. There will also be style manuals for indexers and abstracters. Also, agreements have to be reached between the information provider and the online vendor or CD-ROM publisher who makes the database available to the users. In this way the construction and publication of a database is defined and circumscribed, although there is no clear indication of the degree to which these criteria are enforced.

Work undertaken by EUSIDIC in 1994/5 highlighted a methodology for managing quality in an organization called gap analysis.[12-13] The original work established a conceptual model of a service and identified a total of five potential service quality gaps:

- between management perceptions of customer expectations and actual expectations;
- between service quality specifications and management perceptions of customer expectations;
- between service quality specifications and service delivery;
- between service delivery and external communications to customers;
- between expected service and service as perceived by the customer.

Experience at the Centre for Information Quality Management (CIQM) clearly demonstrates that the first and last of these gaps is frequently found in the information industry, while the existence of the remaining three (which are all located wholly within the information provider's domain) is suggested by much of the publicity material. A review undertaken in late 1995 demonstrated very well that the second and fourth gaps can and do exist. The CD-ROM was publicized as having new software which 'improves the efficiency of your searching, saving you valuable time and money'. But the software took over five minutes to load at each use, each query took minutes to search the indexes, and transitions between the display screens took nearly as long.

The suggestion is that in order to improve quality it is necessary to eliminate the service gaps. One way in which this can be done is by formalizing specification routines and extending them to reach the consumers. Without specifications, users cannot know what it is that they are paying for in anything other than general terms. Many of the larger information providers publicize the fact that they have internal quality management routines in place; some even give guarantees or make specific statements that, for example, all addresses have been verified by telephone interviews; a few even promise to refund monies if users are dissatisfied in any way with the records that are retrieved. While some of these published statements are tantamount to quality assurance, they all fall short of the assurance given by a full specification categorically stating all that a database does and does not do.

Database quality covers every aspect of the product delivered to the user, including the data, the access, the documentation and online/ondisc help and help desks. In Zeithaml's terms this encompasses

- the tangibles (the appearance or physical characteristics);
- reliability (the ability to perform the promised service dependably and accurately);
- responsiveness (the willingness to keep customers satisfied and to provide a prompt service);
- assurance (the knowledge and courtesy of employees and their ability to convey trust and confidence);
- empathy (the caring, possibly individualized, criteria that the firm provides its customers).

In terms of the work of the Centre and of database quality in general this translates into ten areas or criteria originally set out by the Southern California Online User Group (SCOUG) in 1990.[14] These are:

- consistency (of records within a database; of authority control for main indexes);
- coverage and scope (subject and geographical coverage as advertised; gaps in data);
- timeliness (involving updating and currency of material);
- error rate/accuracy (source material, data errors, duplicate records – general 'dirty data');
- ease of use (software facilities and access to the data);
- integration/harmonization (with other like databases);
- output (formatting of records; downloading; aesthetics of delivered records);
- documentation (both print and online help should be current, adequate and accurate);
- customer support and training (includes knowledgeable help desks, training and system support so that changes are not made without warning);
- value-to-cost ratio/charging (records priced for content, good system value, and fair and consistent pricing).

Any specification of a new or existing database needs to include all of these aspects. In terms of the internal specification, this predicates a document of some considerable size with considerable detail of each aspect covered. It is doubtful whether the most meticulous user would plough through several such lengthy sets of documentation in order to decide on the best database for their purposes, and this suggests that for external purposes a shorter, less daunting specification would be more suitable.

Database labelling

As has been noted, the information industry is concerning itself with quality and specifications rather late in the day. There are over 9800 databases available to users around the world and few, if any, have provided their users with a formal specification detailing their capabilities. The average database user is searching a mass of data without any defined parameters from which he or she can judge results. Documentation is intended to teach users how to search a given set of data using a given software; in some cases the tips intended to guide users into getting the best from the product actually disguise existing problems. In the case of some lesser products – often available only on CD-ROM – the documentation extends only to the half dozen pages which will fit inside the jewel case, and quite often does not even describe the coverage or inclusion criteria for items on the database. Users are left without a map to a subset of data selected according to an unknown person's unknown criteria!

At best in the information industry, quality is being dealt with on an ad hoc basis – some companies manage quality and some manage without managing. Even those companies which profess total quality management or quality assurance techniques are not all handling the problem in the same way. In a guest editorial written in January 1993, Peter Jacsó suggested an approach which was analogous to food and drug labelling, and which he called database labelling.[15] In the same way that a tin of soup has its ingredients listed on its side, Jacsó suggested that databases should have a detailed summary of their coverage and content readily available to users and potential users. It is essentially a way in which potential users can determine exactly what is in a database and whether they want to use it – the extent to which they can 'trust' it. A specification designed to a fixed and instantly recognizable layout which would inform the user base of the database parameters. The Centre for Information Quality Management has examined this idea and believes it to have considerable merit. Much of the Centre's work is concerned with the possibilities of database labelling and the methodological problems associated with such a scheme.

Database labels, as foreseen by the Centre, are essentially brief descriptions of a database containing both factual information and quality metrics. They provide users with an up-to-date specification of a product and providers with a set of parameters or a 'standard' against which performance can be measured. Figure 2.1 shows a possible layout for part of a database label with some suggested database quality statements and parameters in place. Labelling is a means of specifying or describing a product or database; labels help to map user/customer expectations to system/product specifications and in so doing they can also form the basis of customer-provider quality agreements. First-time users of databases would know exactly what they were paying for. From the information provider's point of view they offer a baseline from which increases in charges can be argued on the basis of better quality control.

MEDLINE KR Data-Star

January 1996 — Database Label (IQM)

Mission Statement: *One-sentence description of objectives such as:* MEDLINE sets out to provide indexing of all articles of over 1 page in length from the top 6,000 health care journals worldwide.

Subject Coverage: *Series of c.30 Topic Headings such as:* Nursing; Clinical Medicine; Dentistry; Surgery ...

Geographic Coverage: *General but detailed statement such as:* MEDLINE provides international coverage with a primary emphasis on USA and secondary emphasis on Western Europe.

Start Year: 1966
Update time: Weekly for additional records. Annual reloads with corrections

Quality Assurance Policy Statements:
A fixed series of statements such as:
- The average time between journal cover date and inclusion of records is two weeks
- All index terms are checked by a second indexer
- Bibliographic information for all records is checked by supervisor
- Authority files are used for: author names and company names
- All Descriptors are assigned from a thesaurus
- Every 3rd reference is checked in detail against original articles
- Every address is contacted to confirm contact details once per year; no contact possible means address is removed
- Corrections notified by corollary records

*** Dummy Label/Example only – MEDLINE details are *NOT* based on fact, nor are they intended to suggest NLM/KR Data-Star practice ***

MEDLINE KR Data-Star

January 1996 — Database Label (IQM)

Number of Records:

	Total	Last 12m
	8,700,000	61,854
With Abstract (search as: ED=9601 * AB=AB)	5,060,000	99.86% =61,765
With Publication Type (search as ...		
With Publication Year		
With Geog. Coverage		
With Language		

Number of Journals covered: 5,891

Available Fields (* = data compulsory)

Author /AU *	Title /TI *	Controlled Terms /CT *

Geographic Coverage (% of records)

UK	12.1	Australia	1.2
USA	63.4	New Zealand	0.4
W Europe	8.8	South America	0.0
E Europe	2.1	Central America	0.0
Japan	9.0	Russia	1.7
Pacific Rim	1.1	Scandinavia	0.0

Fig. 2.1 *Example of the first pages of a database label. The items included are for demonstration only as no final decisions on content have been made. Please note that both 'MEDLINE' and 'KR Data-Star' have been included for illustration only; the label does not have any factual content*

The standard format or layout of the labels would make them instantly recognizable and simplify the user's assessment of a database. The same database is frequently available on different online hosts or CD-ROMs, having a quite different appearance in each case. Different fields may be made available (with or without abstracts, for example); the indexing is the responsibility of the host; print formats will almost certainly vary and software-related aspects which affect access and ease of use are certain to differ. For these reasons, the label will have to be version-specific and involve the online/CD-ROM vendors in the Label production. A different label for each manifestation of the database will be required.

The label should contain both qualitative and quantitative or factual information about the database. It will thus

- inform users of exactly what a database can and cannot do;
- become a standard/specification to which the information provider will wish to adhere.

From the point of view of the user, the label would immediately show exactly what a database could do for them, leaving them with no unreasonable expectations. The label would become a quality assurance statement demonstrating to what extent the database could be relied upon. The factual information would give unambiguous parameters for coverage while qualitative metrics or indices would demonstrate how well the database functioned within these areas. From the point of view of the information provider, management would be able to use the label to assess quality and conformance to their expectations, thus closing two of the internal gaps in Zeithaml's model.

While no particular data elements or design features have been set for the labels, some preliminary work has been undertaken. On the factual side, the label might be expected to describe the database's coverage by listing between 20 and 50 topic areas, to give the database size, to list the fields available (and when they were introduced), to list numbers of records by year, country, document type and language, and to give some indication of how up-to-date the database was. Quality aspects are less easy to list, but one quality criterion might be an indication of how complete the records were for each indexed field – for example, 'Publication year field' introduced in 1983, since when 98.95% of records contain valid information'.

It is also the intention to provide formulae or search strategies on the label for any factual or quality datum. This means that users can verify the label information and assess any apparent quality complaints against stated parameters.

The label should be generated regularly – ideally to coincide with the normal vendor update cycle – and should be circulated with publicity material and made available on exhibition stands. It should also be published in some form.

The role of the database label can be extended so that, in addition to supplying users with a specification for the database in question, it marks the database as being a quality product. Indeed, without this added value, the label would not necessarily be any more trustworthy than publicity material. The label could become a quality 'flag' or accreditation in its own right. Some form of branding of the label – for example, by incorporating the CIQM logo – would mean that users could readily identify it as an independent label rather than as another piece of sales or marketing literature from the producer.

While the mere provision of a label would be an indication of a responsible attitude towards data provision, it will also be a self-imposed, database-specific standard by which performance can be monitored. In using the term 'standard', care has to be taken to distinguish between a Standard as defined by BSI or ISO procedures and the idea of an entirely local standard which is specific to a given product. The database label would be self-generated, self-imposed and perhaps self-regulated; the information provider would specify database parameters as they pertain to a database at the point when the label is first generated and would then seek to adhere to or better that performance. Thus the so-called standard for EMBASE would be quite different from the standard for ERIC and that for Social Science Abstracts.

Accreditation would effectively 'kite-mark' the quality products and this in turn would bring pressure on other providers to look for accreditation – something that can only be undertaken if their databases live up to certain basic expectations.

Accreditation

A central accreditation agency would function at three levels. Firstly, it would be responsible for making available pro forma labels which could be filled in by information providers and their vendors. The forms would have to be designed to simplify their use as much as possible – if the information industry is to be persuaded of the value of labelling, the mechanics of their creation and updating will need to be as simple and streamlined as possible. The use of scope notes to explain exactly what is needed, and of search strategies to facilitate easy data acquisition, will be of paramount importance. Consideration might be given to the electronic delivery and retrieval of the forms.

Secondly, it will be the role of the agency to validate the form by checking its content against the database in question. Only when this has been done can the form be 'stamped' with the accreditation mark and published. Labels have to be up to date if they are to be of any use. In theory, every version of every database will need to update the label at every update of the database. Clearly, given the rate of updates of some databases, this may not be viable – either for the producers and vendors, or for the accreditation agency – and a standard period may need to be introduced.

The final procedure involves the publication and dissemination of the accredited labels. Distribution to existing users and the provision of copies for use on exhibition stands might become the combined task of the online vendor and the vendor, while the publication of the central store of labels would fall to the agency itself. Again some electronic means, perhaps via the Internet, might be considered. It is interesting to speculate on how long it would take the agency to accredit a label for its own database of labels!

Problems with database labels

Database labelling may provide quality assurance but it can only do so – as has been suggested above – at some cost. Users looking for high-quality databases must expect to be faced with a commensurate rise in charges, and we have yet to see how users will react to this aspect. It has been suggested above that users of the databases of the mid-nineties are paying for unknown entities and that, given this fact, it is unreasonable for information providers and database producers to raise prices in order to improve quality. Most users would think that the costs should be absorbed, as they could reasonably expect to be paying already for a product which meets their expectations.

This remains true, but if charges are raised to meet a clearly defined quality assurance mechanism – as opposed to covering a mechanism to bring quality up to a standard it should already have achieved – users may be more amenable to the increase. Database labelling offers users a means to quality, but it only offers this. No one can make users read the label or take heed of its contents, and in such cases the label will become more of a support for the information provider in case of complaint. So long as the database can be seen to be true to its label, no user can have cause for complaint.

A further consideration is the increasing use of databases distributed over local area networks (for example, in universities); how are the many users to be presented with the labels? Users in any situation cannot be made to read the label but it will be necessary to make users aware of the possibilities for quality control that are open to them. Local training and publicity supplied by library staff can back up efforts made by the information providers, but the most useful tool may well be a logon message asking 'Have you read the label?'

Neither is the work of the accreditation agency free from difficulties. Many of the largest and most-used databases have been available electronically for 20 or more years and in this time have changed considerably. New fields may have been added (for example, an abstract), or fields may have been divided up to provide better access (for example, the source field divided into journal, publication year, volume, issue, etc.); thesaural control may have been introduced at some point, and coverage will almost certainly have improved. Clearly to give a 'score' on the label representing the entirety of the database would give a false or a skewed impression. One solution may be to show the date when fields came into existence and their rating from that date only.

The volume of data to be condensed into a relatively small amount of space – no more than four pages – is also problematic. One possibility is that to balance the short summary labels, documentation could be made available electronically – possibly via the Internet – with links to individual databases. The Internet has already opened up a number of possibilities for conventional-online vendors, and if publication of the labels were to be Internet-based, there is no reason why, for online databases at least, the 'Have you read the label' message should not also have a direct link to the relevant label. The label could, in turn, have links to fuller documentation, but this would fall outside the responsibilities of the accreditation agency.

Database labelling offers exciting opportunities to the database provider who is willing to accept the challenge. As with any new and untried scheme, it is easy to point to difficulties such as those examined briefly here; in reality the advantages to both users and information providers outweigh any disadvantages.

The needs of end-users

It is also easy to suggest that users do not need – and indeed, would not bother to use – an additional level of documentation. The suggestion may have some degree of truth but there is no doubt that some such scheme is needed. In a recent survey of professional database users carried out at the Centre, it became apparent that, on average, between one and two searches in every ten undertaken would unearth a quality problem of some kind. Moreover, such patterns were seen to affect user productivity: nearly half of the respondents reported that they caused them to spend too much time searching, and nearly as many echoed this by reporting a need to repeat searches, while a surprising 31% noted that records located were unusable (perhaps because the reference was at fault or a table was not properly formatted). This is therefore not something to be ignored.

This survey was specifically administered to professional searchers in order to eliminate user searching errors, but the findings suggest that if professional searchers are caused this much aggravation by quality issues, then such issues are likely to cause considerable grief to end-users. And while many end-users will be aware of such problems, many others – those in the 'electronic bedroom', for example – will not. Here, indeed, are the most vulnerable and here is where quality issues become crucially important, because as long as they remain unnoticed they can distort or invalidate research results.

End-users need labelling, both to offer some assurance on the databases they may use and to alert them to unknown dangers lurking in non-labelled databases: here be Dragons!

Conclusion

In a world in which information plays such a major role in everyday professional and leisure activities, we might expect its delivery to ease the impact of the colliding waves of change that Toffler forecast. With the 'third wave' involving information to the extent that it does, users may find an associated undertow in the inadequate or misleading information which is so often delivered. Information has the power to help or subvert and it is crucial to have the outcomes of research guaranteed – at least in so far as the input is concerned!

Today's researchers cannot know to what extent they can trust the information culled from the databanks at their disposal. There is no guarantee. Indeed, the only way to insure the data is to use what is found as a starting point and to validate this personally – which begs a number of questions about the value and cost of information. At the Centre, we have encountered many instances which reinforce this point. In one encyclopaedia there was the photograph of some unknown personage which popped up on the screen in place of the Indonesian president. Then there was the incorrect contact information so frequently discovered the hard way in databases which purported to supply business names and addresses. Such results invariably fail the user in one way or another. Even bibliographic databases are not immune, and references are all too often linked to the wrong journal.

Database labelling will not make such problems disappear overnight but it will offer users a series of statements relating to data acquisition and reliability so that they can assess how much they can rely on. Database producers will also have comparative figures for similar databases and for their own database's past performance, which may spur them to greater, or better, future performance. This is, after all, what quality assurance is all about.

Perhaps society's fourth wave will be exemplified by high quality and low undertow.

References

1   Bell, D., *The coming of post-industrial society: a venture in social forecasting*, London, Heinemann Educational, 1974.
2   Toffler, A., *The Third Wave*, London, Collins, 1980.
3   Needham, C. D., *Organizing knowledge in libraries: an introduction to information retrieval*, 2nd edn, London, André Deutsch, 1971.
4   Jeffcoate, J. and Wesley, I., *Multimedia publishing: market opportunities*, London, Ovum, 1995.
5   Williams, C., 'In search of a perfect host: an end-user goes online', *Information world review*, **107**, October 1995, 32.
6   Stoker, D. and Cooke, A., 'Evaluation of networked information sources'. In A. H. Helal and J. W. Weiss (eds.), *Information superhighway: the role of librarians, information scientists and intermediaries*, Proceedings of the 17th International Essen Symposium 1994, Essen, Universitätsbibliothek Essen, 1995, 287–312.
7   Benn, T., 'Information and democracy' (UKOLUG Annual Lecture, 1994), *The electronic library*, **13** (1), 1995, 57–62.
8   Mantwill, G. H., 'Nutzers Not und Pflichten' (Users' needs and duties), *Cogito*, 3-95, June 1995, 45–9.
9   Minkoff, D., 'Quality: participation plus change'. In *Total Quality Management: based on papers given at a one day conference on Total Quality Management (TQM) in library and information services with additional material*, Hatfield, HERTIS Information and Research, 1992, 70–81.
10 Swindells, N. and Gancedo, I., *A model for the description of large databases*, Paper presented at CODATA International Conference, Chambéry, 1994 (to be published).
11 Alkula, R., 'A framework for database descriptions'. In *Online information 89: 13th international online information meeting* (London, 12–14 December 1989

Proceedings), Oxford, Learned Information, 1989, 77–86.

12 May, N. A., *Methodology for the measurement of quality of electronic databases: a report of work undertaken by EQUIP*, Paper presented at Knowledge Organization and Quality Management, Third International ISKO Conference, 20–24 June 1994, Copenhagen.

13 Zeithaml, V. et al., *Delivering quality service*, New York, The Free Press, 1990.

14 Basch, R., 'Measuring the quality of the data: report on the Fourth Annual SCOUG Retreat', *Database searcher*, **6** (8), 1990, 18–23.

15 Jacsó, Péter, 'A proposal for database "Nutrition And Ingredient" Labelling' (guest editorial), *Database*, **16** (1), 1993, 7–9.

3

Meeting the demand for CD-ROM databases

Case Study 1: Academic libraries
Will Wakeling

Introduction

In books such as this, in which so many of the issues intertwine and are revisited from different viewpoints, a case study needs to display two particular features. It needs to embed the general issues firmly in the practical experience of the case study. It also needs to avoid giving the impression that the only decisions ever made were good ones, and the only users ever catered for were satisfied ones. While what follows dwells on the set of solutions and accommodations that have been developed at Birmingham, there are also plenty of occasions when circumstances, and in particular the tides of change, left us temporarily beached and short of answers.

The changing environment

Over the last decade the changes in the circumstances of the University of Birmingham have been relatively speaking characteristic of the UK higher education sector as a whole. Student numbers have risen by 50% to a total of some 16,000, and demands on library and information services have increased correspondingly. Proportions of distant-learning, part-time and mature students have swollen, requiring fundamental adjustments to the character of information provision. Capital investment to fund extensions and enhancements to the physical space available for library study has failed to keep pace with this growth. The size of our holdings has increased to exceed two million volumes and three million archival items. So we have increasingly placed a premium on fixes (such as programmes for increased relegation to remote, closed-access compact stores, distributed networking of digitized information sources, and greater emphasis on computer-based learning) which encourage the support of teaching and research by non-traditional means, and beyond the walls of the University Library.

At the same time, the University has sensibly sought to make good long-standing under-funding in book and periodicals purchasing by maintaining the Library's non-staff budget at a level sufficient to cover the worst effects of price inflation in that area. It has also encouraged the schools (budget centres) of the University to exploit their freedom under its devolved financial system to supplement from their own resources the funds available to the Library. We realize, I think, that things for us at least could have been a good deal worse.

But in order to exploit the benefits that CD technology has offered, libraries have had to do more than hope for the luxury of stable funding for the purchase of material. The shift at Birmingham, from a single standalone PC with CD drive delivering access to the Library's first CD-ROMs in the late 1980s, to the present range of facilities, has required a range of radical changes in organization and funding that can be seen in academic libraries up and down the country. The resources now on offer include more than 60 CD-ROM databases, of which 35 are available to multiple users across campus and in site libraries via the Library Information Network (LIN) (using Novell, SaberMenu software metering, and three optical servers) on the University's high-speed campus network. Standalone with its laser printer, UMI's Business Periodicals OnDisc alone comprises more than 600 CD-ROM discs. Other groups of databases not viable over the LIN are linked using local CD-changers, while dedicated PCs are available in the Library's main hall and sites for further standalone installations. In delivering access to an ever-widening range of CD-ROM titles (bibliographic, encyclopaedic, multimedia and reference) through a diverse combination of technologies, the University of Birmingham is setting no special trends, but simply adapting like the rest of its species.

Adapting to the new environment

This is not the place to dwell on the most significant expression of the University's evolving information strategy, which is the convergence (from October 1995) of the previously distinct library, computing, television and computer-based learning services into the present single, unified Information Services division. It does, however, exemplify a virtuous trend in higher education institutions seeking to exploit to the full the advantages of bringing together staff with expertise (in networking, data and information handling, and user support) who might otherwise be operating in isolation from each other. It should also ease the process of generating and sustaining a coherent information collection development policy for the University: as a division, Information Services will be in a position to monitor and coordinate the whole range of information-related initiatives campus-wide to ensure, for instance, that Schools acting independently do not unnecessarily duplicate holdings of CD-based and other information sources.

More relevant to this study is the list of inventions, reconfigurings and adaptations to the existing library structure and operations that investment in the CD solution over the last decade has entailed. These include:

- introducing new budgeting arrangements;
- extending the responsibilities of the liaison librarians team;
- creating an Electronic Information Sources group, with project planning

method (milestones);
- creating new forms of product evaluation;
- creating new procedures to cope with the allocation of staff responsibilities in choosing and introducing new products;
- creating new handling procedures for acquiring and putting into stock digitally structured items (CDs and 3.5 inch diskettes);
- major investment and upgrading in IT infrastructure;
- creating and maintaining a file of licensing agreements;
- developing new workstation booking arrangements;
- designing and implementing an effective programme to monitor CD-ROM use.

What follows addresses some of these developments.

Budgetary control

The first investments that academic libraries made in CD-ROM products were, naturally enough, generally specially negotiated and paid for; in this sense, and in others, CD-ROMs were treated as extraordinary. Some major subscription agents made early policy decisions not to handle them. Birmingham's initial commitment to deliver access to CD-based abstracting and indexing titles such as UMI's Dissertation Abstracts and ISI's Citation Indexes was treated as an investment in a value-added new technology which was not simply to be offset by the cancellation of existing hard copy subscriptions – at least not until we had made a longer-term assessment of the benefits to, and take-up by, our academic community. We also needed to address the reservations shared by the academic library community about committing themselves to a relatively unproven medium of uncertain archival permanence, often effectively available only on lease, with all the associated implications of a shift from a 'holdings' to a thoroughly mixed 'holdings and access' collection development policy.

However, in 1991/92 the Library revised its methods of allocating funding for the purchase of information materials, and adopted a fully integrated approach – better suited, we judged, to decision-making in the increasingly variegated information market place. The Schools (budget centres) of the University are each allocated a single all-embracing information fund. Academic colleagues in each School are then charged with agreeing, in full and effective partnership with the Library, the appropriate proportions of annual spending on books, journal subscriptions, non-book items and document delivery from that fund, irrespective of format. This places the issue of decision-making as between CD-based and other (e.g. hard copy) formats squarely into the academic consciousness, so that they are compelled to be involved. Proportions of spending on non-book formats will naturally vary from School to School, depending not least upon the rate at which digital technology has penetrated into the subject area.

Pump-priming and matched funds are available at the Library's discretion, and have been applied to assist, for instance, in financing the start-up costs of some heavily front-loaded CD-ROM subscriptions (e.g. Historical Abstracts on CD), and in taking advantage of the discounted 'current plus archive disc' deals that often accompany start-up. It is also possible to split the attribution of costs between more than one School allocation, reflecting the natural community of interests in many titles. It has to be said that brokering these negotiations can sometimes be a complicated, delicate and long-winded business for the liaison librarians, requiring diplomatic skills not generally taught at library school.

The many academic libraries which have retained separate and undifferentiated periodical funds from which to purchase CD-ROM subscriptions, or which have established and retained a separate fund heading for buying 'electronic information', are spared some of these decisions, but have to make other decisions to ensure that the balance of their collections continues to match the needs of their users. It is clearly of paramount importance, in any case, to avoid committing sums to CD-ROM and related purchases without budgeting for the hardware to read them; many CD-ROM subscriptions, if not properly accessible for six months, will have wasted a four-figure subscription sum in the interim.

The role of liaison librarians, and identifying user needs and demands

At the University of Birmingham a crucial responsibility for identifying and assessing suitable electronic information products rests with the team of academic liaison librarians, who are graduate staff on academic grades – again, a fairly typical academic library arrangement. Organized on a broad subject basis, they themselves originate suggestions for CD-ROM titles, and field them as they arise in the academic departments. They coordinate and undertake their evaluation, calculate the relative merits of new and existing products, and collate information about their financial, technical and operational implications for presentation to academic and library colleagues. They can identify for academic staff the pros and cons of CD products over other format versions, and can back their judgment with the evidence of their regular dealings with staff and student users and the feedback they collect. They are carrying out what Webb has described as the task of the librarian of the future: 'to select the most appropriate information formats according to the content and usage of the information to be acquired. The library will increasingly become a mixture of books, video, CD-ROM, microform, digital and other technologies. Each will have its place in the libraries of the next century.'[1]

Liaison librarians will each typically be the 'lead person' assigned to see a new product through evaluation to implementation (see below). They act as the first line of reference in linking the commercially available CD-ROM sources to the academic teaching and research profile of each school – particularly important when external teaching audits such the AQE (Assessment of

Quality of Education) are laying special emphasis on IT skills training and student access to electronic sources.

A very significant proportion of suggestions for new databases are naturally initiated within academic departments; apart from anything else, publishers are encouraged to ensure that they advertise CD products directly to academics as well as to the Library, as an insurance policy. The network of external contacts which every academic cultivates can also often provide reference sites where CD-ROMs have already been loaded and tested. For example, our acquisition of the New York Public Library's CD catalogue of dance material, *Dance on disc,* and the collection of Latin and Greek texts produced on CD-ROM by the Packard Humanities Institute, both came about following the direct recommendation of academics who had used them either at the source site or some other institution.

Library staff can also be encouraged to indicate when they see that acquiring particular CD-ROM titles will raise the effectiveness of the Library's own internal services – by improving the quality of bibliographic data for book ordering, for instance, or by streamlining the efficiency of placing ILL requests. Installing and networking Book Data's *BookFind* and BLDSC's *Boston Spa serials* on CD-ROM here benefits library users, both in granting them direct searching access and in enhancing the performance of the Library's acquisition and document delivery departments.

The Electronic Information Sources Group

Five years of rapid development, during which the range of the library's CD-ROM resources were augmented to include LAN-based network delivery within the main library, demonstrated that the relevant divisions of our existing operating structure ran the risk of failing to coordinate planning in this area. The problem facing all libraries developing these services is to ensure that expertise in subject and product evaluation, acquisition and technical support is rigorously interlinked, so that commitments to networked titles, for example, are not undertaken without the proper budgeting necessary for additional optical towers, or so that Mac-only CD-ROMs are not purchased by oversight in a wholly PC-based environment.

Birmingham's solution to the handling of these relatively complex interactions was to set up in 1992/93, a cross-divisional Electronic Information Sources group. Its working tool was a standard form: a project action list for each new CD-ROM title by which the group could log and update its progress from the date it was proposed, through evaluation and decision-making on funding and networking, right up to the loading, testing and implementation of software, the preparation of documentation and guides, and the training of staff. Concurrently, the group carried out an important generic function, appropriate to any academic library environment, by steering developments such as the extension of the Library's CD network onto the campus WAN. Such projects have more than a technical significance: they require a programme of liaison, promotion, network registration and changes to levels of licensed concurrent usage, and this in turn needs as much synchronization as the vagaries of the average campus will allow.

Action lists gave an indication of the staff responsible at each stage, and milestones for the completion of steps, up to and including a 'launch date'. Copies could be regularly distributed to liaison staff by way of a progress report. Project-based methods of this type reap their rewards by treating each CD-ROM as a unique (and potentially uniquely troublesome) technical challenge. As platforms have stabilized, and as handling procedures have been regularized to allow for a set of defaults to be agreed and worked to (Windows rather than DOS-based, purchase via an agent/supplier rather than direct from publisher etc.), so the pressure for such a highly differentiated treatment has lessened.

Staff at Birmingham are now kept up to date on prospective purchases and on the arrival of demonstration discs for evaluation via the Library's Pegasus-based bulletin board, while set procedures govern the progress of the discs from unpacking to loading, and also ensure that, for instance, replaced or time-expired discs are destroyed or returned to their origin as required. The EIS group can now devote its attentions to broader issues; developing strategies for acquiring access to the whole gamut of electronic and digital information sources.

Product evaluation

A substantial literature[2] exists on which to ground a local programme of CD-ROM evaluation; the important elements clearly include:

- measures and judgments on the quality of the user interface, overall ease of use, consistency of search methods and data quality;
- analysis of the range of options for tagging, saving and downloading.

A standard and well-constructed evaluation form minimizes subjective variation in the assessment (at Birmingham participation in any one evaluation will typically be open to a range of library reading room and liaison staff, with invitations generally extended to interested user groups). The selection and evaluation process for CD-ROMs is most obviously important when heavy charges are attached to the prospective purchase, and the price of mis-selection is likely to be equally costly. However, with the proliferation of relatively cheap CD and multimedia products the option of arranging comprehensive pre-purchase evaluations in all cases ceases to make practical sense. The data in TFPL's 1995 CD-ROM Directory confirm a near-doubling over the previous year in the number of CD-ROMs costing under £100. The number of titles anticipated in the 1996 edition overall is now some 12,500.

Equally important in this context is the evidence for increased stability in the CD-ROM retrieval software market place; Richards[3] notes that the list of the top 20 CD-ROM retrieval software packages has remained virtually unchanged over 1995, again according to TFPL's data. However, what has not yet apparently happened is that the percentage of software packages associated with a large number of titles has significantly increased. The clear implication is that in many cases careful evaluation has to continue, and librarians have to remain prepared to serve their users by considering moves from one interface to another, in order to see databases better exploited. It was in this context that the University of Birmingham Library switched a collection of heterogeneous networked life science CD-ROMs to CD Plus (Ovid) in 1994, not for financial advantage, but in order to gain the benefit of a preferred common user interface. An evaluation trial also allows systems staff to test the practical networkability under a local configuration of products whose vendors can only otherwise give generalized assurances about network viability, and this is a further reason for continuing the practice, even as the number of such potential purchases rises. For this reason, if no other, there is a natural preference for extended trials as opposed to visiting demonstrations.

Acquisition, processing, licensing and decision-making

In this area the advantages of clearly constructed work-flow models can be very apparent, the more so (as we discovered) when overlaid on previously uncertain practices. We have locally favoured giving a member of staff responsibility for monitoring the progress of CD-ROM trials, which are formalized by the creation of dummy acquisition records while their term and date of completion is tracked in the acquisitions department. Information on standalone and networking costs (the latter for a range of numbers of concurrent users), the availability and cost of back years of serial products, discounts for parallel hard copy subscription, or additional charges for non-subscription to hard copy – this all needs to be gathered at the trial stage. General discounts obtainable through agents have also to be taken into account, and consortium purchasers like CHEST tested for the possibility of subsidized discounts.

CD-ROMS require special and precise treatment as they are put into stock, if accompanying updated manuals and software upgrades are not to go astray on their journey through cataloguing and information systems to their point of access, whether standalone, networked or loanable. Again, we employ the 'lead person' to take responsibility for ensuring that upgrades to software are reflected in product user guides. Practices vary as to how to treat the increasing number of CD-ROMs being produced as supplements to books and journals. With numbers of PCs containing CD drives similarly increasing on-campus and off, we have adopted the local option of issuing supplementary CD-ROMS on loan from a closed-access collection within our lending services, having barcoded them and taken the precaution of adding to each a copyright warning to discourage illicit copying and encourage close study of the Copyright, Designs and Patents Act 1988.

On licensing, the librarian's decisions are not made easier by the complexity and variety that publishers have introduced into their network pricing structures, which effectively prevent like-with-like comparisons. Rowley[4] succinctly outlines the marketing uncertainties that afflict CD suppliers, illustrates some of the tariffs variously applied to standalone, single and multiple concurrent users, and points out the range of interpretations of the term 'site'. Experience teaches that it is never unreasonable to try to negotiate an arrangement that suits one's local circumstances. Real difficulties come with licences that seek to specify numbers of designated network workstations in a campus environment, or where the use of a database is restricted to members of the institution, but physical access within the institution cannot be adequately so controlled.

What can and have been installed in these circumstances are robust and accurate manual booking systems for standalone databases; for these at least-access control is feasible. An important outcome of this sort of control, and of the more sophisticated software that is now widely available to control network use, is the regular analysis of the patterns of usage of CD-ROMS. From monthly accrued statistics, broken down by title and adjusted for term and vacation time, we can detect under-use of expensively networked files, and reach conclusions based on measured traffic about transfers to and from valuable slots in the networked optical towers. It is worth noting here the strong current movement in favour of pre-disk caching (already widely used, including at Birmingham) both to improve performance and replace the purchase of additional multiple CD-drives with general-purpose magnetic disk drives. Locally, this also offers a resolution of long-standing difficulties with networking Windows-based products, which in most other respects clearly represents the preferred interface. Monitoring systems also log occasions when upper licensing limits for concurrent users are reached, so that appropriate adjustments can be negotiated with licensors.

Conclusion

Accommodating to the changing information environment of the last decade, exemplified by the rise of the CD-ROM, has required academic libraries to be flexible and imaginative in their internal organization and in their relationships with users and suppliers. Forthcoming IT developments, such as the high-density optical disc and the cheap CD-R, will present further opportunities for them to demonstrate the adaptive powers developed in the CD-ROM revolution.

References

1   Webb, T. D.,'The frozen library: a model for twenty-first century libraries', *The electronic library*, 13 (1), 1995, 21–6.
2   Harry,V. and Oppenheim, C., 'Evaluations of electronic databases, Part 1: Criteria for testing CD-ROM products', *Online and CD-ROM review*, 17 (4), 1993, 211–22, is but one example.
3   Richards, T., 'Proliferation of CD-ROM retrieval software: stability at last?', *Computers in libraries*, 15 (10), 1995, 61–2.
4   Rowley, J., 'Issues in multiple use and network pricing for CD-ROMs', *The electronic library*, 13 (5), 483–7.

Case study 2: Public libraries
Heather Kirby

Introduction

The earlier history of CD-ROM in Croydon Libraries, and the rationale for introducing the service fully networked, with no standalone experience, was written down and published before full public access had been tested – that is before the opening of the new central library.[1] This new case study begins in October 1993, with the preparations to open the new library, and brings the story up-to-date.

Croydon Central Library is part of a large complex which incorporates a listed Victorian building and offers museum and arts facilities, including three exhibition galleries,workshops and a cinema. The library was designed for IT growth, with raised floors throughout the building, giving the flexibility to move power and data to where it is needed, and maximum opportunity to hook new services on to the LAN (an Ethernet twisted pair network), which is in turn bridged to the council's main network, a facility which would have been prohibitively expensive in the old building. None of this sounds very revolutionary now but it has given us a good start for experiments in wide-area networking, as well as the ability to cope with additional services such as open learning and PCs for hire, which began in March 1995.

The integrated reference and lending stock of half a million items is arranged in broad subject groupings on three of the four public floors (the fifth floor is used entirely for administration and staff facilities). Having the new museum service adjacent to the central library, in the clocktower complex, has increased demand and interest in relevant library resources, in particular the local studies and archives services, with which a shared database of holdings is being created.

The CD-ROM network

Hardware and access

During October 1993 the network was moved to level 3 of the new library, under the supervision of the member of the council's IT department who had usually provided technical support for our CD-ROM service. He was far more worried than we were about the security of the network and the vulnerability of the hardware when we were preparing to open the service to the public, so he loaded the hardware items with security tags, installed large datasafe locks on the floppy drives and locked the software down so tightly that ordinary upgrades became a nightmare to anyone else. Spare mice were ordered in anticipation though this proved quite unjustified as we have lost only one in two years.

At that time (November 1993) we had five public access PCs on the network plus one standalone for use with Extel Financial (because the networking charge for this was higher than we felt able to afford and the software was reputed to cause great problems on a network). Now there are eight public access PCs – seven on the network and still one standalone. In addition there is one PC on level 2 dedicated to Musicmaster (in advance of further extension of the network). Five workstations for staff use are sited in the three workrooms; four PCs in the resources and technical services section access the bibliographical menu on the network, and several senior staff have access to the network from their desks.

Printing

Printing is all done centrally with a very fast network printer in the workroom; users have to come to the desk to claim and pay for their printouts. Fairly soon it will be necessary to install at least one new network printer as additional public workstations are added. This scheme to control and monitor output was first devised to allay publishers' fears that we could not uphold copyright, but it is also an easy method of collecting small change (20p per A4 sheet) to support the service, which is otherwise entirely free.

The problems began with the many different ways of ordering a print on CD-ROMs and the fact that however a notice is worded and wherever it is placed, only a few users will read and act upon it so that a second printout is activated because nothing happened the first time, and so on. Our partially effective solution to this unnecessary waste is to run a print server monitor on which we can easily delete multiple jobs from one workstation as they are added, but before they enter the printer memory. When all the staff are busy, duplicates are not always picked up in time, but even so the system saves a considerable amount of paper and ink.

Centralized printing was also favoured on the grounds that the less hardware available to the public, the fewer the maintenance problems we might have to tackle.

Network upgrades

Soon after moving into the new library we began discussions about upgrading the network server and getting rid of some of the old equipment –at this time we had a Fenwood server with 21 drives and our original Attica tower of ten drives, both running Ultranet software attached to a fileserver with Novell 3.11 netware. It all worked together surprisingly well, but some of the drives in the small tower were dying and we needed expansion space for new titles, so we purchased eight gigabytes of hard disk to go into the new server and began pre-caching existing databases and new disks. The DOS version of Ultranet had a stacker system which contained more than 20 titles on that hard disk, turning pre-caching into a storage space saver which also greatly improved the speed of access. These changes were made during February 1994.

Early in 1995 the server was upgraded again, this time to NT status, with an additional 27 gigabytes of hard disk, which was more than first estimated but enlarged because we seemed to be making a habit of running out of space. The new NT version of Ultranet has proved very friendly to use, operating in Windows and speaking plain language most of the time so that non-technical staff can carry out simple tasks through it. The management information it provides is far more extensive, or perhaps more intelligible than that given by the earlier DOS version, especially the statistics of use, which now tell us daily, weekly, monthly, how frequently and for how long each title is accessed. It also details the activity of each user, and this will become interesting and important as an aid to guessing licensing requirements for the expansion of the network .

Maintenance

In March 1995 an IT Officer was appointed to keep all the public access IT services running efficiently – the CD-ROM network, PCs for hire; open learning and any similar new developments; but excluding the GEAC library management system, which has its own systems librarian. Previously we had been dependent on the council's willing but very busy IT help desk, whereas we now have the benefit of technical knowledge and experience which is consistent and nearly always on hand. This gives the frontline staff confidence and it saves an enormous amount of time – two factors which are becoming increasingly important as the network grows and other services are added round it. The person appointed to this post brought many other skills to the job, and has already been of great assistance in extending the network and planning future developments.

Selecting and buying CD-ROMs

There are now 35 titles and more than 78 discs on the network, arranged in ten subject groups on the menu, for example: company information (*Corporate America, Euro Kompass, Extel financial, Kompass UK, McCarthy* CD-ROM); official publications (*Hansard HC, Statutory instruments SI-CD, UKOP, OSH-UK*); legal (*Weekly law, CCH tax reporter*). Users seem to find it easy to see which sub-menu (and within that which title) they need to search, and there is now no apparent distinction between those discs with a DOS interface and those running in Windows. The new NT server has removed the need for a complicated array of icons, together with all the opportunities for mischief that a desktop screen offered. The new menu still has one unfortunate invitation to exit the system and, although there is very little scope to do anything but ask staff to logon again, we have put on our wish list to Fenwood a request that this could be hidden. Apart from that problem the menu is well designed, clear and the format can be customized to a degree.

Our criteria for selection have so far remained constant – to extend the range and improve the quality of the reference resources we make available through: the superior search facilities offered on a good CD-ROM; economy of data storage; additional content not previously held in this library; the cumulation of updates; the currency of information, which, with weekly and monthly updates, now comes much closer to an online service; and the speed of access to data on a disc. For example: *BNI* (*British newspaper index*) indexes eight important daily and weekly papers; *McCarthy* on CD-ROM provides full text articles on business and industry from journals which we do not stock; *Hansard* stores a complete session of parliament on one disc and renders unnecessary the preservation and binding of daily parts; *CCH tax reporter* updates for us and prevents the unscrupulous from removing useful sections, as they sometimes did from the looseleaf volumes.

With the next expansion phase new criteria will be added to the list to embrace multimedia for all areas, especially for the children's services.

For CD-ROM our acquisitions procedures are less regimented than those we use for book buying. Sometimes publishers write or phone with pre-publication details, wanting to discuss prices and offering demonstrations or trial discs for limited periods, usually at the least convenient times. There is often an element of haggling, which would be unthinkable in our normal stock buying, but has in the past achieved very favourable conditions for us as a public library. Occasionally we discover a new CD-ROM, or reassess an earlier title in response to a user's suggestion, and contact the publishers ourselves to clarify details of software, prices and networking conditions.

In general we would always ask to try a disc before buying, and we keep a standalone CD-ROM drive for this purpose because some publishers are nervous about our test-running discs on the network, though others give full permission. It is very important to ascertain that a disc will run smoothly on a network, so if networking cannot be tested before purchase, there should be a 'money back' guarantee if a network version has been promised. The process takes much longer than choosing a book or serial, and far bigger sums of money are involved in most cases – unfortunately price is the deciding factor far too often, because many titles are quite outside our range, if not absolutely overpriced.

The user response

The enquiry desk on level 3 receives an average of 300 CD-ROM enquiries per month (this is not to be confused with the amount of use made of titles on the network, which is well labelled, can be accessed free, and is open for anyone to approach and start to explore without booking or asking staff). The majority of those coming to the desk ask for help to start searching, or for information on the databases available; some, mainly businesses, request a search to be carried out by staff as a charged service. This last has become popular as a cheap alternative to an online search – clearly inferior in currency and sometimes in the level of detail, but apparently acceptable for some purposes.

Some databases, particularly the company information titles, are in use almost all the 52 hours the library is open, the most notable example being *Kompass UK*, followed closely by *Corporate America*, *McCarthy* and *MAPS*, a market research database.

A steady stream of comment forms comes through, suggesting new titles, asking when we are going to have particular discs, requesting more workstations to access the CD-ROM, and occasionally expressing surprise that we lack a particular title or facility. This is one indication that some sort of revolution has occurred in that many of our users are now taking for granted the availability of the CD-ROM network and all the information it provides to them at first hand, whereas most of them had no previous access to databases and only a few had ever had an online search done. There is a large and growing user base, possessing good search skills and knowledge of the content of many CD-ROM databases. The CD-ROM network has helped many of these regular users to develop a capability for independent research.

During the first few months after the opening of the new library two separate, very small surveys were done with some of the CD-ROM network users: one of these, carried out by Colette Batterbee and mentioned in Chapter 6 of this book,[2] produced even then a cluster of responses asking for more titles to be provided; and in general, very favourable comments on the one-to-one assistance provided by members of the staff. At that early stage some of the staff were themselves struggling to keep up with developments in the new library, since the increase in visits, issues, enrolment and requests had been extraordinarily high from the first month; it has not subsided much since then. They were also still learning to manage the public access side of the CD-ROM service in addition to assimilating a number of new discs, each with different software. It was only about 18 months ago that significant clusters of discs began to form round one piece of software, several of the newspapers being amongst the first of our holdings to take this very sensible step. This process has continued as publishers come to realize that, far from removing the competitive edge of their product, adopting familiar, tried-and-tested software is a strong selling point to a busy librarian, and the benefits will increase as demand supports further work by software developers.

User education

In addition to the very significant commitment on the part of all the staff on level 3 to offering generous one-to-one assistance, the network has been demonstrated extensively, both to visiting groups with very general interests, and to those with specific needs such as school groups with set projects. It is always included in the visit programme for job clubs and training for work schemes, and all these people are very quick to see the potential and eager to use the databases. It is our intention to spread these opportunities by inviting further visits – we are approached for approximately three per month – and also by giving remote access to the network as soon as possible.

Croydon Small Business Club, which meets in the library and is supported by IBC (Information for Business in Croydon; Croydon Libraries' business information service on level 3 of the Central Library), always draws its largest audience for the meetings at which library staff introduce and demonstrate the CD-ROM network, in particular new titles and hints on how to search. It is very difficult to prise members away from the workstations afterwards, even with the lure of refreshments. The response was just as enthusiastic when we invited the Croydon and South London Chamber of Commerce to a similar event.

Demonstrations of the network and presentations about CD-ROM have been given to groups of colleagues from various council departments; to council members; to staff from other sections of Croydon Libraries; and to visiting colleagues from library authorities throughout the UK as well as some from overseas. The response has always been very enthusiastic, both about the resources offered and the functioning of the network.

One of the most exciting (because unexpected) uses of the CD-ROM was as an introduction, for foreign students, to the library and its services. Some of the local tutors of English as a second language courses bring groups of students to be shown the library and some of the stock and facilities which might be relevant to their studies. We are usually asked to teach these people, who are mainly refugees with very little understanding of English, how to use the OPAC and find books in the library, yet there is no recognition of how difficult the terminology on an OPAC can be. On the spur of the moment I showed the Times and Guardian to a few of these students, finding pictures and news about their own countries, and immediately broke through all language barriers. In a matter of minutes they were searching and moving around the entries with great speed and flair, which suggests that the software for these CD-ROMs is far more intuitive, not just better looking than that used for most OPACs. Suddenly the group was relaxed, genuinely busy and eager, so that we began to talk spontaneously, if with few words, about what they should do and see.

There will be many more opportunities for using the CD-ROM network imaginatively in training and user education: the work described above is merely the beginning. A new programme of demonstrations is being put together for 1996, linked with the steps to expand the network to new sites, but such work needs more time than is usually available, together with versatile presentation skills.

Problems

Technical

Technical problems grow as the system grows, with new problems for old on a regular basis. In February 1995 we lost the complication of running three servers but became guinea pigs for the NT installation, which took several weeks instead of several days. Croydon was the first Ultranet NT installation at a UK site. The problem solving went on continuously with data going back and forth between Fenwood and the Austrian base, all done at top speed in order to get us running and stabilized. The network ran but then without warning the public workstations fell over one after another, and for the first time since launching the network we were forced to put up 'out of order' notices, which stayed up for several days. We were near despair as we saw our reputation for solid, reliable running of the network seeping away, and wondered why we had considered upgrading to NT. Whatever was wrong with the DOS version of Ultranet?

Of course, within a week of full functionality staff morale rose to its old level, and continued to rise as we grew accustomed to the transparency of a Windows server and a unified menu, together with greater speed and very reassuring stability. In retrospect one can always say that insufficient testing was done before 'going live' on a public access site, but in our case we can at least say that the commitment and determination of the engineers working on our installation could not have been surpassed.

Previously we had assistance from several of the council's IT staff and now we have our own IT officer. In both cases Fenwood's technical experts have always been very accommodating, willing to discuss problems over the phone, or arrange to visit the site and work with our staff. There was never any difficulty about our taking up only their software maintenance agreement, whilst providing our own hardware support. There are undoubted benefits to library staff in having dedicated technical assistance on site and it is worth saying here how much this person has achieved towards the up-to-dateness and stability of the network. We, and I suppose many other public librarians, have never been able to take such staffing for granted.

Licensing

This has always been a headache. Every publisher has a different idea about their rights, many of them inventing tortuous solutions to non-existent problems – dongles, print credits locally assigned notwithstanding a network licence for three concurrent users; local workstation numbers to unlock the data on a networked disc; new passwords with every monthly update – and some of them clearly expecting librarians to cheat outrageously.

Some publishers still count fixed workstations on a network, rather than concurrent users. Others say that you may network the disc and charge accordingly, even though they have not purchased the network version of the software to make the disc. Some convert to the generally accepted system of bands of concurrent users, but then put up their prices.

For a librarian trying to protect free public access to CD-ROM (which is an ideal medium for the layperson, and perhaps no less ideal for an expert) and attempting to share it efficiently on a network, the only certainty is that prices will rise when they should come down. Chadwyck-Healey for one may have come to regret its generosity to public libraries (for which it was much admired, and promoted by us) as all our recent subscription renewals have come with LAN surcharges for more than one user. Some might say we have been spoilt in the past, having been the first public library in the country to network CD-ROM, but we have also done a fair job of promotion for the publishers of the discs we run since colleagues from nearly all the library authorities in England have talked to us or come to look at our network.

Leasing data and requiring the return of the previous disc is an unattractive practice which has not yet caused us any problems, but might in the future if anything untoward happened to our budgets. Most publishers (examples include Context and ILI) who indulge in this method charge enough for an annual subscription to be able to let a library keep the final disc should the renewal not be affordable every year, but they would probably disagree.

These and many other aspects of licensing and electronic copyright are being researched and discussed widely, and this may lead to some model agreements and conditions of use which could be very beneficial to all libraries.

Software

This has been discussed in relation to the selection of CD-ROM titles. Our users now seem to find much of the software very intuitive and there is less need for any detailed instructions. Those who remember the original DOS interface for the Independent newspaper which required a user to type 'OPEN THE_INDEPENDENT' (and it was case sensitive) can see that progress has been made.

We now provide as a handout a comprehensive annotated list of titles to give users an idea of the content of the discs on the network, and place by the workstations reference copies of very brief hints on how to search, just to get people started. When we began networking CD-ROM we had ten titles and ten quite different interfaces to learn, so written instructions were essential for staff and public.

Upgrades are no longer a problem because we have an expert on hand to load them and sort out the consequences for the network, but some run smoothly and others cause him to phone the producers repeatedly.

Security

As already hinted we have had no real problems in this area. One user with too much spare time managed to write a couple of screens full of free verse on SI-CD and save it so that it came up in the search screen on every workstation, but this was comic rather than threatening. We are helped by the high level of activity in most areas of the library and the popularity of the CD-ROM workstations, which leaves little scope for planned vandalism. Would-be hackers are everywhere, no doubt but we have so far been lucky or beneath contempt. The latter possibility is a very comforting idea.

There will be new areas of concern in the future, as we proceed with plans to wide-area network and to make our CD-ROM available through our community network on the Internet but the details have still to be worked out.

Wide area experiments

Council access

In August 1995, in response to a request from council members, a connection to the CD-ROM network was opened in the Members' Library, following an evening's introduction and demonstration. Twelve Members were assigned user names and passwords, and five more joined during the following few weeks. During this trial period the personal user names have enabled us to evaluate the use made of the network, and not surprisingly, a couple of names have never been logged in while several other members have searched extensively, sometimes out of our opening hours, pointing to an additional benefit of access from their own accommodation.

Since then test sites have been established in several council departments – Environmental Health, Education, and Press and Public Relations. Well-used and popular, they have so far caused no problems and have taken very little of the IT officer's time, beyond half an hour to open the connections and add new users to the network.

The above expansion of the network has been possible without any new costs because the buildings are linked physically and the Central Library's LAN is connected to the council's network, and through that to all the departmental LANs. It has been useful to prove the system in this way, and we will be offering the opportunity to other council departments as soon as possible, but we now need to concentrate on more difficult but very high priority areas.

Local libraries

Plans have been made and budgets are being looked into urgently so that we can begin to deliver some of the electronic resources, at present concentrated in the Central Library, to our 12 local libraries. They are online to the Central Library for the GEAC system but this link, already slower than it should be, needs to be upgraded if it is to carry other services including the CD-ROM network, the Community Information database and Internet access. Already the NT server enables us to run databases other than CD-ROM across the network, such as the Community Information which appears as an ordinary item on the menu. We shall shortly be providing Croydon's Electronic Business Register by the same method as well as making it available on Croydon Online on the Internet.

Other organizations

Several schools and colleges have approached us because they would like to have access to the CD-ROM network in their own libraries. Some of these sites are being included in the first phase of our wide-area plans, to be implemented in parallel with giving access to branch libraries in the same districts of the borough.

The business community, and many organizations in the voluntary sector, are also interested in gaining remote access to our services, including once again the CD-ROM network, but how we make this possible will be the subject matter of the next part of Croydon's case history.

The future of the network

Having established and developed the CD-ROM network, we have created widespread demand for access to it. The future of the network will depend on its evolution as a part of a much larger community network for Croydon and we can say now that we have seen this future and we like it.

References

1   Kirby, H. G., 'Public library case study: CD-ROM at Croydon Central Library'. In Hanson, T. and Day, J. (eds.), *CD-ROM in libraries: management issues*, Bowker-Saur, 1994, 217–32.
2   Batterbee, C., 'Open access CD-ROM in public libraries', *Aslib proceedings*, 47 (3), 1995, 63–72.

Case study 3: Special libraries
Peter Bysouth and Maureen Sullivan

Introduction

Glaxo Wellcome is a major multinational research-based pharmaceutical group of companies whose mission it to discover, develop, manufacture and market innovative, safe and effective medicines.

The published information needs of its UK R&D scientists are met primarily by the information service department, which has a dedicated team of information professionals whose role includes handling specific scientific, technical and business enquiries, providing current awareness services, and training end-users to exploit electronic information sources.

Introduction and use of CD-ROMs

The R&D environment

Within the research-based pharmaceutical industry, the use of information and its value to the organization is of great importance. Further, within the Glaxo Wellcome R&D environment, access to and use of information is vital so that the organization not only keeps up-to-date with developments in the scientific area, but also creates a culture of creativity. That is, a piece of information can be intrinsically useful, but can also cause the germ of other ideas to form. Therefore the argument is that access to the relevant information, by all levels of the organization, will foster that culture of creativity. The core problem has not been access to information, but remains the ease of retrieval and further use of information. Therefore our aim was, and continues to be, to increase the use of published information by the scientific research staff.[1]

End-user searching

When the information services department of Glaxo Research and Development in the UK carried out a preliminary survey, it found that its research scientists had certain reservations about information scientists being barriers to information, and that they would be prepared to carry out searches themselves if the appropriate tools were available. Of a few front-ends available and evaluated[2] at that time, the DIALOG Medical Connection (DMC) was chosen as matching most of the requirements for accessing a restricted number of databases available on the online host DIALOG – amongst the key databases were MEDLINE, Biosis and SciSearch. We initially trained 49 staff and found that most of them aimed to do only quick, simple searching.[3] Because a sample of the scientists accepted this we extended our programme and currently have 150 active users.

Later we considered MEDLINE on CD-ROM as a single source which would meet some of the information needs of a large number of our research scientists. Results from our pilot study of a standalone version of MEDLINE on CD-ROM, situated in each of our two main site libraries, demonstrated a very positive response. So from that start in 1990, we networked MEDLINE in 1992, with unrestricted access to all staff in the UK company.[4] Currently we have a mixed population of end-users. For example, chemists have been trained to search Chemical Abstracts online, and other chemical databases utilizing MDL's REACCS and MACCS software. A number of biologists and chemists still continue to use DMC to access a small number of databases. All staff have access to MEDLINE and some to ENTREZ (both networked) and a number of additional CD-ROMs (on standalone PCs) available in the main UK site libraries.

Impact on information services

Impact on expenditure

One of the initially perceived benefits of the CD-ROM was that it offered a cheap, fixed-price alternative to the traditional pay-as-you-use online information services. This led to its early take-up by many libraries in universities and hospital medical schools. This general perception has not been borne out within our own organization, where despite subscribing to over 30 CD-ROM titles we have not seen our overall online expenditure decrease.

This can partly be explained by the fact that many of the CD-ROM titles that we take do not in fact have an online equivalent. Even with MEDLINE on CD-ROM, many end-user searchers continue to search the online version. In addition, it is certainly true in our environment that CD-ROMs are still far from being the preferred medium for the information professional where a traditional online alternative exists.

It has been our experience over many years that each technological advance – for example end-user menu-driven online searching, standalone CD-ROM and networked CD-ROM – has added further to our expenditure. We have concluded that each advance appears to satisfy the needs and/or aptitudes of a different segment of our end-user population.

Figure 3.3.1 shows an idealized representation of how new technologies have affected spending on, and access to, information within Glaxo Wellcome per se, and the effects on the information experts.

Impact on services

At several times we have evaluated the impact of the introduction of databases on CD-ROM on the level of our services. We have looked more closely at trends in the three areas we considered most likely to be affected. These were our enquiry service, our interlibrary loan service, and our book-buying service.

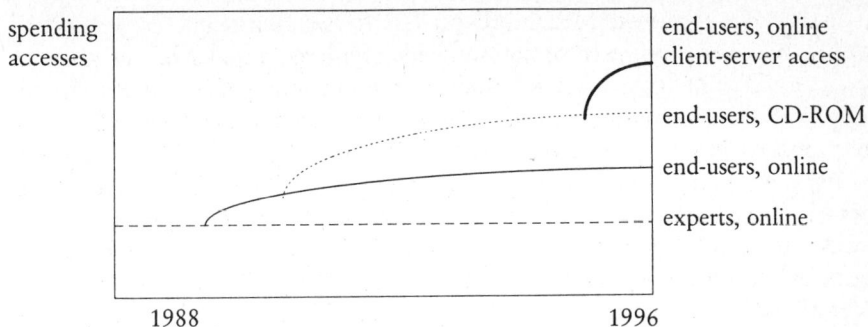

Fig. 3.3.1   *Representation of the effect of new methods to access information*

Enquiry services

When we networked MEDLINE, so removing the 'geographical' barrier, the number of accesses climbed steadily as it was released to more user departments, and it now has approximately seven times as many accesses a month compared to the standalone version. One reason for the growth in usage of the networked MEDLINE is the availability at the user's desktop compared to that in a site library, however short the distance from the work location.

We anticipated that the introduction of MEDLINE on CD-ROM would have a dramatic impact on our enquiry services, in particular its biomedical component. We have seen neither any reduction in requests such as we might have expected, nor any growth as a result of increased awareness of 'information' on the part of the end-users. Instead we have seen a steady levelling of the number of requests, and at the same time a plateauing in the number of accesses to MEDLINE on our standalone PC's.

Figure 3.3.2 shows the increase in the number of accesses to MEDLINE on CD-ROM from when initially launched in July 1990. Note the increased usage seen when the database became available on our network in November 1992, and as it was subsequently released in a phased manner to different departments.

At the time of our introduction of DMC, the increasing demand on our enquiry service since 1989,[3] was slowed, but the subsequent introduction of databases on CD-ROM does not seemed to have reduced demand on the service any further, and over the past three years the demand on our 'expert' enquiry service has remained fairly constant. The reasons for this profile are hard to explain, but do suggest that we have one population of users who will always want to use an intermediary for information retrieval, while a second population will prefer to do it themselves. The use of the database on CD-ROM could also reflect the users' preference for searching for what they consider 'trivial' information, which they would not have asked an intermediary to search for in the past. They may also be more willing to browse electronically through the literature for new ideas.

Reflective number of accesses

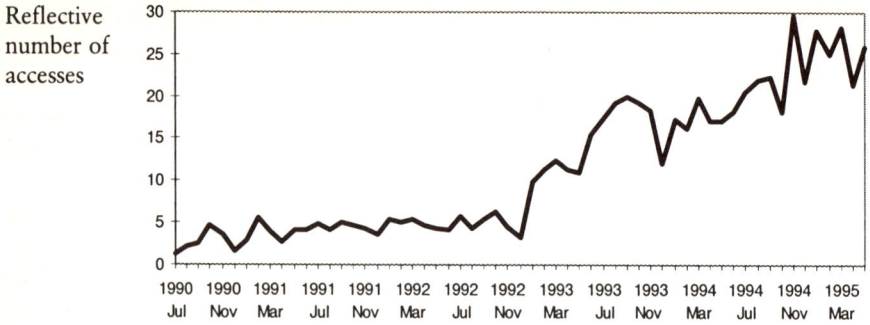

Fig. 3.3.2 *Access to MEDLINE*

We analysed the complexity of enquiries received from the two different populations of end-users in 1991. Enquiries that we carried out for these two groups were classified as being 'simple' or 'complex' by using the following broad criteria: author search, details of a reference, time spent on the search, sources used, free-text *v.* database indexing. The results from the population groups showed that there was a higher percentage of 'simple' enquiries from the group where there was little end-user searching available. From the other group, where there was a large end-user searching population, a higher percentage of 'complex' enquiries was received. The assumption made by us was that the end-users were tackling the simple searches themselves. Overall this has meant that, although the absolute number of enquiries has not increased, we now, as experts, carry out 'complex' ones.

Figure 3.3.3 shows the increases in number of accesses to MEDLINE, compared to the static number of searches carried out by information 'experts'.

Interlibrary loan service

Given the greater access to information, we also looked at the effect this had

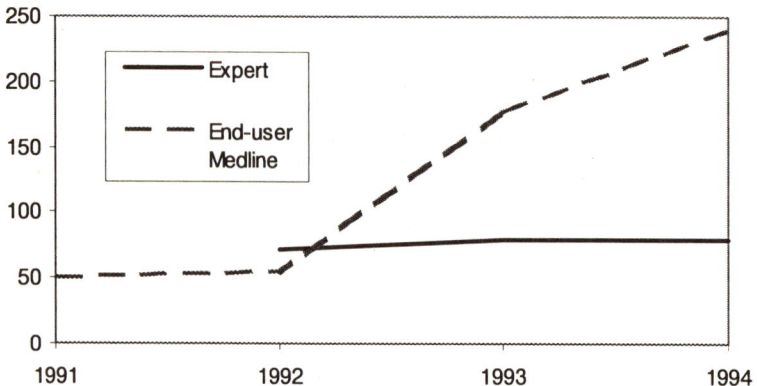

Fig. 3.3.3 *Relative trends in annual totals for Expert searches, and end-user MEDLINE accesses*

on the users' requests for loans of the articles from journals we did not stock in the site libraries. We have found that the actual number of requests over the first few years after allowing our users access to DMC has remained fairly constant. The reasons for this could be either that, of the references retrieved from search, the users only looked at those references already in stock, or that the users now had access to the author abstracts and could therefore make a more informed decision about the value of the references to them. However, since we networked MEDLINE we have seen an increase in loans, which appears to mirror the increase in MEDLINE use directly.

Figure 3.3.4 shows a similar upward trend in both interlibrary loans and MEDLINE accesses over a four year period, suggesting that access to information via MEDLINE resulted in more loans.

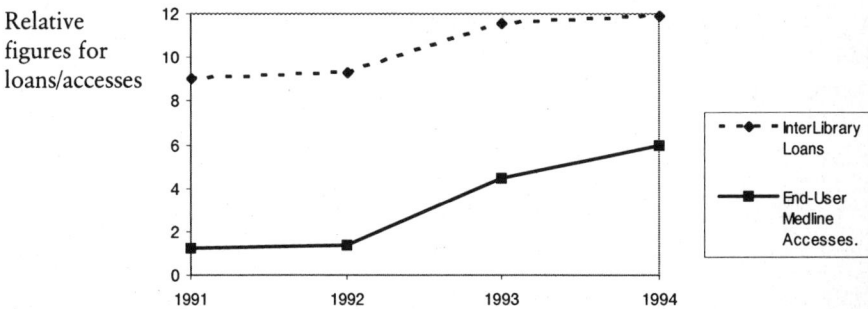

Fig. 3.3.4 *Relative increases in interlibrary loans and MEDLINE accesses*

Book purchasing

Increased awareness of 'information' might also have been reflected in the number of books that the company was buying. This has not in fact happened and the book purchases have not increased dramatically.

Figure 3.3.5 represents the trend in book purchases compared with the trend in access to MEDLINE. Although MEDLINE accesses increased, there was not a similar increase in book purchases.

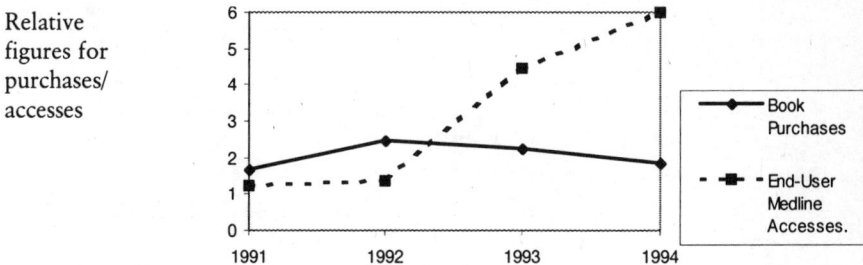

Fig. 3.3.4 *Relative changes in book purchasing compared to MEDLINE accesses*

Impact on the information professional

Just as the initial introduction of end-user online searching had worried our specialist searchers, so the introduction of CD-ROMs caused a second wave of fear to ripple through the information professional's world. Making information available directly to the end-user to search in an attractive manner seemed to suggest that the information professional as intermediary was no longer needed. This has proved unfounded within the company, and after some initial doubts most of the information professionals have had experience of training users in one or several of the CD-ROM packages that we have. Our role as expert intermediary searchers has not been reduced,[5] but as expert searchers we have found that CD-ROM databases do have limitations for our own use.

Two of the greatest strengths that we had as information professionals were knowledge of sources of information and knowledge of our users. The knowledge of sources, and ways to search them to obtain the best results, are now valued by the end-users. Within Glaxo Wellcome in the UK, we have found that it is important to understand the benefits and limitations of the sources, and also to be able to evaluate the software running on the CD-ROM databases. Our information professionals have then applied the knowledge and analysis to other evaluations that we have carried out on other databases and software.

We also had an understanding of our end-users' information needs, but needed to improve this so that we could tailor our training search examples to these needs. Because we have had to impart to the end-user our knowledge of the best way to search a database, training and teaching skills have been added to our armoury of skills. In addition, writing skills have also become valuable, as we have had to compile training manuals and quick guides for the different systems that we use.

We are still in the position of carrying out a significant number of literature searches for users. We took a critical look at our enquiry service and have started to look at ways to add value to the information that we give to our users when answering their enquiries.

Over all we have found a significant shift in what we do as information professionals. The ability to take on new skills is paramount. We play a large role in 'education' in the sense that we carry out training, write guides, devise publicity material, and pass on relevant technical knowledge to our users. A return to online may be the next step, with the introduction of client-server systems, which are now being marketed direct to the end-users. Perhaps we need to be less protective of our jobs and information, and to welcome change and look to ways to enhance our job and help the users manage the volume of information retrieved. Many articles have been written about the threat of the new information age on the information professional, but all of them suggest that instead of accepting extinction, we need to be more welcoming of the new technology. The title of a recent article 'Do or die' hints at extinction for information professionals who are not willing to embrace the changes.[6]

Impact on the end-user

Our users have taken avidly to MEDLINE on CD-ROM. As we have moved from having MEDLINE on standalone PCs, and onto a network, we have seen the use of the database increase dramatically. The decision to network this database was taken primarily because of the scientists' need to access information at their own desktop, and also because the technology allowed users to be more effective and efficient in searching for information. Not surprisingly, we have found this same trend with other databases we have networked – the number of accesses increases considerably. What CD-ROM has done for our end-users is to offer convenient and relatively easy access and simple searching of individual databases.

However, our end-user searchers were quick to spot deficiencies in the system and were soon asking for enhancements such as cross-file searching, a link with our journal holdings, and from there a link to our interlibrary loans system. More importantly, the introduction of CD-ROMs has required a knowledge of different search interfaces and how to exploit them – this may be one of the reasons why our end-users carry out very simple searches since they may remember simple ways to search each of the systems. Bearing all the limitations in mind, we believe our end-users now have access to more and more information.

Networking issues

Technical issues

So many articles have been written about the difficulties of installing CD-ROMs, CD players, and more recently CD networks, that it is astonishing that they have gained the popularity that they have.[7–9] Initially when we introduced MEDLINE on CD-ROM on a standalone PC, we experienced all the technical problems which have been mentioned in many articles, but it has meant that we have had to gain a modicum of new technical skills, which could be re-used when we brought more CD-ROM titles into the company.

We have a dedicated file-server for MEDLINE, and we are fortunate to have been able to call on in-house technical support to fit it into the existing company network topology. This technical support we enjoy is vital, but we have been unable to assess the total costs, which consist of capital expenditure for the equipment, plus ongoing maintenance costs. MEDLINE was the first database that we installed, but it does have drawbacks in that it is such a large database that it is on several discs which the user has to search individually. Further, once the novelty of the CD-ROM has worn off, our users have asked for improvements to the software and the features that it has. As we have introduced more databases on CD-ROM, the users have then been faced with learning the new front-ends so as to be able to get to the information, which is an obvious drawback for the user.

Licensing issues

It is a fact that many CD-ROM products are licensed rather than sold to a would-be purchaser. The licence, however, covering a specific period of time (usually 12 months), will often entitle the subscriber to any periodic updates issued by the publisher during the subscription period.

One should always consult closely the terms and conditions of any such licence[10] as producers can withhold a variety of rights that would normally be granted to a buyer of, say, a book. The rights granted under a specific licence can vary markedly according to whether the subscriber intends the CD-ROM to be for single-user access only or networked either by LAN or WAN.

Once subscribers move to networking CD-ROM products, they are liable to be faced with a plethora of varying metrics used to determine the inevitably increased licence fee. The subscriber may need to know the potential user population for the particular CD-ROM, the number of PCs on their network, and whether their IT colleagues can guarantee that a specified maximum number of simultaneous users cannot be exceeded. These problems are increased, as is the licence fee, for the multisite subscriber, who is faced with a variety of definitions of what actually constitutes a site and with the need to know the radius of the particular site or whether a given PC is within so many miles or kilometres of the server. A subscriber from a multisite, multinational organization operating a WAN that crosses national borders is faced with a particularly challenging licensing situation.

One early frustration for licensees was the necessity, as frequently demanded by the supplier, to return outdated discs to them or face updates being withheld. Gradually this has changed to a more sensible requirement to guarantee that one should physically damage any superseded disc before disposal. Most recently we have experienced the arrival of inbuilt clocks that prevent further usage after the producer-set time limit has expired. This creates a new source of anguish within the information centre as discs can now 'expire' before the producer or distributor delivers the next update!

Pricing issues

It was estimated in 1989 that mastering a CD-ROM cost around $1500 and production and documentation a mere $2 and $1 respectively.[11] However, publishers had to face reduced sales revenue earned from online royalties[12] or hard copy indexes. Thus the increased or even equal pricing for CD-ROM versions of print products is a concept that troubles customers,[13] given their perception of the cheapness and ease with which data, already in electronic form, can be distributed via the silver disc.

One could argue that the pricing of information should be independent of the medium. Many subscribers question the practice of being charged a comparable price twice (even allowing for print-subscriber discounts and search engines on CD-ROM) for taking delivery of the same information on two different media.

The reason most often used to explain the introduction of CD-ROMs is that of cost – they offer a way to control costs, and with changes in technology we have been able to increase access to the CD-ROMs across our networks. Choosing CD-ROM as a delivery medium can be expensive in the 'hidden' costs of hardware, software and licences.[14]

The future of CD-ROMs

As a means to access data in an easy and colourful manner, CD-ROMs have initially been a step forward from online systems, but their existence may now depend on the advances made in accessing online databases via client-server systems. Measured against an 'ideal' specification for a distributed database, databases on CD-ROM have not been able to match up for technological, commercial and practical reasons.[15] Given all the hype when CD-ROM was introduced, it may remain in the library landscape for the medium term, but there are some who now question its long-term future,[15–16] and others who view it as a replacement for printed material rather than an alternative to other forms of electronic information[17] but nevertheless a 'useful and attractive technology'.[14]

The advantages of online in terms of searching speed, currency and range of subject databases means that online may regain its supremacy, providing charging policies for pay-as-you-use are changed. The growth of the Internet (30 million users) shows that end-users are prepared to use new technology to access information, and once the initial novelty has worn off, users will want to be directed to useful sources, and if possible the answers to questions. They will want easy access and simple pricing of the information that they need.[15] SciFinder™ is a client-server system which provides a graphical user interface to Chemical Abstracts online. We have just started using this within the company and will eventually be able to look at the absolute costs per user. What shall we compare them with? The costs of searching hard copy (time)? The costs of searching online (time and money)? The unknown costs of not having the information?

Technological advances have resulted in an increase in the capacity of magnetic discs, so that the advantage that CD-ROMs initially had, in terms of storage capacity, has been reduced. Magnetic discs have other advantages, but the main one is faster access times, so reducing the CD-ROM to a delivery medium.[16]

Discussion

Within Glaxo Wellcome, the use of databases on CD-ROM has been important, and has certainly made information more accessible to our end-users. On closer examination, though, most of the databases are CD-ROM alternatives to print versions of the data, so what CD-ROM has done is to make access to the information easier and more attractive for end-users. There is probably plenty of growth in this area and CD-ROM will remain a viable medium.

It is a different matter when the spotlight is on large databases which have traditionally been available via dial-up to an online host. Here CD-ROM is more limiting because of the variety of front-ends available, and also the access times to the data. Accessibility has been purchased at the expense of standardization of the means to access information. What we have found within the company is that CD-ROM has become more of a delivery mechanism for certain databases. The breadth of databases offered by online hosts has been matched by only a few CD-ROM producers. What users require is a seamless interface to several databases, pointers to which database is suitable for which type of question, and delivery of the information to their desktop. This limitation with CD-ROM sources will remain, and for the professional users online will remain the access method of choice although it too has its limitations.

Perhaps more interesting is the shift on the part of some producers of CD-ROMs into becoming more like traditional online 'hosts'. The issue then returns to the old question of access/response times and availability of sources. Here then, the client-server environment is likely to become more important, and with reasonable pricing policies for the clients and for use of information, online may become the method of choice for end-users who need access to large databases. So CD-ROM is likely to have a place for small libraries, for niche databases, and for directory sources.

References

1 Bysouth, P. T., *End-user searching: the effective gateway to published information,* Aslib, 1990, 93–104.
2 Bysouth, P. T., *End-user searching: the effective gateway to published information,* Aslib, 1990, 105–25.
3 Boyd, T., Warne, K. and Bysouth, P. T., *End-user searching: the effective gateway to published information,* Aslib, 1990, 125–34.
4 Sullivan, M., *Information systems for end-users: research and development issues,* Taylor-Graham, 1992, 71–8.
5 Oppenheim, C., *Librarianship and information work worldwide 1991: an annual survey,* Bowker-Saur, 1991, 1–14.
6 Medhurst, J., 'Do or die: The librarian in the 21st century', *Managing information,* 2 (9), 1995, 30–1.
7 Brakel, P. A., 'Implications of networking CD-ROM databases in a research environment', *South African journal of library and information science,* 61 (1), 1993, 28–34.
8 Cain, M., 'Simple and inexpensive CD-ROM networking: a step-by-step approach', *Information technology and libraries,* 12 (2), 1993, 262–9.
9 Kratzert, M. Y., 'Installation of a CD-ROM local area network: the untold story', *Learned Information: Proceedings 12th National Online Meeting,* 1991, 201–7.
10 Brandt Jensen, M. and Jensen, M. B., 'CD-ROM licenses: what's in the fine or nonexistent print may surprise you', *CD-ROM professional,* 4 (2), 1991, 13–16.
11 Sirkin, A. F., 'Librarians in the 21st century: endangered species or future chief information officer?', *SLA specialist,* 15 (10), 1992, 1–3.

12 Levin, C. S., 'CD-ROM pricing: line for some new ideas. A proposal for a radical restructuring of the pricing of library CD-ROM products', *CD-ROM professional*, 3 (6), 1990, 8–9.
13 Tyckoson, D., 'Access vs. ownership: changing roles for librarians', *Reference librarian*, 34, 1991, 37–45.
14 Stratton, B., 'The transiency of CD-ROM? A reappraisal for the 1990s', *Journal of librarianship and information science*, 26 (3), 1994, 157–64.
15 McSean, T., 'Is CD-ROM a transient technology?', *Library Association record*, 92 (11), 1990, 837–41.
16 Cox, J., Hanson, T., 'CD-ROM: still transient after all these years? Part 2', *Library Association record* , 96 (5), 1994, 271–3.
17 Bevan, N., 'Transient technology? The future of CD-ROMs in libraries', *Program*, 28 (1), 1994, 1–14.

4

Improving user access to
CD-ROM databases

Morag Watson

Introduction

This chapter will address the technical issues in relation to the need to improve user access to information held on CD-ROM. I intend to address these issues from a historical perspective, showing how the technology has developed. I will discuss the technical issues raised by each medium and comment on how these have been addressed by subsequent developments. I shall conclude with a description of the ways in which CD-ROM technology is today being made available to users.

The technical issues discussed here relate almost entirely to DOS or Windows-based CD-ROMs, software and hardware. I have little experience of using Apple Macintosh CD-ROMs and have therefore decided to exclude this from the scope of this chapter, which is based upon my personal experiences of using CD-ROMs gained at the University of Birmingham and the University of Edinburgh.

Background

CD-ROMs were first used in academic libraries in the early 1980s and were greeted enthusiastically by librarians who saw them as a way to improve user access to large indexes and abstracting services. The first CD-ROMs had simple interfaces and were primarily text-based. The CD-ROM discs currently available are much more complex. They can now offer access not just to text but also to graphics, photographs, sound and video – they are now truly multimedia.

From the first, CD-ROM discs, and the many ways of delivering them to users, have offered technical challenges to systems librarians. These challenges have changed as time has passed. However, it is probably fair to say that there is no other technical medium that arouses so much discussion amongst systems librarians, and librarians in general.

Users have liked CD-ROM from the start and have therefore exerted concerted pressure on librarians to provide more CD-ROMs and in ways more appropriate to their needs.

Standalone CD-ROM workstations

In the beginning – the 1980s

The first CD-ROMs were loaded on standalone workstations, using mainly the DOS operating system, with a single CD-ROM disc player attached. Printing facilities were usually provided. At first workstations were located near staff areas so that Library staff could help users to learn the techniques of the new technology. Problems using the new technology were, however, quickly identified.

Technical problems

CD-ROMs were initially produced in High Sierra format, a format that DOS did not recognize and with which it could not communicate. To allow a DOS PC to communicate with a CD-ROM drive the Microsoft extensions (mscdex) needed to be loaded. These types of driver require a substantial amount of free RAM, and that can create hardware problems with the workstation. The lack of memory available at the workstation often caused problems with the software needed to search the CD-ROM.

Multiple-disc databases

Standalone workstations with single CD-ROM players can make large databases hard to use. MEDLINE, for example, has nine discs with each disc holding over 600MB of data. Users have to juggle discs to retrieve all the information they want as each disc has to be loaded and searched separately. This is very time-consuming and frustrating for users. Only one disc can be read at one time unless the workstation has more than one CD-ROM drive attached. It is possible to have a number of CD-ROM drives daisy-chained to each CD-ROM interface card installed in the PC. This increases hardware costs and can be difficult to configure.

Search software

One of the most significant problems with CD-ROM has been the search software provided to interrogate the database information. CD-ROM suppliers each developed their own interface to search the data on the disc. This proved confusing for users as each interface was very different. For example, some suppliers used F5 for printing, while others used F3. Users had to learn the command language for each database they needed to use. There were also differences in the format of search entry screens. Some had forms to fill in while others required the use of a particular command language. Command languages are particularly difficult for users to learn.

The search software for the first CD-ROMs was often idiosyncratic, and the way in which it would work could not be predicted. The real problems often start when software from more than one supplier is loaded onto one micro. CD-ROM software from different suppliers can cause hardware conflicts.

especially memory problems. These can prevent the installation of other databases requiring a lot of RAM at the workstation.

Access

Users must come to the library to use the CD-ROMs. Most libraries use booking systems for standalone discs and users must therefore book to secure a time slot for access. Access is only possible when the library is open. Each CD-ROM disc can only be used by one user at any one time. A partial solution is to ask users to share large databases with multiple discs or more unusually by buying multiple subscriptions to the CD-ROM, which increases costs.

Security

The security of discs and software is a major issue with standalone systems. They are more open to attack from malicious users who break batch files to access the operating system and then delete or damage the installed software. Discs can be damaged or stolen by users who remove them from caddies. When 5¼ in. disks were the standard it was common for systems librarians to have to extract CD-ROM discs from 5¼ in. disk drives. The users having inserted them there after having first carefully removed the disc from the caddie designed to prevent this happening!

The current situation – the 1990s

There have been many software and hardware developments over the last decade since the dawn of the age of CD-ROM. These have alleviated some of the problems of using standalone CD-ROM databases. Some problems have been resolved only to rear their heads again with new developments in hardware. These changes have radically altered the purpose and content of CD-ROMs.

Technical problems

Microsoft extensions are no longer necessary for all CD-ROMs. This is a very positive step as it reduces the need to load these drivers at the workstation and leaves more RAM free for running the database.

Multiple-disc sets

Multiple-disc sets are now more prevalent than they were in the 1980s and the hardware has evolved to cope with them. You can still use daisy-chained CD-ROM drives but there are now also disc-changers available, holding at least six discs in a cassette. Disc-changers can also be daisy-chained to allow up to 36 discs to be available at the workstation. If more storage capacity is required jukeboxes are available that can hold up to 400 discs. There is no longer any need for users to handle discs at standalone workstations, and that makes those discs secure.

Search software

Some progress has been made towards the standardization of DOS-based user interfaces. For example, some search commands are now standard across all databases – for intance, F1 for help, F10 to exit. Most databases now have a range of search screens, and users can choose to use either the form filling approach or command searching, whichever is most appropriate to their needs – for example, BookData.

Supplier interfaces still vary extensively and this still causes problems for users. Libraries have attempted to address this by using the search software as one of the major criteria for selecting databases for purchase. CD-ROM suppliers have grown substantially in the last ten years. Many of them – for example, WILSON, UMI and Silverplatter – now have huge suites of databases from which librarians can select databases required. Now the same databases are often available from a number of different suppliers. This allows the library where possible to standardize on one or two search interfaces, rather than 10 or 20. This standardization aids the user, the user education librarian and the systems librarian.

CD-ROM software used to be primarily DOS-based but in the 1990s there has been a proliferation of Windows databases and multimedia databases. Databases no longer only hold bibliographic and textual information but can hold graphics, maps, photographs, sound, and video. As these databases have all been developed under Windows, one might justifiably assume that they have a similar 'look and feel'. Regrettably this is not the case as there is no concerted approach to how the 'look and feel' works.

The interface of a multimedia database depends very much on the type of data in the database and the ways in which that data can be manipulated. Databases from the same supplier can be very different, as the search software is designed to exploit the uniqueness of the data. For example, Chadwyck-Healey produces both the *English poetry database* and the *Census 1981–91* on CD-ROM, these packages are profoundly different. The *English poetry database* is a full-text poetry database with a search interface used to retrieve the text, which is cross-referenced using hypertext links. The *Census on CD-ROM* is statistical data, and the search interface is used to produce graphs and charts to make that data more usable and user-friendly. The unique problems of mounting certain specialized databases, including charts, graphics, etc., which make multimedia such a good option, make it very hard to customize the functionality of the database.

Networking

In an attempt to address some of the problems of standalone CD-ROMs, university libraries began to consider providing CD-ROM services across local-area networks. Networks were in their infancy when the first CD-ROM networks were installed, but they were a positive move aimed at solving the existing difficulties of user access to CD-ROM.

Local-area networks

The first types of CD-ROM networks were typically within a single building to a limited number of workstations. In Birmingham University the first CD-ROM network (1988) was installed within the main library and then made available to seven workstations on four floors. Each set of workstations had access to a shared printer.

Technical problems

Local area networks helped with some technical issues and exacerbated others. The loading of CD-ROMs was now easier to manage as it was carried out centrally. There were also fewer conflicts between different suppliers' software as it was now downloaded at the workstation as required.

However, other technical problems developed with the software. Database suppliers were now selling special 'network' copies of their software. Unfortunately, this software was often little different from the software supplied for standalone installations.

The most common problems were:

1 Software was supplied for network use with shared disk space that was not shareable. This meant that individual copies of the software needed to be installed for each user or concurrent license.

2 The software would not recognize the network drives and would not install to the server disk space. The software then had either to be fooled into thinking the network drives were local, or modified to make sure that they were pointing to the new location.

3 The software needed a lot of spill space to write temporary files to when running the database. This could be either the server or the local workstation. These packages were supposed to delete all the temporary files when the application was closed. However, this did not always happen, and the local disk drives and the server had to be periodically checked and unwanted files deleted.

4 Technical support from database suppliers was often dire: technical support staff frequently knew nothing about networks and how they worked, and when confronted with the reality of live networking solutions just could not help.

The suppliers' failure to supply real network software caused many additional headaches for systems librarians and made it hard for them to build networks that were secure and suitable for user needs.

Problems still exist with providing the required amounts of free RAM at the workstation. This is made more complex by the need to load network drivers that require a great deal of memory and often leave little for the CD-ROMs themselves. CD-ROMs were and are very memory hungry, and often require tweaking to make them accessible to users.

A major problem with these services has always been the provision of network access to Apple Macintosh users. CD-ROM subject databases are produced in Mac or DOS format. Most CD-ROM networks are DOS-based and therefore are not available to Mac users unless they buy additional software to allow the workstation to emulate a DOS workstation and thus obtain access to the network.

Multiple-disc databases

It is now much easier to handle multi-disc datasets as all discs are now loaded on to the network. There is no longer any necessity for users to mount them manually. In the first instance it was still not possible to search simultaneously across multiple discs but this improved as the search software improved.

Search software

Interfaces for networked databases were generally the same as those for stand-alone discs which was very useful as it meant users did not have to relearn the software.

Access

This type of networking solution increased the number of access points but still meant that users had to come into the library to use the databases. As we noted above, networking does not always address the need for increased access for Apple Macintosh users.

Security

Security is improved when discs are loaded onto a network CD-ROM tower, disc-changer or jukebox which is geographically separate from the user and to which they have no physical access. Discs are then handled less frequently so there is less risk of physical damage.

Once the CD-ROM software is loaded onto a network server it is possible to protect it more thoroughly using the security features of the network operating system. This security is invalidated by CD-ROM suppliers who supply network software that requires users to have full access rights to run the database. This problem is exacerbated by CD-ROM software that allows users to shell to DOS, giving them access to the network operating system.

Windows software is equally problematic, as a standard Windows installation allows users access to changing the hardware configuration of the workstation, and through File Manager access to all the files on the system. This is even more frightening when you are running in a networked environment as windows users then have access to the whole server. One solution to this is to make changes to the progman.ini which removes users' access to Program Manager. It can be useful to delete the icons and programs for the file manager and the DOS prompt.

System security is all about creating an environment that allows users to run all the programs loaded whilst stopping them accessing the operating system of the workstation or network. This is ultimately to ensure that the workstation or network will always work and that users will therefore always be able to access the applications.

Library-wide networks

A logical consequence of the demand for access to CD-ROM databases is to network them and thus increase the number of access points. In academic libraries the network is first broadened to include all the site libraries. This improves access in that users at all site libraries can now have access to databases. This is dependent on the institution having an appropriate network infrastructure.

Campus-wide networks (wide-area networks)

The final step in the networking of CD-ROMs has been the need to make CD-ROM available on wide-area networks, available to all users at the desktop. In theory campus-wide networking should be no more complex than library-wide networking, as you are using the same network server, the same databases and the same network infrastructure for both. The difference lies is in the level of control that the systems librarian now has over the network.

For campus-wide CD-ROM networking to be effective it is important to obtain the support of the university computing service staff. They can then assist with the problems of configuring other networks to access the CD-ROM network and provide support for remote users. The computing service should be involved in developing guidelines for accessing the system remotely. This will make instructions for network supervisors and users more reliable and will help ensure that they configure their networks correctly for accessing the CD-ROM network. With this type of service, systems staff move into a new realm of providing complex services campus-wide and into new areas of cooperation with computing services staff.

Multiple-disc databases

For a database to be made available to users on a network they must be given access to the CD-ROM disc and the search software. This is done by mapping the location of the software to a drive letter and by mapping each CD-ROM disc in the database to a drive letter. For example, the software is installed on sys:databases\umi but will be made available as drive l:. The drive letters used are determined when the software is installed and the same drive letters must always be accessible by the software when it is run. When only workstations on the library networks are accessing the CD-ROMs then this can be guaranteed, as the workstations will be configured according to the library's needs.

The problems arise when users on other network servers want to have access to the CD-ROM databases. These network servers will have been set up for other purposes and may already have used the drive letters that the library has selected for CD-ROM software and disks for running other applications. This can cause many configuration problems, particularly if the network supervisors want their users to attach rather than login to the library network.

Access

Access is vastly improved when CD-ROM networks go campus-wide, as all users can access the system and make use of the databases. Networks can be made available 24 hours a day and users need no longer depend on library opening hours for access. In this case it is very important to provide online documentation to allow users to exploit the databases effectively and provide mechanisms for them to report faults when the library is closed.

The only remaining problem of access is for systems librarians who experience problems in scheduling systems downtime for disk upgrades or for dealing with software and hardware problems.

Licence control

The need to control access to the network so that libraries are not in breach of licensing agreements has been a very important issue. Licensing agreements with publishers for databases in educational institutions often limit access to registered borrowers of that institution. Also, the costs involved meant that libraries usually only purchase a limited number of network licences for each database. Some way must be found to control who accesses the system and to ensure that the licensing limit is not exceeded.

There are software packages that can assist with this, such as Saber Enterprise Application Manager, and Macafee's Sitemeter. These packages allow the systems librarian to monitor the use of the databases and ensure that the licensing limit is not exceeded. In addition users can be made to login to the system, thus ensuring that access is only by registered users as they will need a user ID and password. Saber also sells a complementary package called Saber Lan Workstation that allows the creation of user-friendly menus and in-house help screens, and the use of enhanced security features.

CD-ROM as a delivery mechanism

The most recent development in CD-ROM networking is a move away from the actual networking of CD-ROM discs and towards using the CD-ROM disc solely as a distribution medium. When the CD-ROMs are received the data is downloaded onto local magnetic storage and then made available to users.

Pre-caching

Pre-caching of CD-ROMs is where the data is delivered on CD-ROM and then copied (cached) to disk, on a Novell server, for example. The data is loaded into an 'envelope' on the magnetic disk which holds the same data as on the CD-ROM disc. Multiple disc-sets are pre-cached on to magnetic disk as individual disks, there is no amalgamation of the data and each disk is searched separately. The main supplier of this technology in the United Kingdom is Fenwood Systems.

An advantage of the Fenwood system over CD-ROM networking is that it provides good management utilities, including licensing control. The system gives good response times as the magnetic disk is significantly faster than optical disc. It is also possible to make the pre-cached information available to UNIX and Mac users as well as DOS and Windows users.

UNIX servers

The newest and most exciting development in the use of CD-ROM in libraries is the growing use of UNIX servers. The companies most significantly involved in this area are Silverplatter (Electronic Reference Library or ERL) and Ovid Technologies (OVID). ERL and OVID both use CD-ROMs as a distribution mechanism and the data is then loaded from the CD-ROM onto a UNIX server. ERL is Z39.50 client/server-compliant. Ovid currently markets two UNIX systems, of which one is client/server, while the other is not. The non-client/server product, called Ovidnet for UNIX, is accessed using telnet and the software is run on the UNIX server.

Z39.50 is a standard designed to allow any one client to access any one database. The standard dictates the protocols to both client and server so that instructions and responses can be recognized by both. In theory any client implementing the standard can search and retrieve from any server that has implemented the standard.

Client/server software allows users to load the search software on their local workstations and then use it to search a remote server. Z39.50 implementations usually include a number of clients for different operating systems – for example, DOS, Windows, UNIX. All clients have similar functionality.

The advent of Z39.50 services is a very exciting development for libraries and their users. Once all systems are Z39.50-compliant they will be able to provide users with one client that will access all the information resources provided by the library. This development may be the ultimate solution to the longstanding problem of the user interface. It allows the user to select the retrieval software for the operating system they are most familiar with whilst using their existing computer equipment. The preferred client can then be used to search the housekeeping system, the Internet, national services such as BIDS or EDINA, and services like ERL or OVID. The Z39.50 standard should also permit the seamless integration of library holdings information with subject databases. Users searching subject databases will be able to see at a glance which of the references retrieved are available in their local collections.

Electronic Reference Library (ERL)

Electronic Reference Library supplied by Silverplatter was the first of these services to be available in the UK. Clients currently available on ERL include PC-SPIRS, MacSPIRS, WinSPIRS and UNIX-SPIRS. These are exactly the same as the standalone or CD-ROM network equivalents, making it easier for users to change to the new service. The UNIX client can be mounted on the server and is then accessible by any user who has access to telnet. Server platforms currently available are Sun Solaris and SCO UNIX.

The ERL client and server software is provided free with a subscription to a Silverplatter database. Silverplatter charge the same cost for a single subscription, whether it is made available standalone, on a CD-ROM network or through an ERL server. The ERL software is in the public domain and other suppliers can implement on that platform in collaboration with ERL if they wish.

A current difficulty with ERL is that some of the databases from other suppliers such as UMI are currently more expensive to network on ERL than they are to network on existing CD-ROM networking platforms. This is making it hard for institutions to transfer UMI subscriptions to ERL as it will increase costs substantially.

OVID

OVID on client/server is a newer product – the beta-test version only became available in August 1995. Clients are currently available for Windows and VT100; a Mac client is under development. The VT100 client is usable by anyone who has access to telnet, regardless of the type of workstation or network used. They can therefore be used by Mac and UNIX workstation users to access the service. The Windows and VT100 clients have an interface that has the same basic screen design and keystrokes, making it easy for users to move between platforms. Server platforms supported include Sun Solaris, HP-UX, AIX and OSF1.

OVID Technologies have just begun to offer some full-text services on this platform. Users enter search terms, and from the bibliographic citations retrieved can then move to the full text of the article. Articles include all text and any original colour photographs, illustrations, charts and tables. If the article has other bibliographic citations attached it is possible to select a citation and then link to the full-text article associated with that citation.

Ovid Technologies charge a 'one-time' cost for the client and server software which is not based on the number of licences purchased. Once purchased the client can be installed in as many locations as required without further payment.

Internet services

Academic libraries tend to provide the above services on local hardware and with local support. However, if local hardware or support is not available, institutions can access the databases through the Internet. Silverplatter offer their databases through the Academic Reference Centre at University College London. They have an agreement with UCL whereby UCL maintains the server while Silverplatter manage subscriptions and offer technical support. Ovid offers a similar service called OVID Online that is accessible through the Internet and through other networks like Sprintnet and Tymnet. Ovid Online is available either as a fixed-rate subscription or on a pay as you go basis.

The Internet service is accessed using the same clients that are available for the locally mounted version. The only difference is that the server is being accessed remotely rather than through a local institution. This creates potential problems for response time but it means that smaller institutions or institutions without the technical expertise available can still have access to these services. The Ovid Online pay as you go service should make this option attractive for smaller sites that need occasional access to subject databases but do not make enough use to justify expensive subscriptions.

Technical problems

To use this technology and these database services, users are going to need access to the client software. This raises the question of how the client will be distributed to users. A variety of options are available:

Floppy disk

If the client software is quite small – that is, it does not require much disk space – it can be copied on to a floppy disk and then distributed to users. An exchange programme could be established where users give the library a blank disk and receive in return a disk containing their chosen client.

The UNIX, DOS and Mac clients for ERL are small enough to be distributed in this way. The Windows setup program for ERL is too large to fit on a single floppy disk so another way of making this available to users must be found.

The Windows setup program and VT100 clients for OVID are both small enough to fit on a single disk. There should therefore be no difficulty in making them available by floppy disk.

Network file server

The client software can be installed on networked file servers and all users of that server given access to that one copy of the client. This ensures that the client is properly configured and that all users are using the latest copy of the client software.

Alternatively the network file server can be used as a distribution medium, as users can download the client from there to their local workstations. Users would have to install and configure the client themselves.

File transfer protocol (ftp)

The client software can be installed on the database server and users can then access the server and ftp the software to their local hard disk. They will then need to run the setup program and configure the client as required.

All the clients have to be configured to ensure that they are accessing the correct server. This can be done by the systems librarian before distribution of the client, or by the user after installation. The Windows client is initially downloaded as a setup program and then installed through Windows where the setup program is decompressed. To make certain that the users install the clients correctly, systems librarians will have to ensure that excellent documentation is supplied.

The systems librarian will need to liaise with the computing services staff who maintain the central network file servers if they intend to distribute clients by that method. Computing services staff also have to be briefed on standard installation details so they can install clients for their users.

Silverplatter and Ovid Technologies have recently released Web interfaces and gateways which are compatible with these services. When these are available users will be able to access ERL and OVID with Web browsers like Netscape and Mosaic. As these are already generally available and familiar to users, the problems of distributing clients may soon be solved.

Multiple-disc databases

UNIX servers are ideal for multidisc databases which are loaded on the server in a concatenated form. Users can choose to search over either single discs, or over multiple discs. ERL allows the users to select from a menu of databases whether they wish to search a single disc or a group of discs. OVID offers either the searching of single discs or the searching of groups of discs, depending on the system configuration. The Ovid system manager can choose to create multidisc segments which allow more than one year to be searched.

Search software

Both these services provide databases from more than one supplier. OVID selects its databases according to perceived user need, while ERL databases are mainly Silverplatter, but there are a growing number of disks available from other suppliers, such as UMI, ISI and Elsevier. Disks from different suppliers are mounted under the same search interface and made available using a common set of commands. Users learn one interface and can access all the databases they require within that interface. The OVID and ERL clients can even be used to search each other's databases.

Most users in an academic environment are familiar with Netscape and Web browsers, so when these are being used for database searching this can be even less complex and intimidating for users.

Access

Access to databases is greatly increased by the provision of these systems. Users who have a login to the system can access it from anywhere they wish as long as they have Telnet access. They are not tied to library opening hours, neither are they restricted to the campus or organization. All computer users can use the system, as the proliferation of clients means that the services are now available to Mac and UNIX users as well as DOS and Windows users.

The provision of Web servers will make the service available to any user who has a Web browser such as Netscape or Mosaic, and this will widen access even further.

Licence control

This is still an issue but it has now been addressed by the database suppliers instead of institutions having to purchase separate products for this purpose. ERL contains an administration program called ERLADMIN which is used to manage user accounts, database access, system security and usage statistics. With ERL you can generate reports by database for all users and for individual users to assist the systems librarian assess the needs of the users. OVID provides password control, database metering, security and statistical information using a combination of UNIX utilities.

The provision of more sophisticated usage statistics is important when assessing whether the institution has provided enough licences for each database for its users. Additionally statistics can be used to determine if the institution has bought too many licences and should therefore reduce them. Statistics of database usage can be used to determine if users are making use of the databases, and if not to provide a good case for removing unused databases from the system. This allows librarians to ensure that the limited resources available to them for electronic information are being used most effectively.

The future of CD-ROM provision in academic libraries

As we have seen CD-ROM provision has evolved over time, gradually becoming more sophisticated and less problematic to implement. Unlike evolution, however, these developments have not meant that earlier services have died out, just that the use of them has changed. The method by which a database is now made available to users depends on the perceived usage, cost, the platforms available and the users' requirements.

Standalone CD-ROM workstations, once the sole point of usage, are now being used for databases that are either too costly, too large or too difficult to network. Standalone is also good for databases that are only needed by a small group of users in one location. In this category I would include databases such as Business Periodicals Ondisc, currently only available standalone and with around 600 CD-ROM discs. It would be very expensive to network this either using standard CD-ROM towers or by downloading it on to a UNIX server. The only way to network it would be by using a series of jukeboxes. Multimedia databases are often mounted standalone because of the difficulties of networking sound and video at the present time.

CD-ROM disc networking is appropriate for those databases that are more multidisciplinary and used by more than one group of users. This platform could be used for discs for which substantial but not heavy usage is expected, or for less popular multidisc sets. This category also includes all databases not currently available on ERL or OVID. Here I would include databases like *English poetry database* with five discs, used by more than department and not supplied by OVID Technologies or Silverplatter.

Systems such as ERL and OVID are ideal for larger, heavily used databases to which a majority of users require access. The size of databases installed on these services will be dependent on the amount of disk storage available on the server. One factor in deciding if a database is provided by this method or by CD-ROM will be the relative costs of hard disk storage and CD-ROM drives. Another factor here is the type of workstation to which users have access. It is much easier to make databases available to all users, on all types of workstation, using the UNIX server solutions. ERL and OVID also have the advantage of offering users a common search interface for all the databases no matter how dissimilar they are. Databases that are appropriate for this category are MEDLINE, Inspec, ABI/Inform – multidisc, multidisciplinary databases to which many users will need access to allow them to meet fully their information needs.

Therefore the future will include all aspects of CD-ROM provision with the platform the service is delivered on depending on a number of factors. Some academic libraries already include all these different delivery mediums. Edinburgh University Library currently provides services in site libraries on standalone CD-ROMs and campus-wide using CD-ROM networking and OVID. An ERL server has been ordered to provide campus-wide access to databases not available on OVID. At Edinburgh University Library future developments will centre around making more use of OVID and ERL and other client/server solutions. This will allow us to make more databases available to all our users, with a common interface and in a more user-friendly way.

The development of Z39.50-compliant servers and clients has exciting implications for the way users access systems. It is now possible to imagine a future where users will, from their workstations and using one interface, access a multiplicity of information resources. When the workstation is turned on a menu will be displayed to users; this menu could include OVID and ERL services, but also the local library housekeeping system, external library OPACs, CHEST databases, the World Wide Web or CD-ROM databases. The users need not know where the data is stored or how it is being delivered to them. They will use one interface, with one set of search commands to access these very varied systems and retrieve information.

Other exciting opportunities created by the development of Z39.50-compliant systems concern the potential for resource sharing between different institutions. Both Silverplatter and Ovid Technologies have developed their systems and pricing structures with consortia or regional implementations in mind. Z39.50, ERL and OVID support the installation of servers in distributed sites and the seamless sharing of databases mounted upon them. Institutions that have made an investment in Z39.50, ERL or OVID technology could share this with other local institutions in return for access to each other's systems. Academic sites which have excellent networking facilities and technical support available could provide services to other smaller local organizations. These local institutions may include smaller academic institutions but they could also be schools, public libraries, museums or local businesses.

CD-ROM was one of the most exciting innovations in libraries in the early

1980s. As we approach the millennium it is a technology that is still at the forefront of new developments in library services. The development of Z39.50 that has facilitated the growth of services like ERL and OVID is a challenge to libraries. A challenge to develop services which users need, and in a more effective and user-friendly way than has hitherto been possible.

5

The changing role of the reference librarian

Richard Biddiscombe

Introduction

In the traditional library the reference librarian was, next to the catalogue, the key to the collection. No one was better able to exploit a library's stock and help users to find the answers to their questions. No one had a better overall view of what the collection could offer the user. Conversely there was no better person to assess the needs of the library's clientele, or understand what should be provided to give help and assistance to them. Interestingly, open access collections have made the reference librarian more essential rather than less. Offering users the option to exploit the collections themselves has led to greater demands for information, help and guidance.

Reference librarians can be described, therefore, as intermediaries between the needs of the user and the full potential of the collections they are trying to exploit. Is such a role a wholly benevolent one or has it been created by librarians to cover their inability to organize information for the benefit of users?

According to the latter view, reference librarians are necessary because librarians have arranged collections in such an arcane way that it is difficult for users to find information themselves. They need the help of specially trained librarians to help make sense of libraries. This is an interesting point of view, and if there is some truth in it, how will experienced intermediaries fare in the virtual library environment?

If the former view holds good it could mean that help and guidance from an expert will still be needed. If there was a greater need for assistance when libraries became open access collections, could the same principle apply when end-users have a world of information to choose from? If these end-users do need some assistance to make sense of an increasingly complex information environment, will the traditional skills of the reference librarian be what is required?

The traditional role of the reference librarian

Reference services in libraries are most often defined as direct, personal assistance to readers seeking information.[1] Harrod has suggested that 'Reference work is that branch of a library's service which includes the assistance given to readers in their search for information on various subjects'.[2]

It is this emphasis on helping users locate the information they require which marks out the special role of the reference librarian. The size of the library is not important, for even in the smallest collection users expect some help in finding the answers to their questions as quickly as possible.

Reference librarians have developed, through their training, experience and expertise, a long tradition of helping the user. In most libraries the obvious public face is that of the reference librarian. These front-end staff are responsible, to a large extent, for the image of the library service. There has been much discussion over the years about what qualities such personnel should possess. Katz[3] quotes Robert Taylor[4] as suggesting that the following skills are required:

- the ability to organize data and information for people to use;
- an awareness of the totality of information resources and of the probabilities of success of strategies for searching for information in any specific situation;
- an awareness of, and ability to use, a range of information technologies;
- a sensitivity to use, uses and users of information, and a strong tradition of service, which demands attention to client satisfaction.

Katz[3] does add to these, offering judgement, accuracy and thoroughness as essential too; perseverance is also seen as a necessary quality.

All these qualities are undoubtedly essential but others are growing in importance for a job which is undergoing radical change. Consequently it is increasingly necessary for the reference librarian to have some knowledge of computer technology, networking developments and software packages. This has to be coupled with the ability to communicate to library users, either as part of group tuition or on a one-to-one basis.

More extrovert qualities are being demanded from those who are, or at least have a public image of being, reserved and inward-looking individuals. The age of the generalist is also on the wane, for it becomes increasingly difficult for an individual to keep track of the titles of all major information sources, their different formats and the various front-end software packages used to access them. To provide a better service to the user it is becoming necessary for staff to specialize in particular subject areas and be more computer literate.

The reference librarian and the librarian–client relationship

The qualities demanded of a reference librarian must be seen in the context of the relationship with the client, i.e. 'direct personal assistance to readers seeking information'.[1]

This view suggests that no amount of organizing and retrieval skill will make a good reference librarian unless there is also a good rapport with the client. It is perhaps this key element which has sometimes been missing and has helped to reinforce that public image of the librarian from which the profession has tried so hard to escape.

The basis of this relationship has been seen as having three aspects, these are:

- the reference interview
- follow-up interaction, i.e. a feedback loop
- delivery of the final product that addresses the client's information need.[5]

Much has been written about the complexities of the reference interview and the essential part it plays in finding out what the user's information needs really are.[6, 7] Good interpersonal skills are essential as is the ability to distil an unfashioned request into an answerable, or unanswerable, question and then give help and advice. There is no doubt that the more expert a librarian is in a subject area, the more likelihood there will be that the client will get the information he or she requires.

Abels and Liebscher[5] discuss the transference of these traditional skills in the age of networked communication, but is an intermediary necessary in the new environment? What need is there for a reference interview in the age of the Internet? Users can, after all, input their own search terms and interrogate networks themselves. If an intermediary is required, will it not be some specially developed computer program rather than a reference librarian?

Campbell[8] certainly regards the concept of the reference librarian as outmoded. In his view the term 'access engineers' would better describe their new function. Jennings[9] suggests that reference librarians need to 'regrow' if they are to retain a role in the era of information networks. Both views are quoted by Marcos Silva and Glenn Cartwright[10] in explaining the changing role of the reference librarians at McGill University. Here, and increasingly across other university campuses, the reference librarian's role is to teach others to access the networks and seek answers to their own information needs.

Such new functions make new demands and call for diverse abilities from the reference librarian in the late 20th century. These stem from two factors: firstly the technological revolution, and secondly the changing skills and expectations of the library user.

The reference librarian and the technological revolution

Online searching and the role of the iintermediary

It is undoubtedly true that the introduction of online public access catalogues (OPACs) changed reference librarianship.[11] How far and how much it did so is a matter of debate, but developing user-friendly OPACs needed the expertise of reference librarians if they were to operate effectively.[12] OPACs at first offered nothing very radical and did not change the perceptions of information provision for either library users or staff.

This was partly because their initial introduction brought only a partial change. There was often a lack of investment in retrospective conversion, and consequently the full potential of OPACs was not realized immediately. The introduction of OPACs was often accompanied by the automation of other library services and the introduction of library management systems.

Much of this passed the reference service by. Here there was little change despite the introduction, in the early 1970s, of online searching. Although these online databases offered access to a large amount of data beyond the traditional confines of a single library collection, and required the learning of new skills by the reference librarian, they failed to make a great impact on the reference librarian's traditional role.

Online databases were certainly seen as a natural extension of the resources available to the reference librarian, and the use of online sources to help with the answering of reference enquiries could extend the service in a new way.[13] It was accepted that reference librarians were best placed to exploit this new service, but the difficulties in controlling costs overshadowed its administration and failed to allow it to reach its full potential. The need to pass on charges to the user for online searching resulted in a long debate on the ethical position of doing so.[14–16]

Consequently the high cost of accessing these new online databases ensured that users were usually kept at a safe distance from the technology. Budgets rarely allowed for the possibility of users undertaking their own searches unless there was strict supervision.

Nevertheless, the traditional intermediary role of the reference librarian was used in a new way and to good effect in establishing online search services which exploited the databases on behalf of, and usually alongside, their clientele. Nothing else had ever before expanded the wealth of potentially available and easily accessible information as much as the range of online databases offered by database hosts.

It was noteworthy in other ways as well. It was the first time that most reference librarians had been exposed to the use of computers in any interactive sense. It was, in fact, the start of the networking revolution, though at the time no one could predict its full extent. It was necessary to learn a new set of command languages and cope with the uncertainties of international telecommunications networks. The early primitive interaction, often using a networked printer without a monitor, gradually gave way to the more sophisticated interfaces that are available today.

The possibility of end-user searching was much discussed, but with very little practical application. Some experiments were carried out to examine the possibilities and problems.[17] End-users were few and far between and much sought after to give conference papers. Finding such people was difficult and the search invariably failed.[18]

During this time the wider role of reference librarians in this new world of computerized databases began to emerge. In a number of areas librarians felt

that they could begin exerting their influence on database hosts and other service providers. Various user groups and ad hoc committees began to emerge,
acting as pressure groups in their chosen sectors. In 1984, for example, the UK
Online Coordinating Committee was set up by the Library Association and
others to examine the problems of downloading information from databases.
It produced a statement and made recommendations but there is no evidence
that the commercial hosts responded.[19]

The fight to improve quality has received a better response from the industry. In 1989, after some scattered attempts to improve quality, the Southern
California Online User Group (SCOLUG) was created. It began work on
developing basic principles for judging the quality of the commercial databases and produced a set of criteria which could be applied by information professionals.[20] The momentum that this group created had some success in producing positive responses from online hosts[21] and provided a good role model
for other library user groups around the world.

It was not until the late 1980s that the role of the librarian as intermediary
began to decline. It was around this time that public access to newly acquired
CD-ROM databases began revolutionizing the user's role in the information
process. Some time later BIDS arrived in British academic libraries and administered a further blow to the mediated search. Before long online searching
was regarded as no more than an add-on service.[22]

CD-ROM, the end-user and the reference librarian

The introduction of CD-ROMs to libraries brought the beginnings of the most
profound revolution for the reference librarian. Soon there was little need to
extend a wide search for examples of end-users' experiences.

Most libraries located the new CD-ROM service at the reference desk.
Reference librarians were expected to administer a service which at first sight
was a natural extension to their traditional role as information intermediaries.
There were in essence five main reasons for locating the service at this point:

- to assist users with their information needs;
- to help users with their use of the equipment;
- to control access to the databases;
- to produce any in-house written guidance thought to be necessary for the
  users;
- to ensure security.

Of these, the need to help users find information and to provide appropriate
publications for them was in line with the traditional role of the reference
librarian. However, as we shall discuss later, the extent of the demands made
on staff for these purposes in this new service environment was underestimat-
ed at the time.

Security can also be said to be a legitimate and logical aspect, for reference
librarians have always been concerned with the security of their stock, in what-

ever form. Controlling access to material, however, was a new departure. Drawing up issue systems and demanding evidence of identity from patrons had always been left to colleagues in the lending department. As CD-ROM databases became more popular, and the increase in demand was far more than predicted, the work of the reference desk became distorted by the issuing and return of discs.

At the same time the technical demands on staff were increasing. Few reference staff had much experience of computing, and serious problems could cause the breakdown of the service and lead to workstation reservation problems.

At this time, around the mid to late 1980s, a growing number of microcomputers were being added to library services, both for the public and the staff. Consequently it became more and more evident that a new type of technical expertise was required from the library staff. New posts began to be created for what became known as systems librarians in order to cope with the increasing number of local computer problems. The appointment of these personnel did not, however, mean that reference librarians need no longer worry about computers.

The reference librarian and CD-ROM networking

There were great hopes that the introduction of CD-ROM networking would herald the end of the problems experienced on the reference desk. If CD-ROMs could be networked, some of the peripheral responsibilities the reference desk had taken on would surely disappear.

Libraries started networking CD-ROMs in the early 1990s, a few years after the standalone service had been introduced.[23] A number of advantages resulted for both users and library staff.[24] Access, from the users' point of view, was much improved. There was no longer a need to make a booking, access was quicker and there was the possibility of searching across multiple discs. For staff the pressures of booking were eased and there was better security for the discs.

However, it became evident all too soon that, although some advantages were to be gained, many new problems were arising. Certainly the task of administering the service became less onerous as many of the most popular discs were networked, but the difficulty of networking certain titles and the costs of networking licences meant that it was not possible to network every disc. The days of the standalone service were not at an end, and the reference desk therefore continued to administer this aspect of the service.

As databases became accessible across local networks, other problems arose. How were users to know how to find the databases they wanted across the network? Did users in fact know the names of the databases in their subject areas? From experience at the reference desk it seemed unlikely that many library users could differentiate one database from another. Appropriate networking software was therefore necessary to make sure that the databases could be made accessible in a coherent way, with online help on offer to the networked user if at all possible.

Here the experience of reference librarians, with their retrieval skills and understanding of database searching, could be used in a new way. The networked databases needed menus, online help and database descriptions to guide the end-user. Software such as Sabre provides the means for loading and networking such help. Librarians, who have always produced printed guides to help their users, could now use their expertise in this area to provide online help. Similarly, traditional skills could also be adapted to ensure that helplines and mailboxes were available to answer enquiries and help in problem solving.

The reference librarian and the Internet

With the introduction of CD-ROM databases the reference service was increasingly driven by the needs of the end-user. This change has affected every library and information service in the higher education sector, and will soon be a more accepted part of public library provision. Many users who enthusiastically began their own direct searching on CD-ROM standalone databases later welcomed the opportunity to search them on a networked basis. From searching these locally networked databases they have moved to the wider possibilities of accessing the Internet. The one significant difference with Internet searching is, of course, that end-user searchers do not need any input from the local library.

Is there a legitimate and useful role for librarians in helping end-users search the Internet? In other words, does the intermediary role of reference librarianship have any equivalent here, and if so, what form does it take?

The key to efficient and effective Internet searching is certainly the knowledge of useful and relevant addresses. Those who can find their way around the system can usually locate what they are looking for. Most users are, however, experts, in a narrow subject area. Most Internet users need assistance when starting a new area of interest. They welcome some guidance and key pointers to information, and reference librarians with 'their awareness of the totality of information resources'[3] should be well placed to assist.

Most academic libraries have created library home pages to help library users begin their Internet journeys. Many have provided very detailed lists of addresses for the use of their clientele, but nothing so exemplifies the valuable role that can be played as the BUBL database. BUBL (Bulletin Board for Libraries), with its international reputation, illustrates how traditional skills can be adapted. Its provision of a comprehensive directory to Internet sources, its clear menuing and the continuous maintenance of Telnet links challenges the need for any local equivalents. In a similar way to that in which MARC cataloguing limited the need for local provision, centralized reference services can be held on the Internet and accessed internationally.

While the Internet can be used to point the way to information sources, it can also offer other services if library staff adapt their skills to this new medium. Many libraries are developing other useful aids; directional and informative Web pages and publications are being produced. The development of Web-based OPACs will offer increased scope for improved access to library collections. The creation of Web databases to exploit special collections, or the publication of online journals, is already gaining momentum.

The changing skills and expectations of the library user

In this new and fast developing environment, what exactly is the new role for the reference librarian? Many librarians are feeling uncertain about what the future holds for them. What is certain is that the changes that have already taken place, and that are continuing to do so at an increasing rate, mean that the future will be different and, as has been indicated, traditional skills will have to be used in a different way.

As far as end-users are concerned, their view seems to be that the reputation of librarians has been enhanced rather than undermined or diminished by these changes. This has been shown in a number of studies.[25-7] Nevertheless, reference librarians are beginning to see their work differently, while individual end-users are appreciating their own new power in the provision and organization of information.

Users are not only becoming increasingly computer literate, they are also able to put themselves at the heart of their own information networks. Many users of the Internet are creating their own home pages in which they are able to describe themselves, express their needs and link up the information sources which they find most useful. They can also join like-minded people in newsgroups and on mailing lists.

Through these means, information and help can be offered and exchanged. Subject specialists and enthusiasts in all kinds of areas can communicate, extend their knowledge and improve their information skills. All this can be done without the users leaving their own computers, and certainly without the necessity of consulting an intermediary, who is almost certainly less of an expert than they are in their specialist interest.

These end-users are a fast-growing breed, and the potential offered them in terms of information, entertainment and virtual human contact has not yet reached its limit.

In this rapidly changing environment there is no certain place for the local reference librarian as an information intermediary. Other roles do present themselves, however, for not all information seekers are end-users and not all end-users are self-sufficient in information, especially when it is outside their usual subject area. Librarians have, however, to keep ahead of the game if they are to play any role at all on this information revolution. How is it possible to do that and what wider role have they to play in the process?

The quality of end-user searching

Many librarians have been convinced that the quality of the end-user search cannot be as good as that provided with the librarian as intermediary. This is open to doubt and there is little recent evidence to support the theory.[17] Although it may have been true in the past, when users were unfamiliar with interrogating databases, or even now for those who are not used to using computers, its validity must be questioned as a general principle. With experience – and many surfers of the Internet are building up an extraordinary number of searching hours – search techniques become better and the quality of the result improves.

The quality of the search can, essentially, be judged only by the end-users themselves, and the librarian's search for completeness is not always what is required by the user. The case for the intermediary has always been strongest in the medical area where, it has been argued, a bad search can lead to a wrong diagnosis. Even here, however, the quality of the librarian as intermediary has never been adequately tested.

It is at the outset that each end-user may need help with an explanation of the best techniques and an introduction to the most relevant databases. As Tenopir[28] has pointed out, Boolean logic is not intuitive for most people, and all but a few users would benefit from an introduction to basic principles. The librarian is probably the best person to undertake this role, but once the searcher has been given the basics or has a brief reference tool explaining them, then the librarian's role becomes less clear. There is a need for someone in an advisory role who can be called upon when necessary, perhaps when the end-user changes his or her interest and wants expert advice on the information sources available in a new area. This may be what the term 'reference librarian' should mean in future, i.e. the professional to whom end-users turn for help and advice on search techniques, database quality, database developments and the range of database access that is available.

Whither/wither the reference librarian?

From reference librarian to information specialist

The growing demand for computer expertise to facilitate effective information services has inevitably led to changes in the way services are administered within institutions. As Silva and Cartwright have said, 'Reference librarians have also experienced a radical shift concerning the provision of reference duties arising from the convergence of computer and communication technology. This shift has arisen from an attempt to meet the needs of faculty and students who need to locate, filter and synthesize information'.[29]

It is in the higher education sector that the technological revolution has taken hold to the greatest extent, though changes are beginning to affect public libraries too. For a number of universities this has resulted in the 'convergence' of the library and computing services. The higher investment in networking and computer technology, and the pressures to train greater numbers of students, have inevitably changed the role of some of the library personnel. Often those who have had the necessary skills to adapt to this revolution have been the reference and enquiry staff. Many of them are making the transition into newly created posts, some of which are still, as yet, relatively undefined. Using the intermediary skills learnt at the enquiry desk, these librarians are applying them to the world of end-user searching.

The demands made on reference librarians have therefore become more complex, with fewer now devoted to a static service offered at an enquiry point. The complexity of the services now on offer have increased the demand for training and explanatory publications, and they can only be satisfied effectively by someone with subject expertise.

In a recent survey at the University of Birmingham Main Library[30] the number of long enquiries (i.e. complex questions and help) was only around 2% of the total for an average term. Clearly the use of highly paid staff to perform such a small proportion of professional work has to be seriously questioned, especially when there is much demand for the traditional skills in other areas.

Using the basic skills in new ways; the new reference librarian
The reference role with its four elements[5] has now to be combined with that of trainer and interface developer. All these elements will utilize, in a new and exciting way, the traditional qualities of the reference librarian. It may be appropriate to explore these elements more fully.

Help and advice
There is obviously nothing new in reference librarians being helpful and giving advice on information issues, but traditionally this service has been provided in a library environment. The assistance which is now offered is somewhat different and usually more disparate.

Apart from the traditional forms of communication, telephone helplines and electronic mailboxes offer users additional means by which they can consult librarians. In addition, comments and questions are received over the Internet through library home pages. Requests and comments will therefore not be restricted to the local library environment but may come from the other side of the globe.

Searching techniques and problems
Even though librarians may specialize in particular subject areas, their training and work in information will give them a broader view of available sources than most end-users. Reference librarians are, therefore, in a unique position to offer assistance to them when the need arises. Although end-users may increasingly turn for assistance to their information peer groups through newsgroups and maillists, no one will have such broad overall knowledge of information sources as the librarian. Most users appear to stick to one or two favourite databases and expect them to answer all their information needs. Librarians can usually offer alternative options, some of which may be available only in a different medium.

End-users get hooked on the technology and often disregard the possibility of searching other sources such as CD-ROM and print. Fears have been expressed, for example, at the excessive reliance placed by some chemists in British universities on the BIDS ISI databases. This free online database is often preferred to Chemical Abstracts, despite the fact that it is less comprehensive, because of the convenience it offers.

The reference librarian's overall knowledge of information sources should therefore prove an important asset to the wider community of end-users if and when they seek broader approaches to their problems. Equally, the independence of the library professional is important. As an honest broker in the business of information provision the reference librarian can give unbiased opinions about the advantages and disadvantages of a wide range of databases in a number of mediums and subject areas. In addition this role should enable him or her to discuss the quality of the individual databases.

Database quality

The original debate about the quality of databases began in the USA, most notably with SCOLUG[20] and primarily concerned the provision of online databases. This question has been taken up in the UK by the Library Association and others who have helped create the Centre for Database Quality. Its aim is to receive documentary evidence of poor quality in both online and CD-ROM databases (see Chapter 2).

It is surely the role of the reference librarian in this new environment to act on behalf of the end-user community as a whole in highlighting poor quality and acknowledging excellence when it is found. No other member of the information community, from the professionals to the amateur end-users, is better qualified to undertake this task. It is one which needs to be undertaken on behalf of all database users, many of whom are unaware of the problems that can arise. So many searchers accept what is presented to them without question.

With long-established publishing houses, buyers are usually aware of the standard of product they can expect. At present, however, the average end-user is not as aware as the average book buyer about the reputation of a product's producers, and cannot therefore assess those which can be trusted to offer good-quality databases. As J. A. Large has written, 'Online sources are not easily browsed and it is therefore more difficult to form an opinion of their content than with printed equivalents. Although searches in CD-ROM do not incur direct costs it is still difficult to browse through them and reach conclusions as to the work's authority in quite the way that can be done with printed sources'.[31]

Librarians should have enough knowledge to offer advice and make recommendations on the best products available. The willingness of most database producers to offer free trails of both online and CD-ROM databases gives librarians some opportunity for testing and assessing new products, and of course matching them with the tried-and-tested ones. In 1991 Reva Basch wrote, 'As online professionals we owe it to ourselves, as well as to the mass market of information consumers and those who are marketing them to keep an eye on both the software fixes and real innovation.'[21] The principle is still true even though the concerns now are wider than just online developments.

The reference librarian as trainer

Helping the user with CD-ROM databases has became part of the reference librarian's everyday experience. These are often one-to-one training sessions, especially when the user is unfamiliar with the technology. Pressure has increased at information points as these time-consuming elements detract from the demands of other users. This need to provide adequate training for users, and for library staff themselves, has given rise to a growing role for the reference librarian in organized training.

For academic librarians the days are now past when offers to provide 'user education' sessions were greeted by bemused and unenthusiastic responses by all but the most dedicated library user. The demand for help in searching the wide range of available databases now comes from both students and staff. Library staff are seen as having a vital role to play in training students and academic and library staff.[32]

Such input on all types of courses is increasingly demanded by various funding bodies to show that the information needs of students are being taken seriously. Academic staff, acknowledging that they no longer have the time to teach what has become a complex subject, are now willing to leave teaching to library staff. Librarians take the teaching very seriously. Reporting on the practice at Penn State University, Kalin and Wright claim that 'Organized proactive instruction is viewed as both an opportunity and a responsibility.'[33]

This growing need for information skills training is usually satisfied by those who learned their skills at the reference desk. These training sessions, however, still need to be supplemented by the one-to-one training, often undertaken in an unstructured way by reference desk staff. No amount of organized training will abolish the need for immediate help on an ad hoc basis. This is particularly true in public libraries, where formal education sessions are more difficult to organize, but is also the case in those academic institutions which have to meet the needs of part-time and distance-learning students.

To help with this process, many reference services have produced printed guidance for database users. These publications are often part of a larger publication programme in which the reference librarian plays an important role.

Multimedia publications

Reference librarians have traditionally produced publications which have been designed to help their users access the resources of their libraries. Until the advent of desktop publishing these were often quite primitive, usually either duplicated pages of typed copy or offset litho productions. New computer-based methods of design and production now ensure that good-quality guides can be offered to users, giving help in a number of areas including the basics of database use.

Information technology offers the librarian the possibility of extending the provision of guidance from printed formats into other areas, and many are taking advantage of these possibilities. Some have become involved in the development of library guides using software packages such as Asymetrix Toolbook.[34] Still others have helped develop the library home pages which are springing up on the Internet. Other, fuller publications are also now beginning to make their appearance on the World Wide Web so that network access to them is available for library users at all times.

To augment these some reference librarians are turning their skills to the production of in-house databases in order to exploit their library's resources. In-house CD-ROM projects have been developed to exploit commercially the sources that were previously only available through local catalogues or small-scale publications. Reference librarians have become producers, in some cases developing both CD-ROM and CD audio publications.[35] In addition, the advice and assistance of librarians is sometimes sought from publishers to help create and exploit new CD-ROM and online databases.

Interface developer

Though these new publications often need the expertise of computer software personnel, the types of skills which reference librarians possess are essential if the publication is to be a helpful interface for the user. All those skills demanded by Robert Taylor[4] of the traditional reference librarian have their place in new aspects of information provision. The reference librarian is providing the virtual help necessary for the virtual library.

As we have already seen, the design of database menus and the online database guides is an essential aspect of local area networks. Although not offering that personal interaction which was an essential element of the traditional reference library job, the task is nevertheless vital in directing the user to the information sources they need.

Designing packages for helping the end-user is seen as increasingly important. A number of grants are available from various official bodies for the creation of such products, and many projects have been established for developing them. One of the intentions has been to ensure that pressure is taken off reference desks so that users can identify the information source they need by working through software packages themselves.

The de-skilling of the enquiry desk?

Given the new roles which the traditional reference library staff are developing, and the emphasis on training and software development, what is now happening at the reference desk?

Although most library users are only gradually becoming aware of the extent to which networked services are developing, there is some empirical evidence to suggest that library managements are diverting resources away from their reference and enquiry points. Certainly in UK academic libraries the role of the reference staff is changing as former occupants of the jobs take on their new roles. This too is happening in the US as Whitson[36] has described.

The change in the role of the academic reference desk, and the consequent change in the status of its staff, is taking place for a number of reasons. Reference collections are becoming less important as familiar titles appear in CD-ROM editions and greater access is given to online abstracting and indexing services. Access to library services from outside the library building is increasingly possible, and online help packages can mean there is less need to seek assistance from the librarian at the desk. This is certainly the emerging pattern in academic libraries, where the clientele are heavy users of computer and networked services.

It's not that reference desks are not busy – they are often very busy indeed, and there is little real evidence to support the suggestion that a large number of enquiries are satisfied by networked or standalone workstations. It cannot be denied, however, that the end-user is increasingly aware, often thanks to their information skills training by library staff, of where and how they can find information for themselves.

The service at the reference desk, certainly in academic libraries, is increasingly one which provides support rather than reference services. The balance between these services has now changed so that it is the support services which take most of the staff time. It is here, for example, that user registration for particular databases or workstations is administered; it is the place to go for a library publication offering guidance to a database or service; it provides a back-up to those who use the library's networked services, and of course it is where printer failures or database crashes are most often reported.

Consequently the question of staffing grades and levels inevitably arises. As Whitson[36] says, 'No one in the library can any longer maintain the kind of general competency reference librarians used to take for granted.' If the reference desk is becoming a help desk, then different though related skills are needed. In this changing situation who should staff these service points, and can the professional aspects of their jobs be quantified effectively? The convergence of libraries and computer services highlights the need for considered thought on the training of these new information professionals, the level at which they should be employed, and their possible career structures.

In the same way, those professionals who were formally at reference desks and are now involved in the new tasks we have outlined, need to have their functions formalized. As they are using their old skills in new and different ways, is the term reference librarian now an adequate description for them? There is, as yet, no identifiable title which recognizes these new skills. They are described as information services librarians, Internet librarians, liaison librarians, subject specialists, but none of these adequately describes the range and function of the skills being demanded of them. 'Access engineers'[8] is certainly an accurate description but hardly an attractive possibility.

Conclusion

The development of end-user access, brought about by the huge growth in networking and the relative cheapness of computer hardware and software, is transforming most academic reference services. It is only six or seven years since the initial introduction of CD-ROM standalone services and yet there is now extensive use of networked databases. The traditional role of the reference librarian in most academic libraries has changed decisively over that period. The transformation has been obvious within institutions, but those essential skills needed to make information accessible are finding a place in other, non-library environments.

Though higher education has been in the forefront of this information revolution, public library services are just beginning to see the changes start to affect them. This will result in the need to reskill public reference librarians so they can offer their expertise in a networked information environment. Their new role should be used to provide a new interface to information for the benefit of the wider community. If this is to be achieved it will be essential for new techniques to be learned and new services to be created. Public librarians must take up the challenge and use their undoubted expertise to help bridge the gap between the information rich and poor.

With their established reputation for freely available expert help in finding information, public libraries have a unique role in the community. There is, however, no guarantee that this will continue to be the case unless information skills are brought up-to-date. There are real possibilities that commercial organizations will seize the opportunity if library services do not. For example, the training role could be taken over by private agencies, cyber cafés and franchised services within public libraries themselves could provide public Internet access to the wider community, and specialist network groups could offer the advice and help that, in a traditional environment, would have been available in public libraries.

Information specialists, 'access engineers', or whatever they are to be called, will be in demand from such commercial operations for their important skills. Many may feel that they will not want to be a part of a library service which remains firmly in the print-based era. Librarians will have to rethink their role as part of a wider information profession and accept the importance of the revolutionary changes. Their role as information professionals need not necessarily be wedded to a library service environment.

Such radical changes will need to be reflected in the future educational process, the organization of a professional body and the management structure of individual libraries. In the postmodern world of information provision, it will still be important to retain a sense of professional commitment, built around a strong service ethic. For reference librarians in all types of library, the process of change will continue and its pace will quicken. There are important roles to play in the new environment, but the opportunity must be grasped now if the new information professionals are to have any influence on future developments.

References

1 Galvin, T. J., 'Reference services and libraries'. In *Encyclopedia of library and information science*, 25, New York, Marcel Dekker Inc., 210–26.

2 Harrod, L. M., *Harrod's librarian's glossary of terms used in librarianship, documentation*, 5th edn, London, Gower Press, 1984.

3 Katz, W. A., *Introduction to reference services vol.1: basic information sources*, 4th edn, McGraw Hill, 1982.

4 Taylor, R. S., *Library journal*, 15, 1979, 1873.

5 Abels, E. G. and Liebscher, P., 'A new challenge for intermediary-client communication: the electronic network'. In Kinder, R. (ed.), *Librarians on the Internet*, New York, Haworth Press, 1994, 185–96.

6 Dewdney, P., 'The effective reference interview', *Canadian library journal*, 45 (3), 1988, 183–4.

7 White, M. D., 'Evaluation of the reference interview', *RQ*, 25 (1), 1985, 76–83.

8 Campbell, J. D., 'Skating the conceptual foundations of reference: a perspective', *Reference management*, 20 (Winter), 1992, 29–36.

9 Jennings, L., 'Regrowing staff: managerial priority for the future of university libraries', *Public-access computer systems review*, 3, 4–15.

10 Silva, M. and Cartwright, G. F., 'The Internet and reference librarian: a question of leadership'. In Kinder, R. (ed.), *Librarians on the Internet*, New York, Haworth Press, 1994, 185–96.

11 Carande, R., *Automation in reference library services: a handbook*, Westport CT, Greenwood Press, 1993.

12 Ferguson, D. K., 'Reference and online catalogs: reflections and possibilities'. In Matthews, J. R., *The impact of online catalogues*, New York, London, Neal-Schumann Publishers Inc., 1986, 25–33.

13 Cochrane, M. S., 'Use of online databases at the reference desk'. In Williams, M. E. and Hogan, T. H. (comps.), *National online meeting proceedings, 1981*, Medford, NJ., Learned Information, 1981, 127–32.

14 Crowther, K. N. T., 'Subsidized computer search fees in an academic library'. In Williams, M. E. and Hogan, T. H. (comps.), *National online meeting proceedings 1981*, Medford, NJ., Learned Information, 1981, 151–7.

15 Chene, D. D., 'An analysis of flat fees in an academic library'. In Williams, M. E. and Hogan, T. H. (comps.), *National online meeting proceedings 1981*, Medford NJ., Learned Information, 1981, 161–5.

16 Biddiscombe R. (ed.), *Charging for services in academic libraries: report of the University, College and Research Section Working Party*, UC&R Discussion Paper no. 1, London, Library Association, University, College and Research Section, 1981.

17 Bodtke-Roberts, A., 'Faculty end-user searching of BIOSIS'. In Williams, M. E. and Hogan, T. H. (comps.), *National online meeting proceedings 1983*, Medford, NJ., Learned Information, 1983, 45–53.

18   Summit, R. K. 'Search of the elusive end-user'. In Bysouth, P. T. (ed.), *End-user searching: the effective gateway to published information*, London, Aslib, 1990, 57–63.

19   LA–UK Online Coordinating Committee, *Statement of downloading requirements of users*, London, Library Association, 1984 (unpublished).

20   Tenopir, C., 'Database quality revisited', *Library journal*, October, 1990, 64–7.

21   Basch, R., 'The user wish list and system software for the 90s: how far so far?', *Online*, **15** (November), 1991, 42–7.

22   Biddiscombe, R., 'CD-ROM and the reference librarian: the end of innocence', *Resource sharing and information networks*, 7 (2), 1992, 5–14.

23   Biddiscombe, R., 'Networking CD-ROMs in an academic library environment', *British journal of academic librarianship*, **6** (3), 1991, 175–83.

24   Bradley, P., 'Hardware issues'. In Hanson, T. A. and Day, J. M. (eds.), *CD-ROM in libraries: management issues*, London, Bowker-Saur, 1994, 67–79.

25   Boyd, T. and Warne, K., 'End-user searching within Glaxo Group Research Ltd: an evaluation of the DIALOG Medical Connection'. In Bysouth, P. T. (ed.), *End-user searching: the effective gateway to published information*, London, Aslib, 1990, 125–34.

26   Cassels, R. and Whittall, S. J., 'End-user searching with CD-ROM', London, Aslib, 1990, 153–64.

27   Nicholas, D., Harris, K. and Erbach, G. O., *Online searching: its impact on information users*, London, Mansell Publishing, 1987.

28   Tenopir, C., 'To err is human: seven common searching mistakes', *Library journal*, April, 1984, 635–6.

29   Silva, M. and Cartwright, G. F., 'The Internet and reference librarians: a question of leadership'. In Kinder, R. (ed.), *Libraries on the Internet; impact on reference services*, New York, Haworth Press Inc., 1994, 159–72.

30   University of Birmingham. Information Services, *Main library enquiry statistics, summer term 1995*, University of Birmingham, 1995 (unpublished).

31   Large, J. A. 'Evaluating online and CD-ROM references sources', *Journal of librarianship*, **21** (2), 1989, 87–108.

32   Abbot, C. and Smith, N., 'Resourcing issues'. In Hanson, T. A. and Day, J. M. (eds.), *CD-ROM in libraries: management issues*, London, Bowker-Saur, 1994, 40–5.

33   Kalin, S. and Wright, C., 'Internexus: a partnership for Internet instruction'. In Kinder, R. (ed.), *Libraries on the Internet; impact on reference services*, New York, Haworth Press Inc., 1994, 159–72.

34   Biddiscombe, R. and Watson, M., 'Developing a hypertext guide to an academic library: problems and progress', *Program*, **28** (1), 1994, 29–41.

35   Pelou, P., *'La relation bibliothécaire usager dans le reseau des bibliothèques internationales'* ('The librarian–user relationship in the network of international libraries), Paper given at the Rencontre franco-britannique *L'usager dans la bibliothèque: autonomie et dépendance*, Nice, 7–9 September 1995 (unpublished).

36   Whitson, W. L., 'Differential service: a new reference model', *Journal of academic librarianship*, **21** (2), 1995, 103–10.

6

Training the end-user

Case study 1: Academic libraries
Aileen Wade

We shall not cease from exploration
And the end of all our exploring
Will be to arrive where we started
And know the place for the first time[1]

Introduction

This case study deals with approaches to training end-users at Sheffield Hallam University (SHU) in how to exploit electronic information resources effectively. The training is described in the context of SHU's teaching and learning strategy, using a case study based on the experience of first-year undergraduate science students from 1991 to 1996.

Context

Sheffield Hallam University is one of the largest higher education teaching institutions in the UK. Like many other British universities, it has experienced a rapid expansion in its student numbers during the 1990s and there has been a noticeable shift in emphasis from a lecturer-led towards a student-centred learning environment. As students are increasingly expected to use a huge variety of information resources to support their learning, and to be independent learners, they need to develop their skills in searching for, and exploiting information.

A significant improvement has been made in end-user access to information in the higher education community. This has been achieved by two important but complementary developments. Firstly, it became technologically possible for higher education libraries and information services to network CD-ROMs in the early 1990s. This development was paralleled by the arrival of the Bath Information and Data Services–Institute for Scientific Information (BIDS-ISI) citation databases in February 1991. The BIDS-ISI databases have been made accessible for 24 hours a day, seven days a week, and are free at the point of use for end-users. This has meant that end-users enjoy 'virtually unrestricted access'.[2] There has been a noticeable shift towards a Copernican view, where the library 'is seen as a node in the scholar's information web'[3] rather than as being at the centre of the information retrieval process. Since 1991 a range of other services have been made available from networked PC laboratories across university campuses. The Department of Library and Learning Resources (LLR) at SHU is committed to ensuring the effective exploitation of such information services by its user community.

This case study describes how LLR is achieving this aim and draws heavily on the experience of delivering such provision to students on the programme of degrees in applied sciences.

User education 1979–90: a historical perspective

Sheffield Hallam University (formerly Sheffield City Polytechnic) has a long history of, and continues to have a strong commitment to, undergraduate user education. The subject librarian for science and the course leaders for the BSc degree and Business and Technician Education Council (BTEC) Higher National Diploma/Certificate (HND/C) in applied chemistry developed a library user education programme when these courses were validated in 1979.

The literature for chemistry is both extensive and well organized but can often be complicated to use. All first-year chemists benefited from the programme of instruction, which gave them the necessary skills to exploit a range of reference tools, including dictionaries, handbooks, encyclopaedias, *Chemical abstracts* and the *Science citation index*. Until 1986 this instruction took the form of a series of formal lectures planned and delivered by the subject librarian. The lectures, which drew to some extent on material prepared for The Travelling Workshops *Experiment for chemistry*,[4] were followed by workshop sessions to enable students to put the theory into practice. During a lecture session, the subject librarian showed groups of approximately 30 to 45 chemistry students how to use various search tools, incorporating examples appropriate to their studies. The students were provided with a booklet which gave information on sources for chemistry[5] and were asked to carry out several exercises during the workshops. These exercises were subject-based and were integrated into the curriculum. The assignments tested students' skills in searching for scientific data, locating and verifying references to the chemical literature, and their ability to use up-to-date information to produce a short essay on a chemical topic. Students' attendance was monitored and their work assessed by the subject librarian. A successful assessment contributed to their progression to the second year.

In 1986 the programme of degrees in applied sciences in the Faculty of Technology underwent a validation. The subject librarian for science was invited to be a member of the planning team for the unit entitled Scientific information and literacy. This unit formed part of the core curriculum for all first-year science undergraduates. The tutor for this unit was a member of the Department of Communication Studies who had overall responsibility for its delivery. The unit concentrated on communication, and aimed to develop in the students an understanding of methods of communication, storage of scientific information, information retrieval skills, and oral and written communication skills. Having taken responsibility for library provision for the science programme within the Faculty in 1987, the author continued to be involved in planning the content of the information skills element of the unit, and its delivery. The revision of the unit resulted in science undergraduates attending four information skills sessions, each of two hours' duration, devised to raise their awareness and develop their confidence in finding and using scientific and technical information. In order to ensure that this skills element was appropriate to the needs of the students, the subject librarian developed assessed assignments in close liaison with her academic colleagues in the Faculty.

In the early 1990s a member of the School of Science (as the Faculty became known) assumed responsibility for the unit, which was renamed *Communication of technical information*. From this time, the unit has concentrated on the development of the transferable skills of exploiting information, group working, time management, technical report writing, oral and written presentation, and computing. A planning group was established, comprising subject representatives from the three divisions in the School, a member of the Personal Skills and Qualities Project at the institution, the subject librarian for science and the IT skills tutor. It was created to encourage the promotion of skills acquisition for undergraduate scientists. The group was led by a senior academic, who was responsible for innovations in teaching and learning in the school.

For an understanding of the end-user training approaches adopted by LLR, it is important to have an appreciation of the teaching and learning strategy at Sheffield Hallam University. The University's strategy is centred round an SHU model developed in 1991, which is described in the following section.

The 'three cycle' model at Sheffield Hallam University

> The University's mission is to provide opportunities for the development of intellectual, professional and practical skills and qualities . . . [6]

In 1991 the University formally adopted what has become known as its 'three cycle' model for higher education. The curriculum strategy on which this is based aims to

- support access
- widen opportunity
- increase flexibility.

The model has, as its driving principle, informed and deferred student choice, facilitated by flexible structures and a strong professional focus. Having progressed through higher education foundation programmes, students can then move on to generalist or specialist vocational and professional programmes. Subsequently students may enrol on specialized postgraduate/post-experience programmes. Alternatively they may enter the system at any one of these points. A brief description of each of the cycles follows.

Cycle 1 incorporates pre-higher education and higher education foundation courses – level 0 (access) and level 1 (first year) of a degree programme.

Cycle 2 covers level 2 – final year(s) and above – of undergraduate studies and advanced vocational and professional programmes.

Cycle 3 includes postgraduate and post-experience courses, some of which may not necessarily be more advanced than Cycle 2 studies.[7]

Cycle 1 embraces the development of student self-learning skills and the underpinning of specialist knowledge in the first year. The rationale on which Cycle 1 has been developed is to provide a preliminary and pre-professional course of study-related and transferable skills.[8]

By mid 1994 an SHU cross-subject working group had developed a core skills framework[9] which could be applied to all programmes in the University at all levels, with Cycle 1 as its focus. The framework states that each programme of study at SHU would benefit from the inclusion of the six National Council for Vocational Qualifications (NCVQ) core skills[10] in its learning outcomes, namely:

- communication
- application of number
- information technology
- working with others
- improving own learning and performance
- problem solving

Although the framework failed to receive SHU Academic Board approval, it has informed all subsequent validation and review activities since that time.

Seizing the opportunity – the new science programme

During the academic session 1994/5, when the undergraduate science programme was being planned, the planning team was strongly influenced by the framework document. It was also informed by a report of the Industrial Research and Development Advisory Committee of the Commission of the European Communities entitled *Quality and relevance: the challenge to European education: unlocking Europe's human potential.*[11] This 1994 report draws attention to 'the considerable and continuing advances in information technology (IT) . . . [and] how it is profoundly changing the way we deal with information and data. Information has become a new type of basic material and resource. Undoubtedly, the move towards a more knowledge (and skills) based economy is a direct consequence of this.'[11]

These initiatives contributed to a further development of the School of Science skills unit, which was renamed Scientific Information Technology Communication and Mathematics (SITCoM). SITCoM has been designed to enable students to develop the six General National Vocational Qualifications (GNVQ) core skills within a science-based programme.

Case study 1991–6: approaches to end-user training

Information skills training programme

Many years of experience in library work have repeatedly confirmed the author's firm conviction that the real learning for most, if not all students occurs when they use learning resources for a purpose.

The following case study is drawn from the author's experience of delivering the information skills element of SITCoM from 1991 to 1996. It also describes her experience with students, staff and researchers from other schools, research centres and institutes of the University.

Library and learning resources induction

Students are entitled to receive an introduction to the range of learning support facilities offered by their chosen university. Since the new science undergraduate programme at SHU places a greater emphasis than ever on its students becoming information literate, their need is clear. A general induction session ensures that a large number of students are given the opportunity to learn about the facilities available to them without their having to be seen individually by the library and learning resources staff.

Since 1991 all science undergraduates have received their induction during freshers' week (pre-semester) as part of the skills unit. The method of delivery and the location for this session have both changed in recent years, enabling library and learning resources staff time to be used in a more effective way. Formerly students were seen in small groups in the department and were given a tour of the building. Although the small classroom environment offered the author the opportunity to establish a rapport with her audience and enabled valuable interaction between them, a rapid increase in student numbers in the 1990s made it difficult to continue this approach. This led to a major review of how library and learning resources induction could be delivered. The University's Pennine lecture theatre, with 450 seats, has become the preferred delivery method for large numbers of students. Ten hours of induction time have now been condensed into a one-hour session.

Some 300 science undergraduates gather in this lecture theatre to watch a regularly updated video and see a computer-based presentation on library and learning resources. The induction session concentrates on raising the students' awareness of the facilities and on convincing them that the Department of Library and Learning Resources is a welcoming place. Ticket enrolment is dealt with during the formal university registration process. All the students receive an LLR newspaper and other literature appropriate to their needs at this stage. They receive an introductory assignment, which is planned and assessed by the subject librarian and programme tutors as part of the students' SITCoM work. This requires them to visit the department to find out about its resources. The aims of the assignment are to introduce them to the library catalogue (OPAC) and its various collections, and to develop in them a confidence in using these facilities.

Formal training

During the first semester (September–January) the science students follow three core units: SITCoM, Topics in Science and Functions of Business. The core units and options, offered throughout the first year, involve the students in making extensive use of, and becoming familiar with, a range of library and learning resources.

During freshers' week, the science students receive a guide to SITCoM and are organized into small groups of four to six. Each group is allocated an academic tutor, who offers advice and support for the work they are expected to carry out for the unit. The skills unit requires them to undertake a number of activities: production of a poster, presentation on a scientific topic, and creation of an analytical kit. These activities are undertaken in their groups. An individual student report on the scientific topic is also required. Each group is expected to organize a meeting with its academic tutor during the third week of the semester, and then to continue to meet regularly throughout the first year.

Once the science students have settled into university life and they have some assignment work to complete, they attend SITCoM information skills sessions. These sessions equip them with the necessary skills to carry out their research more effectively. The first, a formal session, is held in the fourth week of the semester. This is followed by two workshops during that week or the subsequent week, and then again in week seven. The subject librarian delivers the initial session, which consists of a one-hour formal presentation in the University's Pennine lecture theatre. The theatre is suitably equipped to enable her to demonstrate a range of information services.

Learning outcomes

The three sessions enable students to achieve the following learning outcomes:

- to understand how learning resources are organized;
- to develop a raised awareness of electronic databases and other information sources held at SHU appropriate for their studies;
- to carry out effective and efficient searching strategies;
- to obtain references found through the searching process (with an emphasis on using locally held material);
- to download (to disk, printout or e-mail) and manipulate information (textual or graphical) in a suitable package (Excel, PowerPoint, Word, Access);
- to present references and make citations correctly;
- to use a suitable bibliographic management package to present references (Word, Reference Manager, Procite, Bibliofile etc.).

The Pennine theatre presentation takes the students through a typical information search for their studies. Appropriate examples are always used, not only to illustrate the process of searching, but to maintain the interest of the students. The presentation includes a mixture of demonstrations of online information services and screen displays to illustrate effective searching techniques. Students receive supporting literature, including a printout of the computer-based presentation, a search strategy sheet, and examples of how to present different types of references and methods of citation. They also have the opportunity to collect other literature on the various services offered by LLR.

The science students are able to use subsequent workshop sessions to search for material on their scientific topic. The assignment work for the unit is completed by the end of the first semester.

Students receive a second formal session in semester two (February–June) which enables them to achieve the following learning outcomes:

- to develop an awareness of the Joint Academic Network (JANET) and networked information resources on the Internet;
- to access information in a variety of ways on the Internet, with particular reference to the SHU Web server and LLR home pages information.

Workshops

Learning is the process whereby knowledge is created through the transformation of experience.[12]

Behaviourist research into adult learning, especially the work of Kolb,[12] suggests that formal instruction has to be reinforced by experience for true learning to take place. In order to ensure this reinforcement the students attend small-group follow-up workshops in library and learning resources or in one of the University's networked computing suites, shortly after the formal session. The hands-on experience is considered to be an indispensable part of their information skills training.

The subject librarian and other LLR staff are present at the workshops to offer their expertise and support. However, as far as possible the students are advised to explore the services. The aim of the sessions is for the students to learn for themselves rather than for LLR staff to carry out the searching on their behalf. The students are asked to refer to the database help screens if they require assistance. This is fundamental to the way in which these workshops are run. The students are also strongly encouraged to draw upon and share with the other group members their own ideas and experiences. Literature is provided to encourage the development of an independent learning attitude.

It is important that the students have specific tasks to carry out using information resources during the workshops to maintain their interest and motivation levels. They use the databases to search for material on their scientific topic. In order to ensure that the students are able to find suitable material, subject team members research the topics beforehand. The subject librarian agrees the list of topics with the academic tutors, who are invited to contact the subject librarian or other subject team members to discuss their respective research topics.

Two one-hour hands-on sessions are organized for group sizes of between 20 and 30 students. Equipment is booked so that students can work individually, or in pairs or small groups. Access to a sufficient number of PCs, and licence arrangements for database use, have to be arranged in advance. The groups are encouraged to read the handouts distributed at the formal session and to discuss their approach to the scientific topic before they attend their workshops. The students meet the subject librarian in the library classroom for the workshops. Each group is given 'quick help sheets' for various services. These are produced by subject team members, in addition to published guides supplied by database providers. Equipped with their topics and search terms, the students access a number of the services during the workshops.

Monitoring effectiveness

As part of the SITCoM unit, the science students produce a number of assignments. This work is assessed by a range of science school staff as well as by the planning group for the unit. All school staff and those who deliver the SITCoM unit are invited to assess, for example, the scientific posters and presentations. The criteria for assessing the work are agreed by the SITCoM planning group.

The science students create a *portfolio* – an academic and professional development record. This provides self-discussed evidence of their skills development during Cycle 1. By continuing the record throughout the students' time at the University, skills enhancements will be logged and developed further throughout their programme. It gives recognition and respectability to skills acquisition, and makes a valid contribution to the academic process.

Support material

In addition to the information skills training programme described above, a range of materials have been produced to enable Cycle 1 science students, or any other library and learning resources users, to learn how to exploit information services effectively. This material, which supports the formal training programme, is described below.

Training packs

Electronic Resources/Information Skills (ERiS)[13–14] has been created by LLR staff specifically to support the University's Cycle 1 programmes. It is an interactive multimedia package and covers computer basics and search skills. The package is available in each of the University's five campus libraries to assist those who, for whatever reason, may require information skills training. Some Cycle 1 students are able to use the package to review how to conduct effective searches. A series of skills packs have also been produced by the Learning and Teaching Institute (LTI) of the University which covers skills enhancement for a range of areas, including searching for and using information.[15–16]

Documentation (guides and leaflets)

Science students at the University are able to search more than 80 databases, some of which are accessible from SHU networked PCs located outside LLR. New services are constantly being added. Unfortunately there is a lack of consistency in how the services are currently presented on the computer screen across the University, and the different interfaces (how a service looks) encountered by users can appear to be rather daunting. Consequently both the selection and use of a service can be problematic for students.

A range of leaflets has been prepared to encourage self-help by the students. Leaflets are produced describing which services may be used for specific subject areas – for example, science, engineering, financial accounting, law and current affairs. This makes the selection of the appropriate services easier.

Quick reference guides, which cover basic and advanced searching techniques, (usually a double sided laminated A4 sheet) are produced. The quick guides are very popular since they enable students to conduct their searches in a database rapidly, working through a logical process.

Printed guides from database providers seem to be less well used unless they have been adapted for SHU users. Important features of a database and sensible search strategies can often be omitted. Material to support the use of the BIDS-ISI databases is a notable exception. The BIDS-ISI self-help guides, and the establishment of a common interface for the BIDS services, have proved invaluable for users. The documentation is located in the five campus libraries and in all the networked computing suites across the University.

Information services documentation produced in-house is progressively being made available electronically on the LLR home pages of the SHU World Wide Web server. A series of home pages have been created which are guides to useful Internet resources based on the subject interests of the University's 11 Schools. These resources have been evaluated and feedback from users is sought constantly by various means including e-mail, in order to improve them. A Networked information services post has recently been created to improve support to Internet users and to coordinate other Internet developments in LLR.

Further training approaches

Personal tutorials

A diverse user population (which includes part-timers, distance learners, mature students, overseas students, combined studies students, researchers, staff) visit library and learning resources at SHU. Some of these users may not be offered any formal training programme like the current Cycle 1 science students, or may find it difficult to attend training. Some final-year project students choose specialist research topics, which may lead to their requiring an individual session with a subject team member. Consequently it is important to provide opportunities for such users to have some dedicated time with subject team members.

Most users receive detailed support via the information desk. Individual appointments can be made with members of the subject team staff by any user. These members of staff also arrange appointments with School staff and researchers for training sessions in a convenient location, often in their offices rather than in LLR. This has two advantages. It enables subject team staff to develop a closer relationship with School staff and it increases the LLR staff's understanding of services available in the Schools and how these services can be accessed.

Drop-in training sessions

In recent years several drop-in training sessions have been offered throughout each semester on a weekly basis. It has been noticeable that the level of demand for these has been decreasing in direct proportion to the increase in the amount of teaching work undertaken by subject librarians. As students move through their respective programmes, their confidence and expertise in using facilities increases.

E-mail and telephone support

An increasing number of students use e-mail to communicate in the University. The BIDS services require the use of e-mail. Consequently science students and other users are encouraged to register as soon as they arrive at SHU. If they need help with information services, they are able to use e-mail for support. At present there are no special e-mail boxes for users to contact but they are given the e-mail address of the appropriate subject librarian or other subject team members. Take-up of this service is minimal at present but likely to grow rapidly.

Telephone support is a normal part of subject team work. However, as more information services are networked across the University, and students are able to gain access to the range of information services both from SHU and remotely, it is likely that this form of assistance will also increase, eventually leading to possible 'round the clock' support. Serious consideration needs to be given as to whether such a level of service is justified.

Relationship with the School of Science

At the present time the majority of the School staff have become involved in the delivery and assessment of the unit. There is much wider acceptance of the need for science students to acquire core skills, and that this is possible through the discipline of science.

Core skills training is now considered an important part of the science students' curriculum rather than as peripheral to their learning experience. This is a view held by members of the School. In addition, School staff are reflecting in their own working practices the skills they expect students to develop. During the planning of the SITCoM unit and throughout its delivery, the planning team, including the subject librarian have met regularly to share ideas and review its progress. They have also monitored the unit by obtaining feedback from the students as they have experienced it. This has enabled the team to respond to feedback when appropriate and introduce amendments in order to improve the learning experience of the students.

The formal information skills training sessions have been challenging, extremely enjoyable and stimulating for the subject team. Its members are regarded as being expert in all issues relating to library and learning resources support. More importantly, they are seen as partners in the process of the programme planning for the School of Science, and are able to make a positive contribution to curriculum content, design, delivery, monitoring and assessment.

Information skills training: key features for success

Any programme is likely to be more effective when the skills training contains certain key features, notably:

- the training is planned and integrated into the curriculum, and at an early stage;
- the training includes subject-based assessed assignments (relevant to each student's area of study);
- assignments are agreed and assessed by the subject librarian and School staff;
- there is an emphasis on hands-on student-centred experience;
- learning outcomes are included;
- monitoring takes place throughout the student's programme;
- feedback and review are part of the process;
- the sessions are part of a student's formal timetable.

Research on the effectiveness with which students are making use of electronic information resources at SHU was recently carried out by library and learning resources and the Sheffield Business School of the University. This confirmed the importance of training and support in information gathering, and provided a set of recommendations which reinforce the author's own view.[17]

Training requirements for networked information resources

In the author's view, the key responsibility of the LLR subject team staff is to assist users to develop the confidence to use information resources effectively. The arrival of electronic and networked information resources does not change the situation; it simply makes it more challenging.

What has altered, however, is the range of skills that SHU science students, and other users, require, and what skills they expect subject team members to possess. For them the level of service they receive from LLR staff to support them in handling electronic information should be the same as for any other service. The fact that this means support in decoding information from the Internet, fixing a PC or printer, or transferring data into a software package to manipulate it, is immaterial to them. Consequently subject team staff continue to play their traditional role whilst extending their range of skills to include increasingly sophisticated computing skills.

In September 1996 Sheffield Hallam University opens the doors of a seven-storey 'learning centre', which will offer its users a flexible learner-support environment. From the user's point of view the services should be seamless. Suitable training to enhance the skills of learning centre staff and its end-users are the key to the establishment of an effective learning environment.

The Electronic Libraries Programme (eLib)[18] of the Higher Education Funding Councils' Joint Information Systems Committee (HEFCs' JISC) will have a major impact on the provision of training for the learning centre staff and its users. Three projects, funded under the training and awareness programme area of eLib, offer a coordinated approach to networked information resources training and are seen as the best method of addressing the higher education community's skill development needs. The projects involve the following:

1 Edulib is creating a nationally recognized and accredited network of library and support staff.

2 NetLinkS is focusing on the establishment of an electronically-mediated professional development and training framework for network learner support.

3 Netskills is developing a programme of training and awareness for higher education community users of information and those supporting them.[18]

The SHU library and learning resources staff are actively participating in these projects

Conclusion

An enlightened attitude at funding council level, combined with technological advances, has led to the 'age of information access' revolution which began in the early 1990s. The revolution in end-user access needs to be accompanied by an end-user training revolution. Users must be equipped with the necessary skills to take advantage of the services offered.

A range of approaches to training end-users in exploiting electronic information resources have been adopted at SHU to accommodate the variety of learning styles needed by the University's diverse user community. Many users still seem to have a preference for a personal tutorial with a member of the subject team, but this level of service cannot be given to all the 20,000 students who attend the University.

The integrated approach to skills training offered by SITCoM ensures that a large group of students has the opportunity to become more efficient at searching for information. Although this inevitably leads to greater demands being made upon subject team members, the students are increasingly making more sophisticated enquiries, which enhances subject team members' job satisfaction. The students develop an awareness of the importance of information, and learn to attribute a greater value to exploiting information services than they might otherwise have done. It is important, however, to negotiate carefully with academic staff in creating an information skills training programme to secure success.

The challenge for information professionals now is to ensure that they equip themselves first with the necessary skills in a constantly changing environment, in order to be able to train their users. If we wish to continue to play an important role in the exploitation of electronic information services, we must influence the direction taken and create our own future.

References

1 Eliot, T. S., *Little Gidding*, 1942 (Four Quartets). In Eliot, T. S., *The complete poems and plays of T. S.Eliot*, London, Faber, 1969, 191–7.
2 East, H. et al., *A huge leap forward: a quantitative and qualitative examination of the development of access to database services by British Universities, 1988–1994*, London, British Library Board, 1995 (Centre for Communication and Information Studies policy paper no. 5/British Library R&D report 6202, May 1995).
3 Sack, J. R. , 'Open systems for open minds: building the libraries without walls', *College and research libraries*, **47** (6), 1986, 535–44.
4 Travelling Workshop Experiment, *Chemistry: a learning package on sources of information*, Newcastle upon Tyne, TWE Newcastle upon Tyne Polytechnic Products Ltd, 1981.
5 Thompson, R., *Chemical information: what it is, where it is, how to find it, what you need*, Sheffield, Sheffield City Polytechnic, 1980.
6 Sheffield Hallam University, *University calendar 1995–96*, Sheffield, SHU, 1995.
7 Cook, M., *Tutor's guide*, Sheffield, SHU, Learning and Teaching Institute, 1995.
8 Sheffield Hallam University, School of Science, *1995 Science programme of four major routes of study in biomedical sciences, chemistry, business & technology, science & technology leading to the awards of University Certificate, University Diploma, BTEC Higher National Diploma, Bachelor of Science (Hons), MSci: Vol. one of three; general introduction*, Sheffield, SHU, 1995.
9 Sheffield Hallam University, Core Skills Working Group, *A core skills framework for the university*, Sheffield, SHU, 1994 (internal document).
10 Oates, T., *Developing and piloting the NCVQ core skill unit: an outline of method and a summary of findings*, London, National Council for Vocational Qualifications, 1993 (NCVQ R&D report no. 16).
11 Industrial Research and Development Advisory Committee of the Commission of the European Communities, *Quality and relevance: the challenge to European education: unlocking Europe's human potential*, Brussels, IRDAC, 1994.
12 Kolb, D. A., *Experiential learning: experience as the source of learning and development*, London, Prentice-Hall, 1984.
13 Hudson, A. et al., *ERiS: electronic resources/information skills: a multimedia package to develop information skills in students: Phase 1 pilot*, Sheffield, SHU, Library & Learning Resources, 1994.
14 Hudson, A. et al., *ERiS: electronic resources/information skills: a multimedia package to develop information skills in students: Phase 2 pilot*, Sheffield, SHU, Library & Learning Resources, 1996 (in preparation).
15 Drew, S. et al., *Student skill pack: gathering and using information: starter pack*, Sheffield, SHU, Learning and Teaching Institute, 1994.

16 Drew, S et al., *Student skill pack: gathering and using information: development pack*, Sheffield, SHU, Learning and Teaching Institute, 1994.

17 Sheffield Hallam University Library and Learning Resources and Sheffield Business School, *Effective use of electronic information resources*, Sheffield, SHU LLR & SBS, 1995.

18 Higher Education Funding Council. Joint Information Systems Committee. *Elib: Electronic Libraries Programme*, Bristol, HEFC, 1995 (folder containing a series of leaflets on eLib and projects).

Case study 2: Public libraries[1]
Colette Batterbee

Introduction

Public libraries face particular problems with training end-users because the general public library user is not necessarily 'information-trained'. As a group public library users have various IT backgrounds, ranging from very little experience of using IT to a few who are reasonably IT experienced. Having such a disparate, heterogeneous group of users makes it difficult for public libraries to provide training. How have public libraries dealt, if at all, with the difficulties of training such a diverse group? Or have they ducked the issue, arguing as so many have done before that CD-ROM is a user-friendly medium and does not require training?

CD-ROM provision in public UK libraries

CD-ROM has made slow inroads into public libraries. In 1990 only 29% of public library authorities (PLAs) had CD-ROMs, though by 1995 the figure had grown to 77% (see Figure 6.2.1).

Despite an increase in the number of PLAs with CD-ROMs, there has been a reluctance to allow users access to the CDs. The number of PLAs providing an open-access CD-ROM service has risen slowly, from only 5% in 1992 to 18% in 1995 (see Figure 6.2.2). If this trend continues as it seems at present, more and more public library users will come into contact with CD-ROMs: meeting their training needs will surely become more and more important.

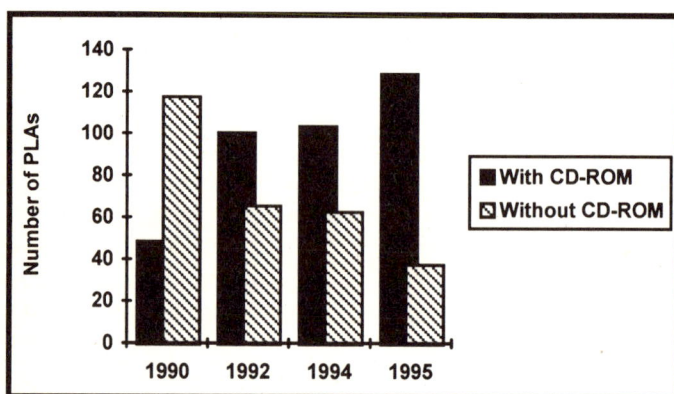

Fig. 6.2.1 *Public library authorities with and without CD-ROM, 1990–95*
Survey sources include: Batt 1990,[2] 1992;[3] Shields, 1993[4]

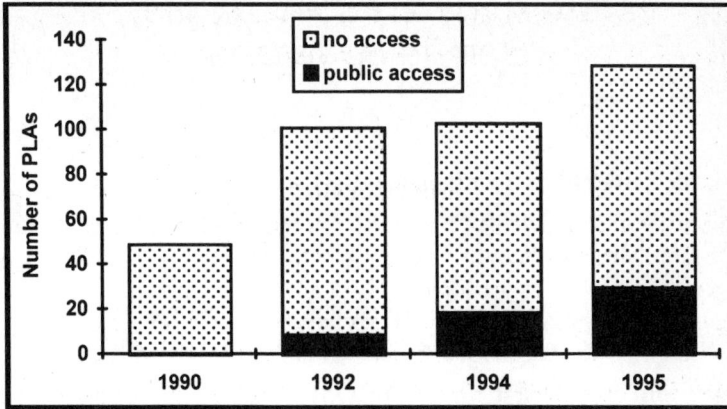

Fig 6.2.2 *Number of PLAs with open access to CD-ROM, 1990–95*
Survey sources include: Batt 1990,[2] 1992;[3] Shields, 1993[4]

Public library CD-ROM users

On the basis of a survey of 87 CD-ROM users in four public libraries, it is possible to ascertain who the end-users are and how they search.

Main overall characteristics

A general profile emerged from the end-user survey.

Occupation

The CD-ROM service attracted a large proportion of students, who accounted for 61% of users; the public library appears to be used as an extension of the college library. Just over a quarter of CD-ROM users (26%) were in employment. The CD-ROM service failed to attract many unemployed library users (9%) or self-employed (3%). Only 1% of users were retired, and there were no users who looked after the home.

Age

The age profile matched the main occupational groups, with young adults as the predominant user group: 61% of users were between 16 and 25 years old. This reflected the large student user group. Users aged between 26 and 35 years accounted for 16% of users, and 13% of users were aged 36–45 years. Only 7% of users were aged between 46 and 65 years. The under-16s were not well represented with only 3% of users. There were no users in the over-65 category.

CD-ROMs were heavily used by younger adults, who would have had contact with IT at school or college, whereas the older age group are less likely to have had contact with computers. Though it is not surprising that not many older people use the CD-ROMs, it is perhaps surprising that children were not well represented. The probable reason is that the range of titles on offer was mainly newspapers, bibliographic or business databases. This begs the question as to whether the range of titles available attracts particular users or whether the selection is determined by the types of user groups.

Sex

The balance between male and female users was fairly even, with only slightly more male users than female users. This was encouraging because in general it is thought that men tend to be the dominant IT users.

CD-ROM experience and usage

Four distinct user groups emerged based on patterns of usage.

1 First time users. First time CD-ROM library users, who had not used CD-ROMs in either the public library or anywhere else, accounted for 18% of users.

2 Regular non-public library CD-ROM users. Users who were using CD-ROMs in the public library for the first time but had used CD-ROMs elsewhere accounted for 21% of users. The places where these users had experience of CD-ROM were:

- college or university (72%)
- school (17%)
- work (5%).

3 Regular public library CD-ROM users. Users who had used CD-ROMs in public libraries before but had not used them elsewhere accounted for 17% of users.

4 Regular public and non-public library CD-ROM users. Users who had used CD-ROMs in public libraries before and had used them elsewhere as well were by far the largest group, with 44% of users. The places used by this group were:

- college or university (59%)
- work (19%)
- school (16%)
- another public library (13%)
- others, such as at home or with friends (5%).

Public library training provision

What kind of training are users getting from their public libraries at the moment? It is not enough for public libraries to provide just physical access to the CD-ROMs, they must also provide the user with the tools to access the information.

Availability of training

Out of the thirty PLAs with an open-access CD-ROM service, 13 provided end-user training, six did not and training provision was unknown within eleven PLAs. There were no obvious connections between availability of end-user training and size of the open access service. The type of CD-ROM service varied considerably from authority to authority. Most CD-ROM services were available at only one site within an authority, providing users with between one and five CD-ROM workstations, users having use of between one and ten databases. Some authorities had networks with a vast range of titles available for public use.

Non-availability of training

The reasons PLAs did not provide end-user training were not a lack of user demand or need but a lack of either staff time, resources or trained staff. One authority couldn't provide user training because of lack of suitable facilities.

Impetus for training provision

The impetus for setting up user training varied from PLA to PLA. There were three main reasons for providing end-user training:

1 **To enable efficient use of CD-ROMs.** Most CD-ROMs weren't easy to use. Most users had never used CD-ROMs before, and some sort of training was necessary in order to access information. PLAs also used training to promote the use of CD-ROMs.

2 **To meet user needs and demands.** Some authorities had anticipated users' training needs and training had formed part of the initial planning of the service. For other authorities training provision had been consumer-led. One authority had identified specific groups or individuals who required training, such as the over-50s.

3 **Staff time.** Staff found that if users were given some initial training it saved staff time in the long run. A trained user was more independent than an untrained one, who could take up a lot of staff time.

Types of training

Formal or informal?

Most PLAs opted for informal training, and only two authorities provided any formal training sessions. The high proportion of informal training was not a surprise. It is perhaps the easiest type of training to provide as it involves a more spontaneous, rather than a planned, approach to meeting users needs. As users book their CD-ROM sessions or collect their discs, the opportunity presents itself for staff to offer short informal training sessions.

One-to-one or group sessions?

Practically all training was delivered on a one-to-one basis, reflecting the informal nature of most training. Group sessions were uncommon. Group training

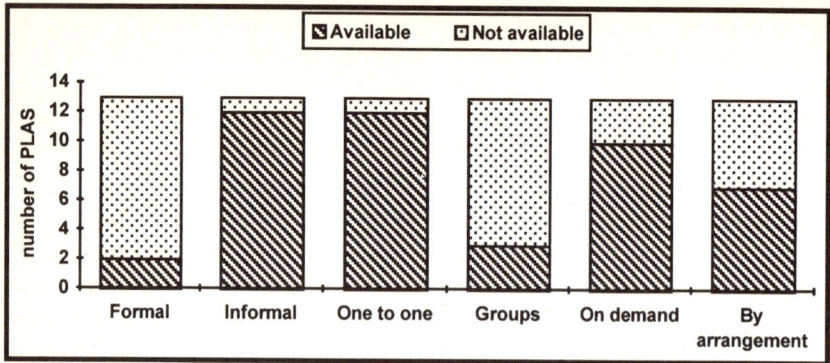

Fig. 6.2.3 *Types of training available*

requires more planning and organizing, involving factors such as time, place, registration and a targeted audience.

On demand or by arrangement?

Most training was available to users on demand. Three PLAs provided training neither on demand nor by arrangement. One can only assume that training was available only when library staff had time and not when the user wanted it! (See Figure 6.2.3.)

Effectiveness of training methods

The effectiveness of the training methods has yet to be evaluated, as the survey only involved PLAs describing their own training provision and did not involve an objective assessment of the training. However, there are plans at City University to include evaluation of various end-user training methods as part of a PhD course. The preliminary findings from the IT POINT project in Solihull indicate that 10–15 mins of one-to-one instruction is an effective method of end-user training. (These findings were discussed by Sue Turner and Gulshan Kayam at an AAL seminar on 5 September 1995 at LibTech International 95.)

Documentation

Ten PLAs provided users with some kind of documentation, usually manuals from suppliers. Only four PLAs went in for anything like simplified user guides or handouts. Only one authority mentioned providing any documentation relating to the training sessions. The end-user survey showed that users had a definite need for documentation. Whether or not PLAs were aware of users' need for documentation is unclear. Pressure on staff time and resources must act as a constraint on producing suitable user guides.

Experience of end-user training

What kind of experiences did PLAs have with providing end users with training? What sorts of problems did they experience? How successful had their training been? PLAs assessed their own service and reported a variety of experiences.

Users' reaction to training

The reaction from users was very positive. Users were happy with about 10 to 15 minutes training sessions of about 10–15 minutes at a time. One authority found it had difficulty meeting the demand, which always outstripped time available. Another authority, whose CD-ROM provision is focused on children, found that children had no problems with computer skills but needed advice on which sources to use to meet their information needs.

Limitations of training

A few authorities did find that the training had its limitations, as it was not possible to provide comprehensive training. For some PLAs, despite training their users, it was still necessary for staff to answer questions as they arose.

Impact on the role of library staff

Providing end-user training had both a positive and negative impact on the roles of various library staff. On the one hand training developed staff skills but on the other hand it increased the work load.

New skills

The greatest impact was the need for staff to learn new skills. Staff required training, not in teaching skills, but in software and hardware systems. Staff increased their knowledge about the CDs. One authority trained all its library staff in order to ensure that a basic level of expertise was available to users at all times.

Teaching role

The shift from the role of gatekeeper to that of teacher was significant. Training users enhanced library staff's status and promoted good relations with users.

Increased workload

Increased demand on staff time seemed to be the major drawback. Time was needed both for initial staff training and for learning about new software. Demands made by users increased workload.

Troubleshooting

Staff become much more involved in troubleshooting, i.e. dealing with the computers, printers and other more technical problems.

Future plans and policies

User training

Only two of the six PLAs who reported no end-user training were considering introducing some sort of training. The other four authorities had no plans to introduce user training, and one of these could only envisage a training programme if staffing levels increased.

Of the 13 PLAs that did provide training, eight were considering further plans for user training. Most plans were linked to the expansion of the service. One authority was considering setting up a user's forum. For one authority, end-user training was regarded as essential for the continuation of the CD-ROM service.

Future of CD-ROM services

The growth of home ownership of multimedia computers was thought to have some impact on the CD-ROM service. Eleven PLAs were planning changes to their CD-ROM provision as a result of home ownership of CD-ROM.

Eight PLAs were contemplating the provision of a CD-ROM loan service. Indeed, one authority was already doing so. In fact several authorities are now providing a CD-ROM loan service in conjunction with the company Ramesis.[5]

Six authorities believed that they would have to expand the number of CD-ROM titles as demand (as well as suggestions) from users increased.

A new role for the library?

The role of the library's CD-ROM service was becoming increasingly important as a result of multimedia home ownership.

1   The library was now being seen as **an informal advisory centre** for the selection and purchase of both software and hardware.

2   Two PLAs from relatively deprived areas felt that it was important to provide **access to CD-ROMs** as very few of their users had access to a computer in the home.

Conclusion

Needs met?

Overall provision

Only 43% of public library authorities with an open-access CD-ROM service provide users with any training in how to use CD-ROM. Not all PLAs could be said to have accepted responsibility for meeting their users' needs. But some PLAs have taken that commitment seriously and are providing training.

CD-ROM users

Hardly any PLAs monitored their CD-ROM service, and there was very little assessment of users' needs or usage levels.[1] Not many public libraries have a clear picture of who their CD-ROM users are or what their searching characteristics are.

Training methods

Most end-user training available in public libraries is basic and haphazard, with very little monitoring of the effectiveness of the training. Most training is of an introductory practical nature.

Documentation

PLAs rely heavily on CD-ROM suppliers' manuals rather than producing simple guides for users.

Constraints

Public libraries have to operate in a very tight financial environment. CD-ROM is not yet a mainstream service, and finding funding for training users is probably hard to justify when library hours are short and book funds low. Public libraries do not have the same funding as academic libraries, where CD-ROM use has flourished.

The main constraints on PLAs providing any training are:

- staffing levels
- staff training
- facilities.

So far many PLAs have relied on the fact that many of their CD-ROM users have used CD-ROM elsewhere and obtained some sort of training already.

References

1   Batterbee, C. and Nicholas, D., 'CD-ROMs in public libraries: a survey', *Aslib proceedings*, 47 (3), March 1995, 63–72.
2   Batt, C., *Information technology in public libraries*, 4th edn, Library Association Publishing, 1992.
3   Batt, C., *Information technology in the public library 1989*, 3rd edn, Public Libraries Research Group, 1990.
4   Shields, W., *Union list of CD-ROMs in London libraries*, Joseph Clarke, 1993.
5   'Public libraries launch CD-ROM lending service', *Managing information*, 2 (12), December 1995, 10.

Further reading

Hanson, T. and Day, J. (eds.), *CD-ROM in libraries: management issues*, Bowker-Saur, 1994.
Johnson, M. E. and Rosen, B. S., 'CD-ROM end-user instruction: a planning model', *Laserdisk professional*, 3 (2), March 1990, 35–40.

Leach, B. A., 'Research notes: Identifying CD-ROM use patterns as a tool for evaluating user instruction', *College and research libraries*, 55 (4), July 1994, 365–71.

Steffey, R. J. and Meyer, N., 'Evaluating user success and satisfaction with CD-ROM', *Laserdisk professional*, 2 (5), September 1989, 35–45.

7

CD-ROM and document delivery

Andrew Cameron

Introduction

Our purpose here is to look at two CD-ROM based document delivery services – ADONIS and Business Periodicals Ondisc (BPO) – as they have been implemented within Aston University Library and Information Services. User reactions, and their effect upon library staff and policies, are considered.

Document delivery seems to be a growth area at present. Many agents and publishers, faced with dwindling subscription numbers, are looking to other means of making money out of the information business. Little wonder, then, that the major players in the field are the large, well-established companies. Their printed periodical operations have decades, if not centuries, of tradition behind them.

The information explosion of the 20th century has rushed the progress of the printed periodical, so that it has taken on the role of ultimate goal – publish or perish. It had been quite a tidy industry until external factors began to rock the boat. The publishers were no longer totally in control. Rising material costs, falling budgets, rising subscription prices and falling subscription numbers all began to erode profits.

On the customers' side, things changed after the boom years of the sixties and seventies. Economics was now the keyword, and public service, educational and R&D budgets were cut back. For libraries, the major area for attention was recurrent costs – periodical subscriptions were an obvious target.

Then along came CD-ROM – hailed as a powerful storage medium for information, at first it threatened the traditional online method of accessing databases. As CD-ROM developed, its potential for image storage was exploited, and the publishers saw new hope.

One of the earliest studies of periodicals in a truly digital era was Project Quartet in 1986, part of which included the fledgling ADONIS system of storing periodicals on CD-ROM. Quite soon after that, the concept of the electronic journal was buzzing around in various forms. Librarians were interested in this new technology, which saved storage space, discouraged vandalism, meant less administrative work for their organization, and could perhaps save them some money. They saw it as little different from the print version of periodicals. Publishers saw a new source of income.

CD-ROM arrived at the right time in the information world. In its handling of bibliographic databases, it was able to establish itself as a reliable character-based medium before Windows and the more graphics-oriented packages became popular. When the world went Windows, CD-ROM was pressed into service as a storage and transmission medium for anything and everything. The electronic journal was with us, even though it was merely a digitized version of the printed format. The true electronic journal was to take some time to develop, and has yet to gain complete acceptance from the academic community.

Document delivery using ADONIS

ADONIS started commercial operations in 1991 – the company is based in Amsterdam. ADONIS discs contain the scanned pages of over 500 biomedical periodicals. New discs arrive weekly, each with a revised cumulative index to what is on the system. ADONIS charges an annual subscription for its service. There is then a royalty to be paid for each article printed out; charging statistics are automatically recorded by the ADONIS software. The charges are set at levels determined by the publisher of each individual periodical, and are broadly in line with copyright clearance charges. Viewing articles is free.

ADONIS was probably the first 'real' CD-ROM based document delivery system. Its early years are well documented by Bradbury,[1] Braid,[2] and Friend.[3] It started out as a research project, carried out between a consortium of publishers (led by Elsevier), and the British Library. The publishers were interested in investigating the economic viability of the ADONIS system, in the face of dwindling subscriptions. This was reported by Clark[4] from the LIRG AGM, and reiterated some years later by McKnight.[5] The ADONIS service is still in use at BLDSC, in its commercial form.

ADONIS was first considered by Aston in 1992. The background to its adoption was not the most ideal. The University Library had to make a considerable budget adjustment in recurrent expenditure, and ADONIS seemed to be a lifeline.

The original aims of ADONIS, however, did not envisage the system being used as a replacement for printed subscriptions in libraries. This may have been a more defensible viewpoint ten years ago, but in the present economic climate any method of reducing costs or getting better value for a shrinking periodicals budget seems fair game to librarians. For producers to be unaware of this factor seems to display extreme ostrich-like tendencies. With little prospect of an improvement in the financial condition of libraries, publishers will surely face even more periodicals cancellations. Librarians might be tempted to think that they would be grateful for any income in the form of royalty payments, and would try to make their material even more easily accessible for end-users without library staff intervention. After all, not every library has enough staff to operate such a mediated document delivery service, given the increase in requests it may generate.

Aston's implementation, therefore, did not match the expectations of the system producer. We were forced to see it in purely financial terms, since we did not have the time to implement a periodicals deselection model. For the cost of its annual subscription, and the royalty payments, we could compensate in a cost-effective manner for the loss of some 75 printed periodicals subscriptions. The 500 periodicals on ADONIS covered subject areas which were peripheral to our teaching and research needs, and it was thought that the royalties would not therefore pose too much of a financial problem. We did not know exactly how much these royalties would cost, and we realized we were taking a risk. This was a matter of great concern to us. If use of the system exceeded our expectations, and we went over our allocated budget, we might have to restrict access to the system. This charging policy is still a concern to us. Many librarians would be uncomfortable to sign up to a system, the exact cost of which was unknown.

Perhaps the problem stems from the origins of ADONIS in the early days, when publishers were familiar with only two factors – subscriptions and copyright clearance charges. But charging for electronic information has changed in the intervening years, especially in academic libraries. Online services are not exclusively pay-as-you-go based, with many offering block subscriptions for so many access hours per year. This type of charging makes library finances much easier to administer and control, and ensures the continuation of a service throughout the academic year. By not providing the means towards a firm financial plan, an open-ended system like ADONIS presents a very real threat to budgetary control. It is interesting to note that BPO, our other CD-ROM document delivery service, does not choose to operate such a charging structure, but favours a one-off inclusive payment.

Consulting the end-user

We consulted our Life Sciences faculty before introducing ADONIS, but no one really knew what we were getting into. Aston was the first academic site for ADONIS in the UK. We had no pool of knowledge to work from. It seemed like just another electronic information system, and we now have over 20 of them. Our policy was (and still is) to have as many systems as possible available as end-user services. ADONIS did not seem any different from the other services we offered. We relied on ADONIS's relatively simple interface to make it accessible to all our users. But ADONIS grew out of a library-oriented project, and much of its testing and implementation had been carried out by library staff within BLDSC. What is acceptable to librarians may not always be suitable for the end-user. After all, librarians have been using complicated command languages in online searching for years, but these are not suitable for an average 'naïve' end-user. When ADONIS went commercial, perhaps they missed the opportunity to revise their software and their product, and to review their potential audience more thoroughly.

The pros and cons of implementing ADONIS have been well discussed recently by Morris,[6] and all the concerns he expresses echo our own experience. It is interesting to note how often the subject of financial considerations comes up in his article, although he did not identify the unpredictable amount of royalty payments as a problem. Aston's own deliberations over the introduction of ADONIS are documented in a conference paper by Smith,[7] and many of the points made then are still valid to us today.

Since we were the first UK academic site for ADONIS, we attracted much attention from other libraries interested in the system. The demand for demonstrations and feedback grew so much that we decided it would be more time-effective if we organized a short seminar at Aston in conjunction with ADONIS. We felt that we could give some useful guidance to others as to how they should think about implementing the system, and perhaps avoid some of the troubles we had encountered. In June 1993, our seminar was attended by over 30 delegates from the UK and elsewhere in Europe. The views of end-users and library staff at Aston, and staff at BLDSC, also appeared in an article by Pilling.[8]

When ADONIS went live at Aston, therefore, it had many negative connotations. It was always linked with periodical cancellations, which may have soured its appeal. We ran awareness and training sessions for academic and research staff, since we considered them the prime users for the system. Initial reaction was mixed. Some academics felt they would miss the portability and browsability of the printed periodicals. Some saw ADONIS as a bonus, providing us with access to over 400 periodicals we did not subscribe to. We realized we would have to monitor its use, and the impressions of the users.

Since our staff time was too limited to embark on an evaluation study, we arranged with Bruce Reid, Senior Lecturer at the School of Information Studies at the University of Central England, for some of his students to base a project on ADONIS. Part of this would involve interviewing users of the system. The students also looked at the ADONIS interface and search procedure, comparing them with other electronic products they had already evaluated. This study was carried out in two separate years. We had also planned to carry out another study, after ADONIS had launched its new Windows-based software, but this second phase has yet to take place.

From the two sets of interviews, and from the impressions of the librarianship students themselves, we derived much useful information about the end-users' perceptions of ADONIS. They fall into two main categories – the interface and the end product.

ADONIS originally used software which had been developed prior to Project Quartet. It was written by their own development team, and was fairly idiosyncratic. It was not Windows-based, but it made extensive use of icons, buttons and graphics screen layout. Being produced in-house, it definitely had a 'feel' of its own, and did not employ some of the conventions which other CD-ROM software used in a fairly standard way. When the product was launched commercially, it would have been prudent of ADONIS to take the opportunity to obtain detailed opinions from potential markets on its interface. Some practical advice from an end-user oriented library might have improved their software dramatically, at an early stage.

After three years with the system, we are not sure that ADONIS can ever really be targeted at end-users in its present state. The system was never designed for end-users, but given current trends in electronic information provision it is rather short-sighted to ignore this method of implementation. Even as early as the final report of Project Quartet in 1990, Tuck et al.[9] were suggesting areas of consideration for the future of ADONIS. Unfortunately, they are very much the same topics as those being raised in this chapter. Little seems to have changed in the past six years.

Its largest (and most profitable) customers are the big document supply outfits, such as BLDSC, and some other national libraries abroad. Its policy for including material supports this observation. ADONIS does not scan the entire periodical. It includes only original articles, and letters. It excludes contents pages, notes for authors, and any advertising material. So for an end-user it is definitely not the same product as the printed form. It has also undergone some form of intellectual censorship, to weed out any material which would not be included in a standard bibliographic database (such as Embase).

Its scanning policy was a big source of irritation to the users we interviewed. For academic staff wishing to submit an article to one of the ADONIS periodicals, it was annoying not to have the instructions for authors, for example. They had to apply through interlibrary loan, to get the paper issue for that. Likewise, the absence of contents pages was seen as a major drawback. Although ADONIS could display the bibliographic details of the contents of an issue, this was not seen as an adequate substitute for the printed contents page. The issue contents list could not be printed, making browsing an on-screen procedure. Myers[10] suggests that this effectively prohibits ADONIS from replacing the printed copy. Both these problems could have been avoided if ADONIS had taken a broader (and more realistic) view of its customer base. Three years before, Line[11] had stated, with reference to current periodicals, 'Reading on screen is unsatisfactory even when a specific article is wanted.' Perhaps it is even more unsatisfactory when scanning lists of potentially useful articles.

Given the funding problems always prevalent in the education system in the UK, it was only a matter of time before academic libraries found their own set of needs from a system such as ADONIS. Firstly, faced by the very pressures which triggered the original ADONIS project (rising subscription costs), academic libraries are moving away from the 'collection' model of information towards an efficient 'access' model. At Aston, we now devote 14% of our acquisitions budget to document delivery, either electronic or 'traditional'. Academic libraries now need fast and cost-effective 'just-in-time' document delivery services, that do not impose additional burdens on already overstretched library staff. Secondly, for many years, the concept of end-user self-service has been commonplace. Librarians have empowered users to perform many hitherto 'restricted' processes. The two concepts seem to blend nicely into a logical solution for an academic environment – the endusers perform the document delivery process themselves. And all the better if that process is a completely local procedure, because then transmission delays are eliminated.

The ADONIS user interface

To paraphrase Line's vision of the future from 1989,[11] CD-ROMs would store vast amounts of literature, making libraries locally self-sufficient. Interlibrary loans would decrease, but publishers, libraries and users would all be the better off. But in complying only with the needs of traditional document delivery organizations, ADONIS lacks many design features which would seem essential to an academic application of the type outlined by Line. For example, users could not easily see the latest issue of a periodical. They had to perform a periodical title search, including year (or volume), and scan through the hit list to find the most recent issue number. It would have been much more acceptable for users to have to enter a periodical title, and hit a 'latest issue' button. While the absence of contents pages was in keeping with the producers' original remit, it seems a pity that they kept their eyes fixed on the same horizon for so long.

One problem with using a graphics-oriented search engine is the opacity of many icons. ADONIS's icons seem particularly obscure, and continue to baffle many end-users. Of course, we don't expect an ISO for icons, but it seems pointless to use them if they do not convey the right information. Two small but different representations of a printer caused a lot of problems – people just didn't know what the difference was meant to be. Buttons with 'Print Article' and 'View Print Queue' might have been more effective. At Aston, we have a policy of not complicating things that are simple. The 'frills' of a system may look easy on the eye, but if they confuse matters, we (and our customers) would rather not have them. In a rare article about design of systems for end-users, McDonald[12] states with admirable common sense, 'The more work the user must do to accommodate the artificially imposed structure of the delivery system, the less effective the delivery system will be . . . [and] . . . the less likely the system is to be used.' This is exactly our experience with ADONIS.

In scientific subject areas, currency is an important factor in information provision. Scientific literature moves forward at high speed, and the academic community expects to be kept abreast of it. In this area, ADONIS was found distinctly lacking. The production process of the CD-ROMs was fragmented over three countries within Europe. This did not help the timeliness of the material on those CD-ROMs. The method of obtaining the articles for inclusion seemed somewhat haphazard. We were told of one publisher whose periodicals for ADONIS were thrown into a big box, which was shipped to ADONIS when it was full. How long the periodicals lay in the box is not known – presumably it depended on how big the box was! In comparison with other electronic services which our users had access to, ADONIS seemed incredibly slow in mounting material.

Many users made comparisons with the ISI databases available on BIDS, which we thought slightly unfair. The two systems provide completely different types of information, and ISI puts much effort into its short turn-around time. We did find many cases, however, when MEDLINE in its monthly updates was well ahead of the weekly ADONIS discs. One thing that many users tactfully 'forgot' when commenting on the slowness of ADONIS was the fact that printed periodicals are sometimes sluggish in finding their way onto library shelves. The problem of timeliness becomes a more serious problem when our major traditional document supply organization (BLDSC) imposes a four-month moratorium on the lending of entire current periodical issues. We are left without an alternative source to ADONIS. The technology seems to have exacerbated the delay in seeing current material. This, of course, applies to BPO as much as ADONIS.

One result of the user interviews came as a surprise to the library staff. The academics admitted that serendipity played an important part in their scanning of the literature. For such a strictly science-based subject area as medicine, this seemed rather odd. But the remark came up time and again, and the academics reported that serendipity suffered using ADONIS. This may have been linked to the policy of not including contents pages, and being unconnected to a proper bibliographic database. ADONIS does have the facility for title word searching, but it lacks the in-depth indexing of something like Embase.

Work is not always carried out in the workplace, and academics frequently take work home with them. This certainly was the case with our interviewees. The ADONIS system, whatever else it is, is definitely not portable. A user could not flip through a periodical issue from ADONIS on the train home. Not unless they had printed it all out beforehand, which costs money and takes time. Time is what they don't have, which is why they read articles on the train.

Perhaps the academic staff at Aston are spoiled, for we allow them to borrow any periodical they want. Some institutions keep their periodicals in the library at all times, so that the portability argument would not be so strong for their academics.

Another important factor in our user perceptions was the quality of images, both on screen and after printing. Medical periodicals include a large amount of illustrative material – graphs, diagrams, half-tones and colour photographs. ADONIS handles line graphs and diagrams well, but there was much adverse comment on its presentation of half-tones. Scientific periodicals tend to be printed on high-quality art paper in order to serve the illustrations as well as possible. In the scanning process, the images suffer quite bad degradation (especially images of electron micrographs). In the subsequent printing process, on normal photocopy-quality paper, the images degrade even more. To our microbiologists this was a real bugbear. On several occasions, we had to get the paper copy on loan from BLDSC for them to see images of satisfactory quality.

Displaying articles on screen does not incur the ADONIS royalty charge. The screen display is not very user-friendly, however. One can see the whole page on screen, but little is legible other than the title, if its font size is large enough. By zooming in, one can read the article, but as it becomes more legible, so less of it can be seen on the screen. The user has then to navigate about the screen using a mouse and scroll bars in order to see the whole page, a segment at a time. As one might expect, this does not encourage users to view articles on screen. The same problem arises with BPO, but the two systems differ at Aston in their users' attitudes towards printing articles. On the ADONIS system, amazingly few users will print out an article without scanning it to assess its quality. On BPO, users printed almost every article, usually without scanning for relevance. Perhaps the charging policies of the two systems have something to do with this. Our cost-conscious academics know well that each ADONIS article incurs a printing royalty, and are perhaps over-cautious lest they run up large bills for the library. BPO's block subscription does not present the same problem.

One very worrying point which came out of our interviews was the fact that users would go to another institution's library to see the paper copy, rather than use the awkward ADONIS screen view. This made little sense to the library staff, because the nearest medical collection to us is a 30-minute car journey away. But the statement was made (and continues to be made) many times, so we have to believe it is true. In that case, someone has misjudged the end market quite drastically. Are librarians the only people to rush to embrace electronic information? If users would spend an hour going somewhere else, rather than use an electronic system, there seems to be a basic mismatch.

It seems to us that the academic community is far more conservative than we thought. In our innocence, we saw no difference between print and electronic versions of a periodical. We thought the information was the most important part of a periodical. What we did not appreciate was that the change may have been too much, too soon. Certainly, given the reactions of our science-based users, we cannot see an overnight move across to electronic journals. Roberts[13] defines the problem as being at the heart of the collection/access model of information: 'The major problem is a lack of acceptance by faculty of document delivery as a substitute for local ownership of even peripheral research journals.' This is a viewpoint with which I concur wholeheartedly, after four years of experience of a CD-ROM document delivery system aimed at end-users. Roberts goes further to say that we may risk losing the support (and even patronage) of faculty by following this road. I think this may be carrying the argument too far. I believe, however, that we as librarians must heed the messages our end-users give to us, and tailor our services accordingly. Any new service which we think may suit their needs must be subject to close scrutiny before introduction, even on a trial basis. We cannot afford to lose the support of our customers.

As a broad generalization, scientific literature relies heavily on periodicals, while the social sciences are perhaps more book-based. This means more demand for scientific periodicals. ADONIS contains 500 scientific periodicals, available on only one terminal. As an end-user service, this creates the possibility of a major bottleneck. This possibility will become more likely as more years are added to the ADONIS collection. Perhaps, in hindsight, our decision to make the system available directly to the end-user was not the best.

The best application of ADONIS may be the provision of a local in-house 'interlibrary loan' service, where users request articles and library staff supply them. But this seems to withdraw completely the browsing and the serendipity which academics stated was so important to them. Of course, there are other ways in which periodicals can be browsed – Current Contents, Uncover, BIDS services. But none of these systems have any link with ADONIS. Not even Embase has a direct link – all it can do is to give the ADONIS accession number for items to be found on that system.

ADONIS revisions

No system remains unchanged, and ADONIS has undergone quite major revisions, partially as a result of feedback from its users. In a recent paper, Compier[14] gives a history of his company's 14-year-old system, saying that 'it should need no introduction' (although Myers[10] recently described it as being one of the 'experiments in document delivery'). Compier outlines the future strategy for ADONIS, and recognizes that the method of charging still needs to be resolved to everyone's satisfaction.

Singleton[15] summarizes ADONIS's situation quite succinctly by saying 'It will have to transform itself almost out of recognition if it is to be successful and significant.' Morris's evaluation[6] led to his rejection of implementing the system. Our own experience at Aston has led to the cancellation of our subscription, for the reasons outlined above.

ADONIS would have been a far better product if it could have combined a database (such as Embase, which is updated weekly, and is owned by Elsevier, historically a leading light of ADONIS) with a link from the bibliographic details to the image.

Business Periodicals Ondisc

This is exactly the system offered in a different subject area by Business Periodicals Ondisc (BPO). Produced by UMI, BPO is an adjunct to the well-known database product from the same company, ABI/INFORM. Images of periodical articles from 1987 onwards are available on around 600 CD-ROMs, updated monthly. For a block subscription, a library can print up to a given limit of articles. Although BPO is linked to ABI/INFORM, it does not deliver every periodical indexed in the database. Of the 800 periodicals scanned for ABI/INFORM, only about 400 of them are available in full-text form on BPO. The database clearly shows if a particular reference is available in full-text by displaying the message 'Availability: CD-ROM' at the foot of the screen. To view such references, the user hits the 'enter' key, and is then told which CD-ROM to insert into the drive; the system then displays the article.

UMI introduced BPO in 1989, by which time the electronic journal concept was not the hot news it had been four years earlier. Contemporary reviews of the new product did not use any of the hyperbole which had been used to describe ADONIS. Halperin and Holley[16] were quite matter-of-fact in their appraisal of the new system. But even writing as early as December 1989, they reported that UMI was geared towards their system being accessed by end-users. UMI had even then taken the idea further than ADONIS has yet to do.

After investigating the possibilities offered by BPO, we agreed to a trial, in financial collaboration with our Business School, in 1994. Its introduction was on the same basis as ADONIS and all our other electronic information services – a machine on public access, devoted exclusively to end-users, without any library staff intervention. Although we were still smarting from the academics' reactions to ADONIS, we were convinced that our philosophy was basically sound, and that this was the way in which such services should be implemented.

BPO compared with ADONIS

Here at Aston, BPO was different from ADONIS from the start. It was introduced as a supplement to our printed collection, and so had none of the negative connotations attached to the introduction of ADONIS. Beyond that, it was a different type of system, for both end-users and library staff.

From the library point of view, there was less 'risk' involved in delivering printouts. BPO charged on a block subscription, whereby for one up-front payment virtually unlimited printouts could be made. There is none of the open-ended pay-as-you-use royalty charge for each document printed. This automatically makes it more attractive to librarians, having to work to a set budget. Whereas ADONIS operates on a 'blank cheque' principle, BPO operates within a defined single payment.

From the end-users viewpoint, it was also more attractive. Not only did it provide the documents, but it also gave easier access to those documents, because it had an in-built database, ABI/INFORM. This meant that on one system, users could perform a proper subject search on the database, and then retrieve a high proportion of them without having to use another source. This has meant that the take-up of BPO has been much more enthusiastic than that of ADONIS.

This difference in approach may be a result of the fact that BPO was a commercial system right from the start. It was an economically thought-out system, attached to an already well-established commercial database. It benefited from using proven and familiar software as a search engine, and operating on a more conventional subscription basis. Because it used a conventional text search engine, it had no need for the somewhat obscure icons of ADONIS's more graphics-oriented package.

With ADONIS, we conducted some research into the end-users' reactions to the system. We have not done the same with BPO, but the users' views of the system have been apparent to us nonetheless.

Many of the problems of updating attributed to ADONIS (weekly updates) may not have the same importance for users of BPO (monthly updates). Because it deals with social sciences material, it may be that the time delays in getting images onto the system do not present the same inconvenience for users. Library staff are aware, however, that delays of up to three months can occur before some issues appear in full-text. Although this has worried some end-users, the social scientists may not have the same urgency for really current material that the pure scientists have. In his review of BPO, Stewart[17] admitted it had been difficult to fulfil his task, because 'students flocked to use it in such numbers.' But he also struck the same note of caution that had been voiced regarding ADONIS. He thought it unwise for a library to discontinue paper versions of periodicals in favour of BPO. But the reason was slightly different – there was no guarantee that a title on BPO would continue to be scanned on it.

This has been true of a few titles already on ADONIS. The detailed print statistics which all subscribers submit easily show which periodical titles are not being looked at. Clearly, time and effort are being wasted by scanning them for input if they are not being looked at by the end-users. ADONIS rightly considers such titles as worthy of deselection. Could this be the start of a rationalization process for periodicals? Will electronic access at last give us accurate information on which articles are read (or at least warrant printing out)?

Although closely linked with the subject database, BPO offers good facilities for browsing through periodical issues, by using a separate periodical database. This is simplicity itself to use. By entering the periodical title, the users can choose an issue, and a hit list of the contents appears. They can then go through the contents of the periodical, one paper at a time, or display the contents page.

Considering the number of titles covered by bibliographic databases in each of the subject areas, the two systems give access to different proportions of available articles. Of the 4000 titles covered by MEDLINE, only 13% are available as image documents on ADONIS. BPO provides images for almost 50% of the titles indexed on ABI/INFORM. This has a lot to do with the publishing patterns in each area, and the subjects the two systems have decided to concentrate on. Biomedicine is comparatively a much larger subject area, and this might explain the comments that ADONIS does not cover 'essential' titles for a large number of academics.

Another major difference between the two systems is the inclusion policy for each. In ADONIS, only the 'real' documents are included – no contents pages, no instructions for authors, no adverts. But BPO offers the whole periodical issue, from front cover to back cover complete. Not everything is indexed in the database, but could we really expect that? Adverts, covers and the rest of the less academically important material cannot be found on the ABI/INFORM database, but they are included, in summary form, in the table of contents for each periodical. Some distinctions, therefore, are made between 'real' documents and other material. But that other material is always included, giving exactly the same periodical in electronic form as we would get in print.

BPO at Aston does not link to a jukebox (which ADONIS does). UMI have been working on their own jukebox, designed specifically for use with BPO. For the time being at Aston, the 600 CD-ROMs are housed in four large rotating carousels, and the user has to insert the appropriate CD-ROM from a screen prompt. This does not seem to cause many problems. Initially, we had been apprehensive that the CD-ROMs would quickly get out of order and be difficult to find. This has not happened. Although not an automatic procedure, it does not seem to cause hardship, especially since each CD-ROM is clearly labelled and already loaded into its own caddy.

From a housekeeping point of view, both systems present librarians with some basic problems. When a library subscribes to ADONIS or BPO, it takes on 400 to 550 periodicals, many of which will be new to that library. There is a major cataloguing implication in this. To conform to other standard periodicals catalogue records, the cataloguing section has to find starting dates and volumes for all the new titles. This is not an easy task, and at Aston we could not contemplate checking each one. So we had to let our standards slip, and exclude volume numbers on the catalogue.

The contracts between libraries and suppliers of electronic services quite often stipulate that they be used only by the staff and students of the library's parent organization. This is a policy we adhere to strictly at Aston. While ADONIS did not impose this restriction, we did not think it wise to operate one access policy for some services and another for the rest. So we decided to make it available only to our own staff and students. Besides being consistent, we did not want students from outside Aston coming in and printing off ADONIS articles, leaving us to pay the not inconsiderable royalty charges. We had to devise a way of alerting our own users to the availability of the periodicals on ADONIS and BPO without entering catalogue records on our union catalogue for other libraries to see. So all CD-ROM periodicals holdings were given purely local cataloguing.

This still means that if outsiders come into our library building, or connect to our OPAC on JANET, they will find the catalogue entries for periodicals to which they have no access. This can cause problems at information points if outsiders find a title through JANET, come to our library, and are then told that they cannot have access to that title. It is a problem which will increase, as more periodicals appear in electronic form. We have to be very careful, in our catalogue entries for all restricted items, to spell out who can use them. On a wider scale, as more libraries take electronic versions of periodicals, local cooperative referral schemes may become less effective, with a proportion of periodicals stock being unavailable for consultation purposes. This is, of course, a direct result of moving from print, which had no such restrictions imposed, to electronic media. This view is in direct opposition to that of King,[18] who states (rather naïvely) that 'Librarians must not allow new licensing agreements, fears about network security or the desire for fee-for-electronic-service to threaten their historical commitment to service and each other.' Librarians have always had respect for legal commitments. Surely now is not the time for them to threaten the livelihood of the copyright owners, or allow the service they provide for their own users to be overloaded?

Another problem is knowing exactly which issues are on the system. By subscribing to a whole block of periodicals to be received in a batch on CD-ROM, we lost the check-in stage which is a normal part of our periodicals routine. Have we got volume 23, issue 3 of the *Journal of hematology* on ADONIS? The only way to find out is to look for it on ADONIS itself. If the producers would care to consult their users, they would find that some libraries actually do like to know what they have available in their stock. (Morris[6] for some reason lists the absence of a check-in procedure as a plus!) Surely it cannot be too difficult for producers to include a delivery note with a listing of issues on each CD-ROM.

Whenever an electronic system is introduced into a library these days, we immediately look to beaming it out of the library, across a network. This is now standard procedure for many institutions. With systems using bitmapped images of periodical pages, this involves sending very large files across the network. The feasibility of this has yet to be proved at Aston, and Myers[10] assumes them to be single-access systems. Instead of networking the images, we opted to make the indexes of the ADONIS system available over our network. The ABI/INFORM database (essentially the index to BPO) was already mounted across campus. The ADONIS indexes needed extensive programming input by our computer officer in order to manipulate them into the required format, and this has been documented by Craft.[19] On the network, users could tag the articles they wanted printed, and submit the request electronically to the library. Library staff would then run a batch program each day to print all requests, and send them through internal mail to the requesters. ABI/INFORM at present cannot offer such a service.

The need for broader-based CD-ROM databases

Despite all the shortcomings of our two 'conglomerate' systems for electronic document delivery, they do have some very positive features. Using only one search engine they allow access to hundreds of periodicals from many different publishers. The increasing trend for publishers to produce CD-ROMs containing only their own periodicals is a very worrying one.

Many major publishers (such as Elsevier), major periodicals (such as *Nature*) and learned societies (such as the American Society for Microbiology) already have their products on CD-ROM. Since there is no standard search engine, each one uses a different one. It is the same problem that libraries encountered some years ago with bibliographic CD-ROM databases. At Aston, we have at least 15 bibliographic search engines to contend with! The prospect of each publisher (or even in some cases each periodical) having its own searching system is one that librarians should view with great concern. Even if these systems are not put out for public access, it is a trainer's nightmare to enable library document delivery staff to become competent in all of them.

The apparent reticence expressed by Myers[10] in accepting CD-ROM as more than an experiment in document delivery is perhaps more than just a slip of the pen. Perhaps the message is not the most important thing, after all – the method of delivering it may be just as important. It could be that we have come too far too soon, and that we are still in a period of end-user culture shock combined with a barrage of publishers panicking in the face of rising subscription costs and diminishing numbers of subscribers.

It seems that the marketing mix is still not quite right. Eiblum,[20] talking on behalf of information brokers about conventional document delivery options, has a fairly chaotic vision of the future: 'the variety of information containers, the expansion of sources and resources and the complexity of ordering options can and will induce more librarians into subcontracting agreements with information brokers.' For librarians, the same gloomy prognosis might also be applied to the proliferation of small specialized electronic document delivery products.

We all know the maxim 'small is beautiful', but how can it be true? If librarians are inundated by a plethora of individual CD-ROM electronic journals, would we not cry out for a single, uniform interface? SilverPlatter have anticipated the impending chaos, and started on their Electronic Reference Library (ERL). They have made quite some headway in providing a single interface to many disparate databases. They claim that over 170 ERL-compliant databases are already available. Yeadon[21] provides an account of how this has been implemented on a limited scale at Imperial College, London. But can one off-the-shelf product provide a single interface to the many varied products that will be available from all these individual publishers? And even if it works now, what will happen when more publishers jump on the bandwagon? Can we be sure that everyone will adhere to an agreed standard (even if there was one)?

It would be a pity if the freedom offered by local storage on CD-ROM actually worked against us, and made the information we hold more complex for our end-users to access. For the user, the basic working of a printed periodical is the same, regardless of publisher or subject. Introducing a variety of computer interfaces for different publishers, or subjects, or periodicals between the user and the words, means that they have to acquire more and more specific new skills. This is perhaps the greatest challenge of the new technology faced by librarians.

We need publishers to be continually aware of the financial strains imposed on libraries, to realize that the rules of the game have changed dramatically in the past ten years, and to accept that individual products which were acceptable in print may not be acceptable as individual electronic services. 'Conglomerate' systems are the ones most likely to appeal to library service providers. This means that publishers have to rethink their traditional enmities. Libraries will want publishers A, B, C, D and E all together in one system, or not at all. Publishers must appreciate that guaranteed profits cannot derive from traditional subscription methods much longer.

Electronic access to periodicals will give an accurate reflection of the value and esteem of the articles they contain. We will have accurate, automatically generated hit lists of articles viewed and printed. We may supply the proof that tolls the knell for certain titles, and encourages them to be disseminated in alternative forms such as electronic discussion groups.

As librarians, we need further to champion the views of our end-users, and to strive to lessen the demands which are imposed upon them as we empower them to fulfil tasks which we traditionally carried out on their behalf.

References

1 Bradbury, D., 'ADONIS – the view of the users', *IFLA journal*, **14** (2), 1988, 132–6.
2 Braid, A., 'Document delivery – the dawn of a new era', *IATUL quarterly*, **3** (4), 1989, 207–13.
3 Friend, F. J., 'ADONIS – a happy medium or falling between two stools?', *IATUL quarterly*, **4** (4), 1990, 239–43.
4 Clark, D., 'ADONIS stands for change', *Library and information research news*, **6** (21), 1983, 15.
5 McKnight, C., 'Electronic journals – past, present . . . and future?', *Aslib proceedings*, **45** (1), 1993, 7–10.
6 Morris, W., 'ADONIS: a document delivery solution? A case study', *Health libraries review*, **11** (1), 1994, 39–51.
7 Smith, N.R., 'ADONIS at Aston: from "just in case" to "just in time" '. In Morley, M. and Woodward, H., *Taming the electronic jungle – electronic information: the collection management issues*, Leeds, National Acquisitions Group, 1993, 96–105.
8 Pilling, S., 'The ADONIS experience: some views', *Serials*, **7** (3), 1994, 249–52.
9 Tuck, B. et al., *Project quartet*, London, British Library, 1990 (Library and Information Research Report No.76).
10 Myers, G., 'Electronic health information services: a review', *Electronic library*, **11** (4/5), 1993, 283–7.
11 Line, M., 'Universal availability of publications in an electronic age', *IATUL quarterly*, **3** (4), 1989, 214–23.
12 McDonald, M., 'Paper versus screen: evaluating different design metaphors for electronic document delivery systems'. In Raitt, D. I. and Jeapes, B., *Online Information 94: 18th International Online Information Meeting Proceedings, London, 6–8 December 1994*, Oxford, Learned Information, 1995, 285–92.
13 Roberts, E. P., 'ILL/document delivery as an alternative to local ownership of seldom-used scientific journals', *Journal of academic librarianship*, **18** (1), 1992, 30–4.

14 Compier, H. and Campbell, R., 'ADONIS gathers momentum and faces some new problems', *Interlending and document supply*, **23** (3), 1995, 22–5.

15 Singleton, A., *The scientific journal: present trends and likely futures – their impact on library and information services*, LITC, London, 1994 (Information UK Outlooks, No.7).

16 Halperin, M. and Holley, B.A., 'Business collection and Business Periodicals Ondisc: streamlining periodical retrieval', *Database*, **12** (6), 1989, 28–43.

17 Stewart, J. A., 'Business Periodicals Ondisc: ABI/Inform on CD-ROM', *Information today*, **8** (9), 1991, 21–3.

18 King, H., 'Walls around the electronic library', *Electronic library*, **11** (3), 1993, 165–74.

19 Craft, E. J., 'Distributed ADONIS indexing – the Aston LIS solution', *ADONIS news*, **4** (1), 1993, 1–3.

20 Eiblum, P., 'The coming of age of document delivery', *Bulletin of the American Society for Information Science*, **21** (3), 1995, 21–2.

21 Yeadon, J., 'Experiences with SilverPlatter Electronic Reference Library at Imperial College', *Program*, **29** (2), 1995, 169–75.

8

Developing in-house
CD-ROM databases

Case study 1: the RAM Database
at Nottingham Trent University
Jim Corlett

Introduction
In this chapter we shall consider why CDs have been chosen as a key part of
the development of the Recent Advances in Manufacturing (RAM) Project at
The Nottingham Trent University, and how user access has been improved by
this choice. Future developments will also be indicated. The RAM project
involves commercially available in-house products, and the dual nature of
RAM will affect the following discussion.

The Nottingham Trent University, one of the most popular higher education establishments in the UK as far as applications are concerned, has 26
departments grouped into nine faculties. It has some 15,400 people studying
on full-time and sandwich courses, and 5200 on over 90 part-time courses. In
addition, it runs an increasing number of short courses, conferences and continuing education programmes. The three libraries comprising the Library and
Information Services (LIS) stock over 400,000 books, 2500 periodicals, audio-
visual materials and electronic databases. A brand-new learning resource centre is currently being planned. The RAM project is the major entrepreneurial
activity run from within LIS.

Dilemmas raised by entrepreneurial projects in an academic library environment have been addressed and four universally applicable tenets identified
to assist in answering them:

1 Any entrepreneurial project should be compatible with the library's and
the institution's objectives.

2 Entrepreneurial projects must be managed in such a way that they do not
undermine or put at risk the mainstream activities of the library and information service.

3 Institutional support, at the highest level, is essential for all but the smallest of initiatives.

4 Everybody must realize from the start that risk is involved, and must
accept the likely consequences of failure, in both financial and human terms.[1]

Assuming these tenets have been recognized and addressed, projects such as RAM offer several inherent advantages, besides the potential for 'blood, toil, tears and sweat' and the increased management burden and stress involved in risk-taking.[2] One of these advantages is the exploitation of (often expensive) items of library material and the rationalization of interlibrary loan material: that is, ensuring that items contained in in-house material are easily found, and that this material is explored first before the option is taken to obtain items through interlibrary loan. Another benefit is the underpinning and enhancement of services to internal users on the back of the commercial developments. More general reasons for wanting to create an in-house CD-ROM are discussed by Hallgren.[3]

What is RAM?

> One of the most useful services which any information unit can offer to any firm, large or small, is a selective 'current awareness' bulletin derived from scanning sources of new information. Preferably this should lead to the building-up of a database of special relevance to a firm or closely-related group of firms.[4]

Applied also to an academic context, this quotation describes perfectly the conviction which lies behind the RAM project. RAM consists of the production, promotion and distribution of a series of commercial bibliographic products addressing the area of manufacturing. These products bring together the engineering/technological and managerial/organizational aspects of manufacturing. This is seen as a niche area not explicitly addressed by other commercial products. Its aim is to provide a one-stop source of information in an area which would otherwise require searches across several different types of sources. While not covering a vast range of information (some 3000 items are added annually, although this may shortly increase), it is a first-stop source which will provide sufficient information for many needs.

The structure of RAM aims to follow a logical path through the manufacturing cycle, from general items on manufacturing industry as a whole, through management concerns, product development, manufacturing systems and processes, manufacturing planning and control, to maintenance, monitoring and inspection. Advanced technologies, such as communications and control, artificial intelligence, and simulation, are covered as they are applied to manufacturing. Training and educational aspects also appear. Details of books, conference proceedings and videos in any of the above areas are provided.

Within these broad headings, items detailing current developments are included if they are likely to be of interest to manufacturing firms, even if not exclusively so. Thus, to give a flavour of the project, reviews of issues such as business process reengineering, total quality management, and environmental management are included, as well as topics such as manufacturing strategy, logistics, production planning and control, and process planning. Within product development, areas including concurrent engineering, product design and design for X, and rapid prototyping, are addressed. Advanced manufacturing systems – computer-integrated manufacturing, flexible manufacturing, cellular manufacturing systems etc. – are covered, together with (usually automated) developments in processes such as machining, assembly, materials handling etc. Robotics, both theory and applications, is explored in some depth. Advanced technologies considered when applied to manufacturing include neural networks, knowledge-based systems, fuzzy logic, genetic algorithms and virtual reality.

RAM grew out of a current awareness service initially designed to collate information on the microprocessor/computer revolution in the early 1980s. With the increasing impact of automation in the manufacturing domain, a service dedicated to this area was separated from the original service in 1984. The initial medium was a monthly printed bulletin. This was supplemented by a PC database in 1989, at which time the products were offered commercially to outside users.

The reasons for offering the products commercially stemmed from the demand both internally (which suggested that it could be of use to other academic institutions) and externally (initially often from students going into the workplace and finding no alternative/preferable product). Given an initial clientele, their loyalty to (and comments on) the products suggest that it is worthwhile to maintain them in the market-place.

The existing product range consists of:

- a current awareness bulletin (RAMB)
- a PC database (RAM-PC)
- a CD-ROM (RAM-CD).

The last two of these offer both DOS and MS Windows platforms and a networking option. The database products are built around the Idealist software from Blackwell Scientific. The products are produced and distributed by Library and Information Services at The Nottingham Trent University, They are promoted worldwide by Research Information Ltd of Hemel Hempstead.

Why CD-ROM for RAM?

I remain convinced that CD-ROM is, at bottom, a crap technology that is temporarily filling a gap.[5]

Recent sources are more sanguine about the temporary nature of CDs, quoting a future of 15–20 years,[6] and highlighting the likely increase in cost advantage over online distribution together with the fact that some of the technologies set to challenge CD are a decade away from fruition.[7, 8]

Indeed, there has been a spectacular growth curve for CD-ROM and multimedia titles,[9] and surveys indicate the rapid adoption of CD-ROM technologies by libraries and organizations.[10, 11] The 1995 CD-ROM Directory[12] notes that there are now 'over 8,000 titles contained within CD-ROMs in Print. Titles released in 1994 represent over a quarter of all titles ever published.'

Thus the CD-ROM, for all its much-quoted limitations, has become a staple part of our libraries' information diet. Adoption has been driven to a large extent by the enthusiasm of librarians.[13] Certainly, the choice of compact disc as an information medium for RAM has been dictated both by its current popularity and by the enthusiasm for CD as opposed to alternatives such as a printed, cumulative version of the current awareness bulletin (RAMB) or an online version. The strengths of the CD-ROM revolve around four key factors:

- fixed costs
- easy interfaces
- accessibility, flexibility and power
- portability.

The introduction of CD-ROM databases, and the opportunities which they have provided for the development and expansion of new information services, have also resulted in greater prestige and enhanced status with the parent organization. The recent RAM-CD launch at Nottingham Trent was accompanied by an event featuring the Pro-Vice Chancellor and Deans/Heads of Department, with attendant in-house and external press publicity. Despite the fact that CD-ROMs have proved so popular in libraries (The Nottingham Trent University LIS currently subscribes to more than 40 titles), there are limitations both in terms of the medium itself and in relations between libraries and the other players in the market. However, despite these limitations, the alternatives to CD-ROM do not offer particularly attractive options to a small bibliographic database like RAM, mainly on grounds of costs. The primary alternatives consist of various online access strategies or local solutions.

RAM has in the past been available on an online commercial host, Data-Star (for two years, 1990–92), but was removed for strategic reasons. A general economic analysis of CD-ROM versus online[14] suggests that, thanks largely to the dynamism of CD-ROM technology, today's information delivery system is practical, cheap and rapidly improving, while for the foreseeable future online services of all kinds will depend on large computer installations, whose costs must be passed on to the customer. The situation within the UK has been studied,[15] and confirms the CD challenge to online.

The option of using the services available on JANET for RAM were considered, but rejected on grounds of cost. As far as the Internet is concerned, this is an attractive option, which is being actively explored at present. RAM currently appears on the Department of Manufacturing's World Wide Web home page, and it will shortly have a home page of its own.

Moreover, the EEVL (Edinburgh Engineering Virtual Library) project, part of the Electronic Libraries Programme, has as part of its brief to 'encourage the provision of new sources of relevant data . . . and [to encourage] copyright owners to make available all or part of their data or texts.' RAM fits into this strategy, and it is intended, at the time of writing, that the RAM database should become available on the Internet via the gateway to quality information resources which the EEVL project is building; this will facilitate access to high quality information resources in engineering.

The original rationale behind the RAM project involved offering a PC-based product that would provide a quality interface to readily-available information. PCs were (in 1989) becoming common on the desktop and in the library (the latter attached to a CD drive, but with hard disk space available). Therefore, a PC database at an affordable price, with source documents only a fax, e-mail or phone call away, had the potential to fill what was perceived as a niche in the market. This strategy was hit hard by the recession, and funding problems both in industry and academia.

In the meantime, the pace of development in the PC market-place has meant that many PC systems are now purchased incorporating a CD drive, and by the year 2000 it is estimated that the installation of CD-ROM drives will be in excess of 65 million worldwide. A Benchmark Research study reveals that 55% of manufacturing sites employing more than 50 people are now equipped to use CD-ROM; in 1994, the figure was 29%.

In the light of the market-place, apart from any other consideration, it is seen as important for the RAM project to have a CD product available. Other reasons for producing a CD version of RAM included the strategies being adopted by libraries in constructing information provision where CD-ROMs featured as a primary building block, together with the CD-ROM based programmes being developed by libraries for networking information. This is happening despite the problems with CD-ROM software, trying to 'network the unnetworkable'. It is, indeed, the scenario at Nottingham Trent, where phase one of a CD networking programme has seen 15 CD-ROM titles put up on the academic computing network, with phase two now starting.

The ability to network the product has obvious advantages in terms of remote access, either on the desktop or at least within the immediate place of work/study, and simultaneous usage. This is advantageous to RAM, since, despite its overall coherence, there are individual areas which are of interest to different groups. In an academic environment, for example, courses covering specific areas, such as design, textiles, management, quality, computing, control, electrical and integrated engineering, will access relevant parts of the database and find material.

RAM CD-ROM production

'It is felt that CD-ROM is a suitable medium for smaller databases'.[16] Despite this comment, a variety of reasons have also been identified why academic institutions are not generally interested in commercial CD-ROM publishing. In the early years, the constraints on the RAM project mirrored these, including the lack of resources to support in-house publication. However, the situation changed dramatically with the advent, in the Art and Design Faculty, of the Fashion Information Service (FIS), headed by Professor Stephen Gray.

This multimedia project quickly won international renown, and fulfilled a need for short runs of CD-ROMs which would also be updatable. The needs of FIS were similar to those of RAM, and the existence of equipment to support such a service, along with the willingness of Professor Gray to hire it out, made the production of RAM-CD a feasible proposition.

Cost of development

A very rough guide to the absolute lowest costs which might be expected to produce a single 100Mb database has been produced.[17] The costs fall under the following headings:

- administration
- data preparation
- database design
- retrieval software
- artwork
- documentation
- build
- mastering
- replication
- shipping and handling
- printing
- support
- sales and marketing.

The total estimated cost came to $125,000, although it will have probably come down in the years since this estimate was published. The pump-priming necessary to launch such a service would be beyond the scope and justification of most libraries. RAM-CD survives and prospers by utilizing in-house resources and expertise to keep costs to a minimum, while negotiating a commission-based contract for marketing services.

One of the primary aims of the RAM project is to exploit existing resources and existing equipment. The raw material for the Project exists in the current journal subscriptions which already support the academic courses run at the University. The major development costs lie in the use of staff. These costs fall under five main headings:

- scanning
- bibliographic framework inputting
- abstracting
- data conversion
- administrative assistance.

The advantages involved in commercializing already existing in-house products, already alluded to, are seen here in that some of the staff activities (scanning especially) are undertaken in the line of normal duties, and this is recognized in the project costings, together with the fact that RAM already provided a service to University staff before it was commercialized, and continues to do so.

The scanning and abstracting duties require the services of a professional information specialist, while the bibliographic details are input by support staff. The bibliographic records are input into a DBaseIV format, which then needs to be converted to a desktop publishing system for bulletin production, and into an Idealist format for the database.

These conversion activities are undertaken by an outside specialist, who designed the initial system while working for the company with whom the commercial products were originally launched as a joint venture. Although the company has ceased to trade, the specialist continues to develop the service on the University's behalf.

The regular time allotted to the project from within the library amounts to:

- five hours/week scanning and abstracting
- three hours/week for the framework inputting
- one hour/week for administrative assistance.

Flexibility is achieved by providing the facilities for inputting off-site and outside working hours when necessary. The conversion from the RAM-PC database to CD-ROM proved a relatively simple task (see below) and no major development costs were incurred. The CD-ROMs are currently produced within the University as and when required (bearing in mind the very recent launch of RAM-CD and the consequently fairly small current volume of sales). In addition, support is available from the LIS Publicity and Display Department, from the Finance and Postal Services departments, and from the University's commercial arm, Nottingham Consultants Ltd. A management consultant with a longstanding knowledge of the project is also called on when this is considered necessary.

Development costs are thus primarily incurred from within the institution, with the notable exception of the data conversion and the management consultant.

Equipment costs and ease of production

Inputting to the RAM-PC database and data conversion are undertaken using a standard PC configuration. The CDs are produced using an Optistore CDR, which cost £5000 at time of purchase, but which is much less than half that cost in today's market. Converting the RAM-PC database to CD-ROM proved a relatively simple task. The Optistore CDR acts as a standard CD player, but also has writing facilities. Each blank CD now costs less than £10 and it is possible to write up to some 650Mb of data. The advantage of this system is that data can be written in sections over a period of time, which is ideal for extending the information content when the core data is unchanging.

The main purpose of the system is to support the Fashion Information

Service (FIS), previously described. The technology is a WORM (Write Once, Read Many) concept and a full CD takes about 60 minutes to write, so the system is only suitable for short runs or for creating master copies for later mass production. FIS use the system mainly for producing demos (including text and pictures), which are dispatched in small quantities. This obviously suits the RAM project as its CD-ROM gets off the ground. If RAM-CD customer numbers expand sufficiently, a commercial CD pressing plant will be employed to generate the CD-ROM discs in bulk.

The Idealist software used by RAM was already suitable for use on a CD-ROM system, and so the main task was to write a suitable program to install the search software and associated files from the CD to the hard disk of a PC. The installation routine, system files and data files were then transferred to the PC attached to the CD-ROM 'burner' by means of a series of diskettes.

A file-compression program (PKZIP) was used to keep the number of diskettes (and hence the manual handling) required to a minimum. Each recordable CD-ROM has space for 650Mb of data; a full set of RAM-PC, when expanded, currently occupies some 30Mb. In the initial stages of the RAM-CD programme, therefore, it is planned that each customer will be assigned two recordable discs. These will be cycled back and forth, and updates will be added alternately to each disc.

To ensure that the installation of Windows-based CD-ROMs proceeds smoothly, particularly where demo discs are concerned, a useful set of guide-lines[18] has been provided, which basically call for non-intrusive installation and performance routines which respect end-user system requirements and limitations. These have been the aims of both the DOS and Windows versions of the RAM database.

Copyright

Questions of copyright arise in several areas. Answers to some basic questions are fairly straightforward – for example:

> 148   Question: Can they [abstracts] be used in information bulletins?
> Answer: Yes. They can be duplicated, printed, given away or sold, either free or by licence.

In fact, most abstracts used in the RAM project are customized to suit the project's style, although some are very close to the original. Efforts are made to maintain a uniform style of abstract for the project.

> 113   Question: What about databases stored on CD-ROM?
> Answer: CD-ROMs are not cable programs so any data stored on a CD-ROM is protected as a literary work and is available under the same rules of fair dealing.[19]

A bibliography compiled by someone is protected just as if it were a book, and if the author created a work as a part of his job, then his employer is usually the copyright owner; in the case of RAM-CD, the copyright rests with the University's commercial arm, Nottingham Consultants Ltd.

Document supply is a more difficult issue. RAM does not advertise a document supply service, although it is currently investigating the feasibility of doing so. Letters have been written to publishers to obtain permission to copy articles, and this continues to be done as and when requests are made for source documents. To date, there has been little or no response from the publishers. This represents a limiting factor on the database's usefulness, since access to source documents would constitute a valuable addition to the service, particularly in those areas of the world where obtaining documents is not as easy as in the UK. Cornish[20] discusses various regulations covering copying and charging, and interlibrary copying.

The forthcoming EU directive on legal protection of commercial databases will obviously have an impact on the RAM project. Recommendations for action to be included in this directive have been put forward by Wall,[21] among others.

User reaction

There are a good number of studies which document the popularity of CD-ROM products with both students and academic staff;[22-5] The views expressed in one questionnaire's results would seem to sum up user reaction in general:

- end-users find the CD-ROM easy or very easy to use
- end-users like doing their own searching with CD-ROM
- end-users find the CD-ROM user-friendly
- end-users' main concern is the subject and journal coverage of the database.[26]

Another reaction highlights a further strength: 'A rather vague request can be turned into a finely tuned result after the effective and serendipitous browsing of a CD-ROM session . . . No one should underestimate the value of such a learning aid.[27] However, there are implications which flow from the popularity of CD-ROMs. The CD-ROM revolution is changing the nature of patron-librarian interaction. One key issue is the loss of control the information specialist has experienced as a result of end-user searching. As an intermediary in the online searching process, the information specialist would keep abreast of information needs, since they would be expressed in terms of a search strategy each time an online search was undertaken. End-user searching has meant that other ways must be found to maintain an overview of the current state of users' interests.

Another implication is the use of inappropriate databases by end-users, for a variety of reasons.[28] Firstly there is a tendency to trust electronic sources over a printed source even when the latter may be more appropriate. Also, many end-users fail to understand a database's coverage limitations. RAM does not, for example, cover many sources on materials, since there is a major database, Metadex, devoted to this subject – yet users are still found vainly searching RAM for this area, despite clear statements of what is and is not covered.

Then there is the question of the accessibility of particular sources. Studies have shown that, for users in one of the major RAM subject areas (engineering), accessibility is the key determinant of the overall extent to which a particular information channel or source is used.[29] 'When significant information is not readily available to any organization, there is a serious risk of ignorance and non-use of important data through the "human inertia" which accompanies non-availability on the spot.'[30] Certainly, empirical observation shows that users prefer to access a networked database from their nearest terminal, rather than consult a more relevant standalone source housed in the library across the road.

The fact that RAM has been a PC- rather than a CD-based product has been transparent to the internal user. It is selected from a menu in the same way as the CDs. The advent of RAM-CD rather than RAM-PC at Nottingham Trent should not therefore have a significant impact on the user. It does, however, bring RAM within the general strategy of LIS information provision, where it sits more happily than it did in the past. This would also seem to be true of external academic institutions, where reaction has shown that customers in this sector are much more comfortable with a CD-ROM than with the PC version.

Training the user

Documentation

Some form of user training is offered by 94% of UK and Eire libraries and by over 98% of US and Canadian libraries.[31] The majority of libraries offer a mixture of home-produced documentation and materials from the database suppliers.

User guides for RAM-CD have been prepared covering all the basic areas of searching, browsing and printing/exporting. The imminent networking of RAM will entail wider circulation of such documentation. The Windows version of the database has a pull-down help screen for both Idealist and for RAM. Separate guides (on creating search strategies, citing references, etc.) have also been produced.

Information skills programme

LIS recently won the prestigious Digital Equipment Company Prize, part of the annual Partnership Awards, for the implementation of its information skills programme. For the engineering departments, this consists of a series of drop-in workshops, whereby students from all levels are invited to 90-minute sessions featuring several workstations, to try out the various standalone and networked services available. Qualified staff are on hand to help out where required, although the emphasis is very much hands-on. At the same time, a more structured programme of information skills is being incorporated into courses in the first and final years.

RAM features in these sessions, and is highlighted because of its subject coverage and the immediacy of source document access. It also appears as part of the Business Studies, Textiles and Design information skills programmes.

Two main problems with training the user in CD-ROM search skills are the lack of standardization and the proliferation of databases. For anyone but a regular user, it is easy to forget the various search strategies and symbols for each database. The RAM user guides and on-screen help aim to reduce this problem. It is a function of the help available at the workshops, and of the worksheets for first-years, to lead the student through the options available.

Although in its basic form, the Idealist software used by RAM is very user-friendly and is simple to configure, a minority of options need explaining, and one or two commands are not particularly intuitive. The main problems come with complex searches involving more than one set of qualifications to a word/term (e.g. [a or b or c] and [d or e or f]). In the DOS version, a function key is used to copy (save) the basic search (a or b or c) to a different level, on which other alternatives can be used to narrow the original down, returning to the original and copying back to the different level as many times as necessary. In the MS Windows version, the basic search is stacked (saved), and a subsequent search is then merged to narrow the basic search down. On the DOS version, each record consists of two screens, unless high-resolution is used, and users need to be made aware of this. (On MS Windows, each record appears on only one screen). A limiting function of the software is the fact that only single words may be truncated. However, these non-intuitive and limiting aspects seem minor when compared to the ease of use of the database as a whole, as suggested by the experiences of users who find their way around the system with ease. The basic search commands are simple to use.

The problems of proliferation have already been mentioned (inappropriate database use). RAM's one-stop niche subject coverage aims to address this problem in its own particular area, and one of the key functions of the information skills programme is to make users aware of the range and coverage of what is available. Electronic and paper versions of a subject index to the CD-ROM database collection are being prepared.

The future

The pace of development in electronic information provision has gathered such momentum that is difficult to judge with any certainty what the scenario will be by the year 2000, except to say that it will be radically different from today.[32-4] Research under the umbrella of the likes of the Electronic Libraries Programme (ELP) will mean that the current somewhat chaotic approach to development will take on a more organized form. ELP programme areas cover electronic journals, electronic document delivery, training and awareness, on-demand publishing, and access to network resources.

The position of CD-ROMs within the electronic library environment is equally difficult to predict. On the one hand, highly competitive ventures attempting to penetrate the broad desktop market in CD-Recorder (CD-R) systems are already being noted, and the advent of such systems will make many more applications economically viable.[35-7] Moreover, the marriage of CD-ROM and multimedia is getting over its honeymoon phase, and the technology is maturing fast.[38] With CD-ROM systems already well established, the technology may prove difficult to dislodge in the short term.

However, in the longer term, 'If we take the best of all the options described and assign equal importance to all the features, then it is clear that CD-ROM cannot be the strategic long-term option because of its weaknesses in speed, limited capacity and updating arrangements'.[39] As far as the RAM-CD project is concerned, discussions are being held with internal multimedia experts to explore ways of exploiting the technology, to make it more user-friendly and attractive, and to ensure that it is competitive in the market-place. Cooperation with other synergistic small databases is being considered, so that a number of related databases can be offered on a single CD-ROM.

The database will also be offered over the Internet, and other options will have to be examined as traditional bibliographic databases are replaced by full-text services, although there will still be a place for comparatively low-cost niche products. RAM aims to continue to make a contribution through its CD-ROM project to The Nottingham Trent University, both in terms of its income and internal information provision, and as regards its reputation at home and abroad.

References

1   Nicholson, H., 'Uncomfortable bedfellows: enterprise and academic libraries', *Journal of librarianship and information science*, 24 (1), 1992, 9–13.
2   Nicholson, op. cit.
3   Hallgren, S., 'Developing your own CD-ROM', *Electronic library*, 8 (5), 1990, 331–5.
4   Wall, R., 'Copyright and information service for small firms', *Managing information*, 2 (1/2), 1995, 25–31.
5   McSeán, T., 'Networking CDs – why bother?'. In *CD-ROM networking seminar*, 1991, 71–4.
6   Ward, S., *Networked CD-ROMs as academic information sources*, London, British Library Board, 1993, 24.
7   Wiedemer, J. D. and Boelio, D. B., 'CD-ROM versus online: an economic analysis for publishers', *CD-ROM professional*, 8 (4), 1995, 36–42.
8   Hanson, T., 'A future for CD-ROM as a strategic technology?'. In Hanson, T. and Day, J. (eds.), *CD-ROMs in libraries: management issues*, London, Bowker Saur, 1994, 241–53.
9   Stoneman, G., 'Worldwide trends in CD-ROM publishing', *Electronic library*, 11 (4/5), 1993, 299–302.
10 Arbour, D., 'Information technology in the US library market: what the numbers tell us', *Electronic library*, 12 (6), 1994, 367–9.

11 Ronen, E., 'Internet CD-ROM survey', *Electronic Library*, **12** (6), 1994, 372–3.
12 Anon., *The CD-ROM Directory*, 1995, London, TFPL, 1995.
13 Ward, op. cit., 2–3.
14 Wiedemer, op. cit.
15 Hollis, R., 'CD-ROM versus online: the UK perspective', *Electronic library*, **11** (4/5), 1993, 307–9.
16 Ward, op. cit., 25–6.
17 Rhind-Tutt, S., 'CD-ROM publishing: should you do-it-yourself or contract with a commercial publisher?', *CD-ROM professional*, **6** (3), 1993, 119–21.
18 Crawford, W., 'Those installation, demonstration, possible defenestration blues, or, is your demo disc a demon?', *CD-ROM professional*, **8** (7), 1995, 56–7.
19 Cornish, G. P., *Copyright: interpreting the law for libraries and archives*, London, Library Association, 1990.
20 Cornish, op. cit.
21 Wall, op.cit.
22 Schultz, K. and Salomon, K., 'End-users respond to CD-ROM', *Library journal*, **115** (2), 1990, 56–7.
23 Gillian, A., 'Patron response to bibliographic databases on CD-ROM', *RQ*, **29** (1), 103–10.
24 Steffey, R. J. and Meyer, N., 'Evaluating user success and satisfaction with CD-ROM', *Laserdisk professional*, **2** (5), 1989, 35–45.
25 Dyson, R. and Carey, K.' 'User preference for CD-ROMs: implications for library planners', *CD-ROM professional*, **6** (3), 1993, 86–9.
26 Cassells, R. and Whittall, S. J., 'End-user searching with CD-ROM'. In Bysouth, P.T. (ed.), *End-user searching: the effective gateway to published information*, London, Aslib, 1990, 153–64.
27 Lewis, M., 'Academic library case study: CD-ROM at the University of Sussex'. In Hanson, T. and Day, J. (eds.), *CD-ROMs in libraries: management issues*, London, Bowker Saur, 1994, 207–16.
28 Dyson, op. cit.
29 Pinelli, T. E. et al., 'Technological innovation and technical communications: their place in aerospace engineering curricula; a survey of European, Japanese and US aerospace engineers and scientists', *European journal of engineering education*, **16** (4), 1991, 337–51.
30 Wall, op. cit.
31 Ward, op. cit., 17–18.
32 Steele, C., 'Millennial libraries: management changes in an electronic environment', *Electronic library*, **11** (6), 1993, 393–402.
33 Barker, P., 'Electronic libraries – visions of the future', *Electronic library*, **12** (4), 1994, 221–9.
34 Steele, C., 'The frozen library: a model for the twenty- first century', *Electronic library*, **13** (1), 1995, 21–6
35 Carlton, T., 'CD-R on the cheap', *CD-ROM professional*, **8** (4), 1995, 20–7.
36 Udell, J., 'Start the presses', *Byte*, **18** (2), 1993, 116–34.
37 Falk, H., 'CD-ROM recording for every library', *Electronic library*, **12** (5), 1994, 304–7.
38 Hudson, B. and White, D., 'The art and science of business multimedia development', *CD-ROM professional*, **8** (7), 1995, 44–54.
39 Hanson, op. cit.

Case study 2: *Glasgow on disc*
David Buri and Robert Anderson

Introduction

Glasgow on disc is one of the world's first city architectural guides on CD-ROM. It has been produced by Architecture on Disc, a company formed by Robert Anderson and David Buri, Information Technology Librarian and Architecture Librarian respectively at Glasgow School of Art. The CD-ROM is an interactive multimedia guide to the architecture of Glasgow. It provides 250 high quality colour images of 160 of the city's finest buildings from medieval times to the present day. The images are accompanied by informative text about each building, and biographical information is provided about each architect whose work is featured. The CD-ROM can be searched by the name of the architect or building, the type of building, period of construction, or by clicking on a map of the city. The images and text can be printed out or downloaded for use elsewhere, and the product runs on both Apple Macs and Windows-based PCs.

The concept behind *Glasgow on disc*

In the summer of 1993, the Joint Information Systems Committee of the Higher Education Funding Councils invited bids for grants under the New Technology Initiative. Their intention was to identify and promote key information technologies and to make these open to students and researchers who might not otherwise have these available to them. We conceived the idea of a Scottish architectural image database on CD-ROM which would comprise images from the slide collections of the four Scottish art schools in Glasgow, Edinburgh, Dundee and Aberdeen respectively. It was envisaged that the library of each institution would contribute architectural images of their own city, which would then be digitized and transferred to CD-ROM using Kodak's new Photo CD technology. A product such as Shoebox, also from Kodak, would be used to create a catalogue to search the images. Although the database was viewed mainly as an in-house tool which would improve the image collections of each participating library, it was was felt that the CD-ROM might also have some commercial potential. If successful it would be expanded to include other Scottish towns and cities. It was also hoped that improvements in technology would enable the database to be networked so that, for example, lecturers in each institution could download images to create their own slide shows.

In early 1994 we heard that our bid for funding had been unsuccessful, despite its having been shortlisted. As no other funds were forthcoming and the project could not progress under existing budgets, the idea had to be completely dropped by the four institutions.

Despite this setback we felt that the idea of an architectural guide on CD-ROM was worth pursuing by ourselves in some form, particularly as the technology for creating and using such a product was rapidly becoming less expensive and more accessible. Kodak had recently introduced Photo CD in the hope of persuading the public to digitize their photographs and replay them through their television sets. For us, this meant that 35mm slides could be digitized relatively cheaply. In the world of personal computing, colour screens were now widely available, and an explosive growth was taking place in the manufacture of personal computers with CD-ROM drives as a standard feature. From here, it was but a short step to the idea of developing a more selective image database by ourselves which would cover just Glasgow, and so *Glasgow on disc* was born.

The development of *Glasgow on disc*

As we had decided to go it alone, and to finance and develop *Glasgow on disc* ourselves, we realized that we would have to create a commercial, rather than an academic product. It is worth stressing that the market for a product greatly affects, or should affect, its content and design. We envisaged our market to be similar to that of a printed architectural guidebook – i.e. the interested lay person – but we also hoped that the CD-ROM format would broaden its attraction to include schools and colleges. To appeal to these markets we decided that our database would have to contain a large element of visual information, with hypertext links and other features to give a very interactive feel when using it. We realized that we would need to create a very high quality product if it was to sell alongside the CD-ROM titles which were emerging from publishers such as Dorling Kindersley and Microsoft.

Selecting the information to be included

The first step was to select the information to be included on the CD-ROM. The original Scottish architectural image database had envisaged a very rigorous, almost building-by-building coverage of each city. For our more commercial purposes, this approach seemed unnecessarily thorough. We decided to limit ourselves to the major works of the key architects, plus some of the more interesting buildings produced by other less well-known designers. To compile our final selection, totalling around 150 buildings designed by 80 architects, we relied on a combination of our own knowledge plus the opinions of printed architectural guides to Glasgow.

Copyright

The problem of copyright had to be addressed quite early on. We had little option but to arrange to photograph the buildings for the database ourselves. Attempting to obtain copyright clearance for existing images would have been very time-consuming and possibly expensive. An added problem was that copyright owners become particularly nervous at the thought of their images being converted into an electronic format, which is difficult to control and police. Our solution was to employ a photographer to photograph the buildings that we required, having first obtained his agreement to assign the copyright of his photographs to us.

Gathering the information

Photography commenced in the spring of 1994, and at the same time we began the process of gathering the textual information about each of the buildings and their architects. We used the many printed architectural guides to Glasgow as the starting point for our research. These were supplemented by biographical dictionaries of architects, and primary sources such as obituaries and articles in contemporary architectural journals. There were problems caused by discrepancies in the literature as to dates of construction of buildings, birth and death dates of architects, and even the names and addresses of buildings. We felt that one Glasgow architectural guide stood out from the rest as being the most thoroughly researched, and so we relied on its information to resolve these anomalies.

Despite this, considerable research on the ground was still necessary to ensure that very recent alterations to buildings were properly reflected in the text. For example, we found that prominent decorative features described in a guidebook had sometimes been removed from a building, or that new additions had substantially changed the setting or appearance of a structure. One building which we intended to feature was even demolished while we were compiling the text.

A further unforeseen and potentially serious problem occurred at the photographic stage. In common with many other cities, Glasgow is undertaking an extensive programme to restore and stoneclean its architecture. This meant that a number of key buildings were shrouded in scaffolding while work was in progress, including the Glasgow School of Art, designed by Charles Rennie Mackintosh and the city's most internationally renowned building. To resolve this we were eventually able to obtain some images of sufficient quality from architectural staff at Glasgow School of Art, together with permission to reproduce them.

Organizing the information

In organizing the information, our principal challenge was to design the product to satisfy a broad range of potential end-users. The CD-ROM had to be suitable for groups as diverse as primary school children, the general public and architecture students. We felt that the most intuitive way for users to access the CD-ROM was through an easy-to-use point-and-click interface. This meant that all interaction with the CD-ROM was through a mouse rather than a keyboard. This simple approach would also enable us to adapt the product for use in a public access kiosk.

The information on the CD-ROM is split into several facets: architect, building name, building type, date of construction, and location. The home page, which presents the option to search the CD-ROM by each of these facets is shown in Figure 8.2.1.

Within the CD-ROM the screen is split into three elements. The strip at the top of each screen indicates the user's location within the database. This is an essential feature, as users of CD-ROM can easily become 'lost' within a database during a search.

The toolbar at the bottom of each screen incorporates a number of buttons that are on constant display: 'Help', 'Print', 'Go Back', 'Next Page', 'See Also' and 'Home'. These permit navigation through the CD-ROM and perform common functions. A noteworthy feature is the option to return to the home page with a single click from any point within the disc, enabling a new search to be quickly started.

The middle of each screen is reserved for the actual textual and pictorial information. The text features hypertext links that allow the user to jump quickly between related architects and buildings (see Figure 8.2.2).

Digitizing the images

The 35mm slides of the buildings were transferred onto Kodak Photo CD, which we found to be a very economical way to digitize a large number of

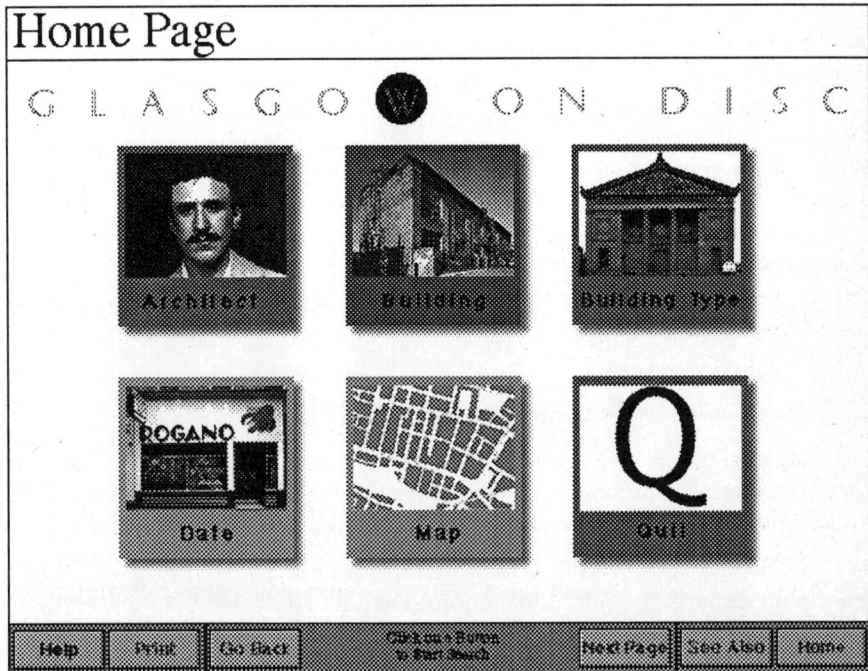

Fig. 8.2.1   *The home page of Glasgow on disc, showing the location indication ('Home Page') and the toolbar*

Atlantic Quay

Buildings

Building Design Partnership

1988–90

Broomielaw

Comprises a group of three office buildings with a total area of 275,000 square feet.

They form the first phase of a development to regenerate the Broomielaw, a historic former manufacturing and warehousing area on land sloping down to the Clyde south of Argyle Street.

Building Design Partnership were commissioned to masterplan the East Broomielaw area with the aim of extending the city's commercial core into the Broomielaw.

cont..

| Help | Print | Go Back | 1 of 2 Pages on Atlantic Quay Buildings A - Z | Next Page | See Also | Home |

Fig. 8.2.2   *A typical screen display in Glasgow on disc*

images. The images were then imported into Adobe Photoshop, and cropped and resized. Photoshop was also used to manipulate the colour palette of each image, thereby enabling photographic quality images to be displayed on standard 256 colour monitors.

Software development

Our market research had demonstrated that in order for *Glasgow on disc* to be commercially viable it would have to run on both Apple Macs and Windows-based PCs. This restricted the number of development tools that we could reasonably use, and after much testing we chose Macromedia Director. This product gave us the necessary colour palette control, and enabled us to reuse our programming code on both platforms, thus saving a considerable amount of time.

Production of *Glasgow on disc*

Although low-cost CD-ROM writers are now available, we felt that we did not possess the expertise required for the production of a dual-format master disc. We therefore subcontracted the Scottish Council for Educational Technology (SCET) to prepare the master from our hard disks. Once the master had been extensively beta-tested it was sent to a London-based CD-replication firm for mass-production.

Although many retailers prefer CD-ROMs to be packaged in book-sized cardboard boxes, we felt that the cost of their production for our relatively small print run could not be justified. Instead we designed full-colour inlay cards for both the front and back of the jewel case.

Recent improvements in the ease of use and speed of CD-ROM writers now mean that in-house production of a master disc and very small print runs are now viable.

Marketing *Glasgow on disc*

By the early summer of 1995, *Glasgow on disc* was complete. We felt confident that we had created an excellent product, but were less certain about how to market it effectively to ensure that it reached its full potential. One of the principal obstacles to be overcome was the fact that we were an unknown name in a market-place which was being swamped with other multimedia products.

We had always envisaged our main user group as being schools and colleges, plus those interested individuals who might otherwise purchase a printed architectural guidebook. Although we felt that we could reach some of these customers by direct selling ourselves, we realized that we would need to form partnerships with organizetions with a greater selling power if we were to reach the wider market beyond Glasgow.

Accordingly, our first step was to contract a local specialist multimedia representative to distribute *Glasgow on disc* to bookshops throughout the UK. With hindsight, we overestimated the role played by bookshops in the CD-ROM market. Few of them seemed organized to sell these products. There was often no computer equipment to enable potential purchasers to view the disc, and booksellers were so concerned about theft of the discs that they failed to display them properly.

At the same time we attempted some direct selling of *Glasgow on disc* to colleges and libraries, but with mixed results. The typical success rate of direct selling is less than 5%, and our efforts were no exception. We were more successful in selling to schools in and around Glasgow, as we were fortunate to find a 'product champion' in Strathclyde Regional Council's Education Department, who undertook a mailshot to all schools on our behalf and was generally very encouraging.

However, it remains the case that in the UK most CD-ROMs are not sold through traditional channels such as booksellers, but through CD-ROM magazines and by mail order. We have contacted a number of these organizations, most of whom require to see a copy of the disc for evaluation before agreeing to publicize it. At the time of writing it is too early to give any indication of our success in this method of selling.

Review copies of *Glasgow on disc* were also sent to the architectural, library and computing press, but with rather disappointing results. To the newspapers and computer magazines, we were probably producing just another CD-ROM, and our publicity was rather overshadowed by the unveiling of Windows 95. Reviews, particularly in the architectural press, can take a year or more to appear in print, and we are still hoping for coverage at a future date.

The future of *Glasgow on disc*

Because the data is held in digital form, it will be relatively easy to reengineer it and adapt it to changing and emerging technologies. *Glasgow on disc* is particularly suitable for conversion into a public access kiosk, and we have successfully done this for Glasgow's architecture centre, where it is being used to stimulate public interest in the run-up to the UK Festival of Architecture and Design 1999, to be hosted by Glasgow.

We have also used some of the digitized data to create our own World Wide Web site on the Internet (http://www.colloquium.co.uk/aod/). We have included sample screens from *Glasgow on disc* together with information about ourselves and our future plans. It will be interesting to see how frequently the site is visited and whether it generates any sales, particularly to the large North American market.

Conclusion

User reactions to *Glasgow on disc* have been overwhelmingly positive, and we feel assured that the disc has succeeded in its aims of presenting Glasgow's architecture in an innovative and stimulating way. The ease of use of the product has probably made a significant contribution to its success, as both adults and children can immediately use it without the need for training or a manual.

Our experience with *Glasgow on disc* has shown that it is possible to produce a CD-ROM largely in-house within a short timescale. Multimedia publishing does, however, require an unusual combination of skills: the ability to gather and organize a large quantity of information; a good knowledge of hardware and software; and graphic design skills to create a product which is pleasing to the eye.

During the next few years, end-users of CD-ROM will increasingly demand television-quality productions, incorporating features such as video, music and narration. This will mean that the production of even a small-scale CD-ROM will require a large team with a range of highly-specialized skills.

9

Networking and the end-user revolution

Richard Biddiscombe

Introduction

The easier the access to a database, the more it will be used, and the cheaper the access, the more intensively it will be used. Networks offer easy access to databases and can make them available at the most convenient place for the user.

The cost of accessing databases is one of the key factors in the use that databases will receive. It has been free or low-cost network access which has been a vital element in the development of end-user searching. In those areas where access is free the end-user culture has thrived. There is evidence for this in the higher education sector. It is also borne out in the US where there has been a faster rate of growth in the use of the Internet by the general public, reflecting the fact that local US telephone calls are usually free.

To most people outside academic institutions the concept of information networks is still relatively new. It is only in the recent past that the wider community has begun to embrace, or has been embraced by, the Internet. Thanks to the growing market in personal computers and the improved accessibility of networking software, demand for network access has been growing. Commercial companies, individuals and others have been linking up and logging on in ever greater numbers.

There is a social, and economic, need to widen such Internet access so that the whole community can enjoy the benefits of a networked environment. To make this possible some public money, or at least government encouragement for the provision of private resources, is necessary. Public libraries ought to play an important part in this community provision and this has been recognized in a number of countries.

From the higher education community's experience, in the UK through JISC for example, it is also evident that a central coordinating body can smooth the path to an end-user environment by using the skills of information professionals in libraries. For, although informal discussion groups can generate ideas and offer support on a communal basis, an official organization providing central direction on an agreed basis can play a much more effective role in facilitating network access and encouraging research into future possibilities and potential projects.

The encourgement of research into such areas should be seen as an essential element in identifying the options which are opening up. A number of types of organization, both publicly and cooperatively funded, are pursuing various possibilities. In addition, of course, companies are seeking to identify what is likely to be commercially viable and potentially threatening.

The end-user revolution has already had profound effects on academic libraries and is also now bringing new challenges to information professionals in other sectors. Although the role of libraries has already been important in developing end-user provision, for the individual end-user the identity of an information provider is not always apparent. Academic libraries, as the user survey in this chapter reveals, are seen by users as important information providers at present, but this may not continue to be the case.

Networked information and social change

The first wide-area networks (WANS) were created with the introduction of telegraph and telephones, and changed the way the world was viewed. Until the first telegraph and railway humans could not move nor communicate faster than the sun travelled across the earth. Communities were therefore governed by local time and had no need to change this age-old system. Some greater uniformity was required once technology made fast communication possible.

The early demand for telecommunications resulted in a rapid expansion of telephone networks. In 1872, for example, there were 2000 telephone subscribers in London; by 1938 this had grown to over 800,000. In just over 50 years a complex wide-area network had been established capable of linking every house, factory and institution. The continued growth of the communications infrastructure, the improvements in technology, and the application of agreed standards, means that we now live, for better or worse, in what has been described as a global village.

Essentially this same street-level network is still the means of bringing computerized services to homes and offices, though the old copper wire cables are from another technological era. More recently, cable companies have begun linking homes and businesses to bring additional or competing services using coaxial cabling. In a few years' time satellite links will make even more efficient communication possible.

Online databases

Libraries were in advance of most of the rest of the community in their use of the computer and telephone interface for communicating information. Online database hosts began in the US with BRS in 1965, and DIALOG followed a year later. In the UK online search services were introduced into libraries in the mid-seventies with BLAISE-LINK, which started in 1971.[1]

There are now over 5000 online databases, searchable through a large number of hosts. Many of these offer easy-to-use, menu-driven interface options for novice searchers. There is consequently less mystique surrounding the search procedure, and the necessity for calling in the aid of an experienced intermediary is much reduced.

In the USA BRS After Dark was the first 'out-of-hours' service catering for the home user, and in 1982 DIALOG launched Knowledge Index.[1] Both these offered reduced rate access, encouraging home-based end-user access. In France, Minitel has been was an important experiment in end-user searching, encouraging millions of people to go online. Although the service is being eclipsed by the Internet it has given end-users nationwide experience in the use of database searching and online communication.

The beginnings of the Internet

Much has been written about the start of the Internet and the early part played by the US Defense Department in linking a number of computers to form ARPANET. Briefly, this strategic decision, and the subsequent establishment of NSFNET, began the linking of universities across the US and formed the backbone of the present US network.

Over the years other networks have been linked to it in order to provide the essential elements of the Internet structure. In parallel to these American networks, similar ones have been created in other countries. Through telecommunication gateways at national boundaries, these different networks are joined to provide the international network known as the Internet.

In the UK one of the major networks making up the backbone of the British network is JANET (the Joint Academic Network), one of the original intentions of which was to link academic institutions in a similar way to NSFNET in the US. It was inaugurated in 1984, 'replacing a variety of networks that had been established over the previous ten years to serve the scientific community'.[2] Transmission protocols were changed in 1991 so that JANET could operate as part of the Internet. As the university sector has grown, so JANET has expanded too, and now links all the universities in the UK. Some of the original restrictions on its franchise have also been eased so that it now includes a number of other non-profit-making institutions. It presently links over 250 institutions in the UK.

JANET is not a public network. It is designed essentially for use by students and staff in higher education, and they have free access to the service. The costs are met by higher education funding bodies and individual universities. To ensure its continued success, SuperJANET is being established. A more advanced network, this will eventually replace the existing JANET and provide a wider band-width, enabling faster and more innovative services such as video conferencing, full-text documents and improved document delivery.

As the development of JANET has shown, the original concept of the Internet has been transformed from an institutional arrangement to a global network of connected individuals. It is difficult to assess accurately the present size of the Internet. There are many estimates, some of which suggest that, at the present growth rate, all the world's literate people will be connected to the Internet by the year 2004. There are now reported to be about 30 million regular users across 152 countries.

The World Wide Web and the transformation of the Internet

Gopher menus and Veronicas, allowing the possibility of interrogating the Internet, enabled easier end-user access to the network. Their use, however, while making searching possible, did nothing to make it attractive. Endless look-alike menus to choose from, with long waits for typescript documents, demanded the patience of either the enthusiast or the very determined.

The hypertext options offered by the World Wide Web transformed this dull and somewhat dreary experience into a fascinating pleasure. Certainly the waiting is not always taken out of the wanting, but it is possible to see the extent to which a document is being retrieved. The browser technology offered through Mosaic, Netscape and others has also done much to improve accessibility and acceptability.

This accessibility is evidenced by the way end-users can easily communicate and create their own home pages. The ease with which HTML, the browser language, can be learned and applied, coupled with the simplicity of creating one's own home page, has opened up new possibilities. End-users can now become information providers, offering their own databases on the Internet.

The development of Adobe Acrobat and Adobe Capture software has created new possibilities for Internet publishing. The incorporation of Acrobat into future editions of HTML will widen the opportunity for creating high quality documents on the Web. Such developments offer exciting opportunities for creating networked editions of existing publications by established publishers. They also promise the advent of entirely novel publications from other sources. These possibilities, which are so exercising the publishing industry at the present time, also have profound implications for libraries in general and information professionals in particular.

The demand for networking

The promise of easy accessibility to networked databases has attracted an increasing number of users, with the seemingly insatiable demand for improved access to more databases. Since the moment library users began using electronic databases directly, they have wanted more convenient access. That has inevitably meant network access. From the establishing of OPACs through to their growing dependence on the Internet, libraries are being transformed from static depositories to dynamic information hubs.

Networking CD-ROMs

From their first introduction into libraries CD-ROMs proved to be very popular. In academic libraries both library staff and users were agreed that investment in CD-ROMs was a good thing. On the one hand, library staff found them easier to manage financially than online searching. On the other, users were able to undertake their own database searches without the need for an intermediary. Even so, users were soon dissatisfied with the access which was offered, and were pressing for some form of networking.

Within a remarkably short time networked access to CD-ROM databases was being introduced. Some of these networks were more reliable than others. At present, although CD-ROM networks are widespread, there is little uniformity in their construction or accessibility. In academic libraries the situation differs from campus to campus. Some academic institutions are able to claim their CD-ROM network is accessible from every part of the campus. Others have only managed to network them in their libraries. Some have failed to find the investment necessary to offer Windows-based databases or provide the option of multidisc searching across multiple-disc databases.

Networking has therefore been a mixed blessing, but the demand created by CD-ROM databases has become difficult to satisfy. The mixed results that were obtained by in-house networking, the administrative costs of providing networked slots for each additional networked database, and the negotiation of adequate licensing agreements, have all conspired to lessen the enthusiasm of some library staff for such provision. Libraries, certainly those without any networking expertise, are seeking other solutions such as Silverplatter's ERA service.

Other options such as the loading of large-scale databases on a central server for faster local searching are too expensive for the average British university. The arithmetic only makes sense in large organizations such as the federally structured universities in the US.

Wide-area networking in higher education

In the UK another solution needed to be found if end-user searching was to grow and meet the latent demand. This was done by treating the individual universities as a type of federal structure under the auspices of the national funding body, now called the HEFC (the Higher Education Funding Council). Under its auspices JISC (Joint Information Services Committee) was established and was able to create a suitable environment for such a development.

The role of JISC

JISC is at the heart of networked information provision in the British academic community, for it is the body which funds JANET and manages it through UKERNA, the UK Education and Research Networking Association. JISC also has a wider role in encouraging the provision of adequate information services at national and local levels.

At the national level it has done more than any other organization to establish and encourage end-user searching. Working through its Information Services Sub-Committee (ISSC) it manages a number of information services which have helped to transform the work of university students and staff. At the local level it has sought to influence the way information provision should be managed, publishing in December 1995 a set of guidelines for the creation of an information strategy in academic institutions.[3]

The JISC home page describes its functions as 'funding a number of national information services and initiatives which benefit the higher education and research community in the UK. These include: online bibliographic databases; bulletin boards; software archives; data archives; socio-economic, scientific and digital map databases; electronic mail; discussion lists, and the arranging of discount offers on quality commercial software support for graphics, visualization and multimedia.' The providers of these services, some of which are described below, have a forum in JASPER, an organization seeking to coordinate the training, marketing and user needs of the all these JISC-based services.

Some services supported by JISC

The development of JISC services has involved academic librarians at all levels. Librarians at the service level have sought improvements on behalf of their clients through user groups. Participation at a local level has also been encouraged by BUBL. Pressure for easier network access, improved database quality, and better interfaces and connectivity, have all been matters which have exercised the user groups.

Information services

NISS describes itself on its home page as 'a collection of resources that include data, papers, circulars and reports from councils and committees concerned with funding, management, research and associated activities within the UK HE community.' It also has a wider role, as 'a collection of resources that include catalogues of computer software and indexes to data archives.'

Mailbase has been established to support the British higher education and research community in their use of networks by offering a discussion and information sharing service, largely based on the provision of academic mail-lists. It also offers training, both online and on a seminar basis, in the use of networks and networked services.

BUBL was originally set up as the Bulletin Board for Libraries, with aims to 'inform, support and educate, and represent the interests of the UK LIS community'.[4] This important service now has an international reputation and is useful to all Internet users. It provides an index to Internet resources by subject, a current awareness service for information professionals, and access to library catalogues and other network searching tools.

UKOLN is jointly funded by JISC and the British Library. This body was originally established in the late 1970s and went through various name changes to become UKOLN – the UK Office for Library and Information Networking – in 1992. Its remit is not just limited to the academic community but supports the wider UK library and information communities through research, network services and awareness raising in the area of network infor-mation management. It is concerned with: bibliographic management; public library networking; information quality control; and the development of end-user services. In 1995 it conducted a survey which provided a unique picture of the state of Internet provision in UK public libraries. In the same year it launched an online journal, the *ARIADNE newsletter*, to report on Internet issues for librarians.

Online databases

BIDS it is now taken for granted on the British academic scene, but it was a revolutionary concept when it was launched in 1991. Establishing the service required vision and courage, and could not have been done without the man-agement of a central agency.

BIDS currently provides the following databases: Citation Indexes from ISI; EMBASE; Compendex Plus and Page One; Inside Information from the British Library, and IBSS from the British Library of Political and Economic Science. It operates a document delivery service for these databases through the British Library. In addition it offers access to the specialized datasets EcoFlora and Legumeline, and gateway access to other services, such as the CARL UnCover.

EDINA, which was launched in January 1996, is based at the Edinburgh University Data Library. It offers network access to a library of data, informa-tion and research resources for the academic community in the UK. Amongst the services it offers or plans to offer are: BIOSIS Previews; Periodicals Contents Index (PCI), and Palmers Index to the Times.

OCLC Firstsearch is a database service offered by OCLC to the British higher education community through the auspices of JISC. Established in the US, it has been offered in the UK since 1993, and works on a similar basis to BIDS in offering networked access to all registered users. Access is offered to the databases in the US. By means of a set of options various databases are offered on a subscription basis.

The combination of BIDS, EDINA and Firstsearch gives a wide choice of databases to universities in the UK. Their provision has broadened the end-user base, and given staff and students an understanding of online information provision whilst teaching them new transferable skills.

Other aspects of JISC

Another of JISC's functions is to organize the distribution of resources fol-lowing on the recommendations of the Follett Report.[5] A sub-committee called the Follett Implementation Group on Information Technology (FIGIT) was established to distribute grants to schemes whose aims were to enhance the quality of technology in information services in support of teaching, learn-ing and research. In 1994/95 a total of 4.75 million pounds sterling was allo-cated to these projects, which have been set up to examine a number of aspects of this broad remit, and in many cases advance the cause, both directly and indirectly, of the end-user. A number of these projects point the way in which libraries can use networking technology to benefit the end-user.

In the US a positive coordinating role is being increasingly provided by the RLG (Research Libraries Group), which is not only offering access to ARLAN, its union catalogue, but is also encouraging cooperation at other levels. Studies in Scarlet, for example, is an international project which is creating a digitalized library of materials on marriage and sexuality between 1815 and 1915. RLG sees itself as building a 'global digital library' with 'carefree access to global resources'. Although it does not itself depend on public resources this consortium of research libraries is taking the lead in developing networked resources in a similar way to JISC in the UK.

Networked services at the local level

Academic libraries

In many universities the library service has been, or is proving to be, the leading force for change in approaches to networked information. Many academic libraries have installed their own LANs for CD-ROM networking whilst also taking advantage of the free network access offered by JANET. Through these local means, and backed by the enlightened work of JISC, they have made significant progress in offering networked services to their students and staff.

They have also been in the lead in the creation of home pages for their institutions and their own libraries. In addition, librarians are heavily involved in using the Internet as part of the education process. Enterprising libraries have already taken advantage of the universal accessibility offered by the World Wide Web to create new information opportunities. Library guides and study skills packages are just the beginning of online information skills programmes, while the prospect of distance learning offers the possibility of the virtual university.

In line with the traditional need for librarians to meet and share experiences, groups of interested academic librarians are discussing the needs and possibilities presented by networked information. For example, in late 1995, the Regional Focus Group for Networked Information was set up in the English Midlands. They produced a document outlining the current state of the art in universities stretching from Leeds to Birmingham. Many projects are described in the document[6] and show that all the nine universities that are represented have a broad-based and developing interest in WWW projects. A number have appointed Networked Information Librarians or Internet Information Specialists to oversee such developments.

Public libraries

Lacking the free access to networks enjoyed by universities, public libraries in the UK have been at a disadvantage. They have not been able, apart from some notable exceptions, to move forward in this area. Yet there is a role for them in the networked information environment, and this will be taken over by others unless public librarians take a positive, pro-active approach.

There are a number of ways in which public libraries could create a new, and perhaps more relevant role, once they have repositioned themselves in the network environment. Using network access they could, for example, offer the Internet to the wider community, helping to reduce the divisions between information rich and information poor; they could also use the network to improve their present services by giving each small community library access to internal and external information sources; and finally, they could become increasingly pro-active information providers themselves by exploiting their own resources – in local history, for example. With the likely prospect of an increasingly commercialized Internet, public libraries should play a part in providing unbiased help and freely available training packages for their users.

In the US some useful progress is now being made in linking public libraries to the Internet. This has been due to the 1993 Clinton-Gore initiative on the National Information Infrastructure (NII). In Europe the Bangemann Report[7] in 1994 discussed the information industry in the EU and on 30 June 1995 the European Commission approved the INFO2000 programme. As reported by de Bruine,[8] this has three long-term objectives:

- to facilitate the development of the European content industry
- to optimize the contribution of the new information services to growth, competitiveness and employment in Europe
- to maximize the contribution of the advanced information services to the professional, social and cultural development of the citizens of Europe.

Although there is great stress on the commercial potential of information networking, as indicated above, the community aspects are also covered. Public libraries, although not specifically mentioned, could play an important part in applications such as those in Distance Learning and City Information Highways[7] if the full potential of these opportunities is to be realized.

The European Libraries Programme under the EU's DGXIII Libraries Unit is also a possible source of European funding. PUBLICA is expected to be launched in March 1996. This will actively seek to encourage public libraries to become involved in the Libraries Programme, which also intends to create an information resource centre for public libraries on the World Wide Web.

The Library 2000 project in Singapore is another example of where governments are encouraging better information provision for the whole community. Here the intention is to provide better access to libraries, and information networks to the whole community by the beginning of the new millennium. The Library 2000 Review Committee was established in 1992 with the task of formulating a library master plan which would position them to play a greater role in establishing Singapore as an international information hub.[9] It reported in 1995, promising to increase the role of public libraries in providing community access to information networks.

There is a strong social argument – accepted, it seems, by a number of governments – for extending to the wider community the end-user access which is now so vital to the academic sector. Despite the launch in February 1996 of the DTI's Information Society Initiative (ISI), the UK government has made no firm commitment to helping the public library sector in this way, and so coherent progress is impossible at present. A major survey entitled The Public Library and the Information superhighway was undertaken by UKOLN on behalf of the UK's Department of National Heritage in 1995. The existence of JANET and the work of JISC in the British academic sector is thrown into relief by the obvious need for a parallel arrangement on the public library side.

Although progress has been made in the US there is still a major problem of funding. Many public libraries are having to seek financial support from their local communities to keep the service running. The Library Association's millennium bid, if accepted in 1995, will help to kick-start the process in the UK, but long term commitment is needed from both funding bodies and librarians themselves. Given the continued decline in the lending of books from public libraries,[10] and with financial restrictions on future developments set to continue, public librarians need to refocus on the new opportunities that are awaiting them. It will not be an easy option but offers a more relevant and interesting future than simply the management of decline.

User views of networks

Whereas the academic information community regards developments, such as BIDS, as essential parts of an information strategy, do the users themselves see this access as vital? Surprisingly little has been done to ascertain the views of users, though there are some notable exceptions. The work of Sheppard and East, for example,[11] found that the general reaction of users in individual libraries towards end-user searching was favourable. Only a small minority objected to the rapid changes that have been taking place, though those who did seemed to hold their views strongly.

The views of library users on their experiences of networked databases should be a legitimate and rich source of information on the best ways of developing such services. User feedback should be sought at both a local and national level so that librarians can assess user reaction and make effective responses.

Responsiveness at the local level, coupled with pressure for improved quality and access at the national level, are necessary if librarians are to retain a role in future development. Libraries are, after all, presently at the centre of a number of networked activities, especially in higher education, and it is important, not least for the user, that this continues to be so. This role may not be as the provider of networked services, for libraries are, even now, often only the agent. In UK academic libraries, for example, BIDS was brought about by the library community and is seen as an adjunct to library services, but this pattern will not necessarily always be the case.

Users are beginning to have difficulty in identifying who is offering the networked service they are using. Equally, is it possible to say that users of networks provided by the library are library users? Those who are registered for using networked services may use the library, or the converged service, only to register for network access; that may be their only contact with the library service. Similarly, though network users may attend training courses run by libraries, that doesn't mean that other library services are used. Interestingly, Sheppard and East[11] found that those searchers of BIDS who had their own offices were less likely to attend a BIDS training course than those who used public space facilities. They also found that this group is less likely to ask for help from library staff if they get into difficulties.

If this is true, then as more individuals have their own computers and depend increasingly on networked information, there will be fewer people dependent on communal services and library support for their needs. As the information providers become less and less identifiable to users, then any part played by the library will not be a significant factor for them. Indeed, as the role of the library changes its very virtuality may rob it of a significant identity.

International survey of academic library networked services

How aware are users of library networked service? Do they in fact see libraries as providing them? If so, has it enhanced the reputation of a library service as an information provider? These are some of the questions that our questionnaire sought to answer (see below). Other questions follow on. What training, if any, should be provided by libraries for the accessing and best use of these databases? Have present users found that they needed training at all? Did they use the library or did they seek help from others in their quest for information? Are there still users who would prefer there to be a librarian as an intermediary?

Answers to these questions could provide better information on the role of libraries in the developing networked environment. Our questionnaire posed such questions, but a more comprehensive survey of particular libraries would be a useful guide to the attitude of users in a given campus, community or country.

This survey, undertaken for the purpose of this chapter, is intended to give no more than a snapshot of the use of networks by library users. Given the traditionally different roles of libraries in mainland Europe from those in the UK and the US, it was thought interesting to see if views on library networking and the role of the libraries themselves would differ to any noticeable extent.

Six libraries participated in the survey. The participants were: three technological universities, one each in Germany, Norway and Belgium; a broadbased traditional university in the UK; an American college; and a French scientific research library. The names of the libraries, in which the questionnaire was completed during the summer/autumn of 1995, are as follows:

- University of Edinburgh, UK;
- Universitätsbibliothek Hannover und Technische Informationbibliothek Hannover, Germany;
- The Library, Black Hawk College, Moline, Illinois, USA;
- Université Libre de Bruxelles (ULB), Brussels, Belgium;
- Bibliothèque Interuniversitaire Scientifique Jessieu, Géologie-Recherche, Paris, France;
- The Technical University Library of Norway at the University of Trondheim, and the Norwegian Institute of Technology Institute.

The international nature of this survey of selected academic libraries meant that the questionnaire had to be kept short. It was originally in English but a French translation was made for the survey in Paris. In total 25 questionnaires were despatched to each of the universities; 110 were completed and returned. The total return figures for each institution are as follows: UK 25, Belgium 29, USA 21, Germany 10, France 13, and Norway 12.

Summary of responses

Do you search networked databases yourself?
Yes: 97.2%; No: 2.7%
It is evident that access to network databases is now a common feature for most universities across Europe as well as in the US. It would seem that academic library users have come to expect these services to be available.

Are these networked services provided/facilitated by your library/information service?
Yes: 84.54%; No: 5.4%; Don't know: 6.3%; No response: 3.6%
Most academic library users obviously associate the service they access with the library as the provider. As the number and variety of networked services increase there will be more uncertainty about who is providing the access. In this situation, libraries must consider ways in which they can raise their public profiles as important information providers.

Do you see the library as an important information provider?
Yes: 98.1%; No: 0.9%; Don't know: 0.9%
The overwhelming view is that the library is still at the centre of the academic community. It is doubtful whether such a response would have been received in a survey about public libraries. Had not academic libraries taken the lead in encouraging the end-user, it is doubtful whether such a good response would have been received, as the next question indicates.

If yes, has your view been enhanced since the introduction of networked databases?
Yes: 88.1%; No: 7.2%; No response: 4.5%
Many respondents took the opportunity to make some comment at this point, most referring to the advantages of database searching rather than their general opinion of the library networked services. The major reasons given were:

easier searching for information, both in terms of the wider range of databases and in the ability to search by keyword; the time saved through using one interface; and the ability to search the catalogues of other libraries.

More specifically there were the following comments:

Now everybody has good access to any information wanted. It is much easier now to get an overview over the state of the art in certain subjects and it's easy to find very special information. (Germany)

Students are using the system more and incorporating more researched material in their writing. (USA)

I have always used library systems as resources for information; however, with the advent of computerized tools the information available has increased dramatically. (USA)

The discovery of references from unexpected sources. (France)

For the most part those few who answered 'no' protested that their view of the library had not changed as a result of the introduction of networked services. Though one person from the UK felt that the 'direct library role has been diminished', most were more positive:

I have always held [the library] in high esteem [it is] the heart of the college with or without computers. (USA)

The library has always been vital. (Germany)

Library always important, value increased by database searching, more complete, successful. (Germany)

Information concerning history = library. (Germany)

In general are you satisfied with the results you obtain from your database searching?
Yes: 79.0%; No: 19.0%; No response: 1.8%
Although the vast majority are obviously happy about their searching, one fifth were not and this sizeable group obviously would welcome help. The respondents who answered 'no' were asked to state why this was. Was it:

- *because they needed more training?*   50%
- *because they wanted better written help?*   31.8%
- *because a helpline was needed?*   18.2%

The responses speak for themselves and underline the new role which information professionals need to adopt if they have not already done so. The need for better written help was underlined by one German respondent who wanted 'written help to take home and read.'

Other reasons for a negative response were a desire for one database to cover all subjects, and complaints that databases are incomplete. From the US came this comment:

I have certainly found that computer databases speed the process. Not only is there quick access, the print is more readable and one can obtain copies of desired resources with the pressing of a key. That's a real advantage. However, one's ability to assess information is absolutely dependent on the design of the database. Some are better than others and some subjects are easier to search than others. I have found that I must be rather divergent in thinking how to get at significant keywords (in either expanding or limiting the search). However, when I think back to my usage of a bound index I think the same challenge occurred. The difference is that we expect that a computer-based index will streamline the process dramatically and for the most part it really does!

Do you think you would obtain better results if you had the help of a librarian as an intermediary when searching networked databases?
Yes: 56.3%; No: 30.9%; Don't know: 3.6; No response: 9.0%
This question seems to have been largely misinterpreted, for most respondents did not seem to understand 'intermediary' in the sense in which it is used by librarians in a mediated online search. It appears to have been interpreted as having help on hand from an expert; would they use it?

> Possibly: might be useful if [one] could submit proposed search terms and get feedback from, e.g., the appropriate subject librarian. (UK)

> Depends on the nature of my search, I think the answer for most is that help from a librarian is invaluable. (USA)

The comments do suggest a vote of confidence in the ability of librarians to offer advice and assistance. In general the belief is that librarians are available to help if called upon and that the quality of the help is appreciated. 'They would have assisted if I'd asked' was one comment from the US.

Those who said 'no' and made a comment were, as one could expect, strongly of the opinion that they could manage without help.

Did you receive any initial retraining in the use of networked databases?
Yes: 52.2%; No: 45.4%; No response: 2.7%
There are obviously a large number of database users who have failed to take up, or have not been offered training. It is not possible to tell, without a much more comprehensive survey, whether this is an opportunity missed by the users or by the library staff. Judging from the comments and the responses it would seem that it is more likely to be the latter. The survey indicated that there was more training offered by the UK institution than elsewhere.

If training was offered was it by library staff?
Yes: 50.9%; No: 40.0%; No response: 9.0%
If yes, what sort of training was it?

- *formal training sessions?*   47.9%
- *one-to-one tuition?*   30.2%
- *other?*   21.9%

The formal training seemed most available (or at least known about) in Edinburgh. Here 13 of the 25 respondents had received training from the library, though it is also true that one-to-one tuition also featured strongly here.

In the US academic staff seemed to have received instruction indirectly, for example:

> Attended library orientations with my students.

> Usually when I bring my students I learn something new!

There seems to be more need for considering the librarian's role in training in Belgium and France. For example, in Belgium the following comment was offered:

> At the open of this building, a person from the library explained it to our class.

If no, then who provided it?

- *other colleagues?*   6.6%
- *other students?*   24.4%
- *a friend?*   26.7%
- *another database user?*   11.1%
- *other?*   31.2%

Other comments mainly concerned self-tuition, with comments from the USA including: 'self taught but with library assistance'; 'computer prompts plus trial and error'; 'worked through it myself with the help of a librarian as needed'.

In Belgium and France it is clear that others are providing database training. In Brussels three said that a lecturer had helped them, while in France a computer scientist had trained someone. It was the plaintive cry from someone in Belgium which underlines the need for librarians to accept the formal training role:

> No-one helped me; I had to find out by myself.

What other help do you think the library can provide to help you in your search of networked databases?
The following options were presented:

- *database guides?*   57.1%
- *help with searching skills?* 33.1%
- *other?*   9.8%

When asked to offer any other comments, were made more demands for single databases to cover all subject areas, and demands to network particular databases. The more interesting comments included:

> Database guides but using previous users' experiences. (UK)

> An updated list (with short descriptions) of databases available/existing. (Germany)

Create better database guides explaining where to find the databases that are available. (Belgium)

Other comments

Asked for some final comments, a number of respondents did so. Many repeated some of the demands they had made earlier, for more unified databases or additional titles. Others praised the work of the library staff of their institution. Amongst the more original comments were:

A lot of searching skills are picked up by experience but training is useful as it shows one more unusual features. (UK)

The problem of the networked databases is that we know a book exists but we can't reach it. The library should foresee a service which can procure us all the books of all the networked databases. (Belgium)

Quality of databases e.g. correct spelling of databases should be improved. (Germany)

The use of computers has been a tremendous stride forward for users as well as librarians. BHC's relatively small library is expanded through its connections with other colleges and universities by computer. (USA)

I rely heavily on the library staff to assist me in researching materials for my teaching, moreover, the staff works very closely with my students. Our librarians are truly teachers. (USA)

Survey summary

It is difficult to draw too specific a conclusion from such a cursory glance at academic libraries across such a wide spectrum, but a number of things seem evident:

1 It would appear that networking databases and providing access to them for all students and staff of an institution is now a common feature of modern academic libraries. This fact seems to be very much appreciated by their clientele.

2 Libraries have enhanced their reputation as important information providers by their networked information provision.

3 The role library staff should play in this environment is one which facilitates the better access to information. This should be done principally through offering training in some form, either in formal groups or in one-to-one situations.

4 The need for a common database interface is a heartfelt demand from users. Some progress in this area would obviously be welcomed. There is, however, an obvious need to explain about the organization of information sources. Many users still feel that there should be a one-stop shop for the answer to all their information needs. Though common interfaces may help ease search problems, better education may provide some enlightenment on the broader issues.

Conclusion

As the user survey has revealed, librarians are held in high regard for their dedication and integrity. Users trust them to give good advice and offer informed help. This good relationship has, if anything, been strengthened by the educative part played by librarians in introducing their users to networked information. This is a strong basis on which to build at a time when information professionals are seeking to redefine their future role in the academic community and beyond.

Academic libraries and librarians have had to adapt to the changes brought about by the networking environment. Indeed, in many ways they have been leaders in their own institutions. They have taken a lead in the wider context too, often taking the initiative at a national level.

The networked environment, however, means that there is a wider international dimension which also needs to be considered and any new initiatives should take this into account. The creation of research projects into digitization, on-demand publishing, and electronic document and article delivery, are necessary for an informed approach to future progress. Such projects are under way in the UK but there is surely a danger that limiting them to a narrow national remit will render them less authoritative. Organizations such as the RLG are presently developing their international role, though for the most part partnering only English-speaking institutions. It is, at least, a start to the process of international dialogue and cooperation.

Individual contact is, of course, maintained by librarians through access to discussion lists across the world. User groups have, for example, learned from each other in their fight for better database quality. Such informal contact is vital, but for research and development projects a more formal bank of documents and information would help keep information professionals aware of what is being done where, by whom and with what support. What is missing, however, is an effective international body or database which would record and advise on current research projects and provide pointers to published papers and reports. This may not be easy to establish, but it would be an extremely helpful source of information and data.

There is no doubt that the individual end-users in our libraries are starting to appreciate the potential of networked information. Information professionals at all levels have already used their expertise to develop new organizations and help facilitate easier provision; they have also worked on improving the quality of what is offered. There are, however, still a number of important tasks to be done. Amongst these are: the broadening of networked access to the wider community; fighting to ensure that networked information remains free from censorship; and the creation of an international database of research and development projects.

The very dimension of these tasks reflects the wider role that information professionals need to undertake in the interests of their users. If the world has become a global village, librarians need to join together as global gatekeepers.

References

1 Coney, J., *Online information retrieval: an introductory manual of principles and practice*, 3rd edn, London, Clive Bingley 1989.
2 Stone, P., *JANET: a report on its use for libraries*, London, British Library Research and Development Department, 1990 (British Library Research Paper 77).
3 Joint Information Systems Committee, Guidelines for developing an information strategy, JISC 1995.
4 *The BUBL leaflet*, BUBL, 1994.
5 Joint Funding Council Libraries Review Group, *Report*, Bristol, HEFC, 1994 (Follett Report).
6 Vickery, B. (ed.), *Summaries of the current state of networked information at participating institutions*, Nottingham, Regional Focus Group for Networked Information, 1995.
7 *Europe and the global information society: recommendations to the European Council*, Brussels, European Council, 1994 (Bangemann Report).
8 de Bruine, F. R., 'INFO2000: from scribe to screen – which cars on the infobahn?', *I&T magazine*, 18, October 1995, 10–13.
9 Pong, L. Y., 'Library 2000: expanding our nation's capacity to learn', *Library times international*, 11 (3), January 1995, 29–30.
10 'Library loans tumble again', *The Bookseller*, 12 January 1995.
11 Sheppard, E. and East, H., 'Access to wide area networked bibliographic databases: end-users' behaviour and perceptions'. In *Online Information 95: 19th International Online Information Meeting Proceedings*, London, 5–7 December 1995, 109–125.

Acknowledgements

My grateful thanks are due to the following people, without whose help the user survey would not have been possible:

Margaret Dowling, University of Edinburgh, UK.

Claudine Kleb and Elizabeth Noel, Bibliothèque Interuniversitaire Scientifique Jessieu, Géologie-Recherche, Paris, France.

Hardy Warlich, Universitätsbibliothek Hannover und Technische Informationbibliothek Hannover, Germany.

Charlet Key, Library, Black Hawk College, Moline, Illinois, US.

Claudine Kellinckx, Université Libre de Bruxelles (ULB), Bruxelles, Belgium.

Roar Storleer, The Technical University of Norway, University of Trondheim and The Norwegian Institute of Technology.

In addition I am very grateful to Tony Snape, good friend and freelance journalist based in Brussels, for his groundwork in the city.

10

The changing role of professional education for information professionals

Bruce Reid and Pauline Rafferty Brown

Introduction

Other chapters in this book demonstrate clearly how radically the recent rapid changes in information technology and its applications have affected the relationships between information, its users and information professionals. It is obvious that the new role and skills required of professionals, now and in the future, have comprehensive implications for the role, content and style of information and library service (ILS) education, both for first professional and for postgraduate and research qualifications.

In this chapter we attempt to establish the nature of the main technological and economic changes impinging on the profession; to identify the knowledge and skills required by information practitioners in their new role; and to outline some of the principal ways in which university schools of information and library studies (SILS) are responding to these needs.

Changes in the information environment

The new key principle on which virtually all else depends is the clearly observable convergence of core information professional knowledge and computing. The topic now has its own journal.[1] The word 'convergence' has been used ambiguously in recent professional literature – sometimes to mean this external phenomenon, sometimes to connote the actual managerial integration of previously separate library and computing services.[2] In our view, and certainly for the purposes of this chapter, a clearer usage is to reserve 'convergence' for the irreversible phenomenon affecting these areas of theoretical knowledge and practice, and to use 'integration' or 'merging' when referring to deliberate decisions to bring together service units, personnel, courses or indeed subjects of study.[3-5] For SILS it is the former external trend affecting the whole discipline which is of paramount importance, and the managerial strategy adopted to respond to it is just one of the many issues it raises for the style and content of professional courses.

A second important strand in the changing environment is the drive towards end-user empowerment in the accessing of information. There are a number of distinct forces at work in this, but they all prevail in the same direction. There is the 'pull' of increasingly user-friendly interfaces and of readier access to electronic databases, and the 'push' of users anxious to do it for themselves. Then there is the management imperative to maintain services with dwindling resources, and the inability of service staff to cope with demand in a role of total mediation, leading to a concern to equip customers to help themselves without a decline in the quality of the final result.

These broad changes can only be properly appreciated, particularly in their implications for the information profession, in the context of particular technological innovations, new modes of communication, and new and competing product development, which have all had profound effects on both information service provision and document delivery. A brief overview of these innovative modes and products will give some indication of the complex and unstable (though not chaotic) situation which faces the post-modern users of information and the professionals alike.

Online searching of remote databases (mostly bibliographic) via the international packet switching system was, of course, the first significant innovation. It was relatively slow to spread and even slower to be regarded as an alternative to print equivalents. Just as demand for mediated online provision in well-financed and publicized services began to outstrip the professional time to maintain them, CD-ROM (at first bibliographic) appeared. In time this accommodated demand but raised new problems of choice, installation, maintenance, training (especially of users), comparative costs and access. This last was eventually solved (but at the additional cost of special surcharges) by the emergence of CD-ROM networks.[6] Financial decisions became even more a matter for fine (and informed) judgement, especially with the spread of campus-wide information networks (CWIS) and the possibility of networking to more than one site.

In parallel, CD-ROMs were being applied to document delivery[7] as an alternative first to photocopying and interlibrary lending, then to local print periodical holdings. ADONIS and Business Periodicals on Disc (University Microfilms International) are two widely used examples which began to blur the distinction between information service and document delivery, and raised all kinds of questions about the 'true' cost of print periodical subscriptions, the adequacy of print on demand, and the cost and value of browsability versus increased local electronic holdings. Some libraries even networked the indexing to such collections to increase their local accessibility.[8] Meanwhile, the acceptance of non-bibliographic CD-ROMs of a reference and directory nature, for which the cost comparisons with print were frequently more favourable, was widespread, especially in schools, where multimedia enhancements facilitated the learning process.[9, 10]

National and international networks now began to realize their information potential, but also to further complicate an already complex situation. JANET, previously important for bulletin boards, mail-lists, software exchange, gateways to remote hosts, and access to the OPACs of other libraries, took on a new dimension with the advent of BIDS (Bath Information and Data Services) in 1991. Its publicity describes it accurately as 'a national service providing widespread network access to commercially supplied bibliographic databases **free at the point of delivery**' (emphasis ours). Like CD-ROMs, BIDS allows unlimited searching once a subscription has been paid. Its innovative feature, however, is that it allows this at the desktop for all users connected to the institution's local-area network. Such access immediately raised a range of issues for information professionals: the viability of retaining 'BIDS databases' in other formats, the usability of BIDS by end-users, the training requirements, the monitoring of use and effectiveness and the role of the LIS. There was also the question of the link with document delivery, since BIDS permits direct ordering of documents.

All of the above developments provided an added impetus to the growing use of personal bibliographic software (PBS), as users of electronic bibliographic databases sought to download retrieved references onto their own machine, reformat them and use them for their own purposes. Increasingly information professionals were expected to be able to recommend a package and instruct in its use. Since at least four of these are widely used (Procite, Reference Manager, End-Note and Papyrus) this requires some evaluative skills.[11]

A further product type to cut across the old categories of information service and document delivery is what the literature appears to call current awareness services/individual article services (CAS/IAS).[12] Examples of these are Inside Information (British Library Document Supply Centre), Right Pages (Springer Electronic Media), Swetscan (Swets Subscription Service), EBSCO and Uncover (B. H. Blackwell and Carl Systems Inc.). Briefly these are current databases of details of articles published in a very large number (10–20 thousand) of journal titles. They are backed by document delivery services, are accessible variously on BIDS, the Internet and by subscription. and offer a variety of refinements such as searching regularly to a user profile and tagging journals held by the customer institutions, all at a wide range of costs. A further raft of issues is raised for the information practitioner by these services. Comparisons are invited not only with full-text subscriptions but also with other discipline-based information services – though since these products are hybrids, straight and simple comparison is neither possible nor valid.

Finally (for the moment) there is the gradually increasing importance of the Internet and its proliferating resource access, detection, and retrieval (RADAR) tools. Its potential for access to the world's OPACs, to document delivery (via systems such as Ariel)[13] and to bibliographic databases and full-text systems has effected a profound and permanent change in the information environment. Internet development is progressing in parallel with an increasing proliferation and globalization of the information industry itself. Examples are the acquisition of Uncover by Knight Ridder[14] and the introduction of Internet resource access and detection tools bundled with existing products by some of the major players. OCLC is planning to distribute NetFirst via its online services FirstSearch and EPIC[15] while Microsoft has found itself accused of unfair competition as a result of offering Microsoft net (MSN) free with the release of Windows 95.[16]

Impetus has been given to the involvement of information professionals in the assessment, development, integration, encouragement and use of these various innovations, products and services by several official reports and further reports funded by the British Library Research and Development Department. The Follett Report[17, 18] identified the shift from the view of the library as a single repository of information to the emphasis on information and information access, stressing the need for strategic information planning, and proposed a series of development projects over three years designed to further the use of IT in selective areas. Among the areas recommended were: on-demand publishing, electronic document and article delivery, electronic journals, a database and dataset strategy, investment in navigational tools and the further development of library automation and management systems. Subsequently FIGIT (Follett Implementation Group for Information Technology) set up eLib (the Electronic Libraries Programme) – a coordinated set of research, training and awareness projects in which SILS are participating.

Even before Follett, projects such as ELINOR (Electronic Library Information Online Retrieval) at the Milton Keynes campus of De Montfort University had pointed the way towards the resolution of the problems of increasing demand for information from increasing numbers of students through the development of new relationships between publishers and librarians and the wider use of networks.[19, 20] The Fielden Report,[21] – part of the Follett process but published separately from the main Group report – addresses the very important area of human resource management in academic libraries. For SILS the important recommendations were that professional staff should be expected to play a greater role in learner support and academic liaison, that staff must know how to access/navigate in electronic databases, that subject librarians will have to understand teaching/learning skills, and that customer care and service attitudes will have to be widely applied. Library schools and academic library employers were also urged to work more closely together at national level to address the curricular implications of the pending changes. That this advice need not be given only to academic employers has been illustrated by projects such as Croydon Libraries Internet Project (CLIP).[22] In the longer term, all information professionals will find their role greatly changed by the evolving new global information environment outlined in this section.

New role: new knowledge, new skills

That this new role is emerging for the information worker seems almost to have become received opinion. The exact nature of that role is, however, subject to rather less agreement, but some salient features are appearing. A more proactive relationship with publishers and other providers of information seems to be necessary in an environment where, as we have seen, publishers are experimenting with new storage and transmission media, pricing and the user market at least as much as information workers are. In our view, and that of the practitioners we consulted[23] while designing the new BA (Hons) Information Studies Programme at the University of Central England, the main areas in which information professionals require new and extended knowledge and skills are: managerial, financial, research, and training/advisory, with IT skills pervading all of them.

This consultation was formal and wide-ranging, but unstructured and open-ended. We chose 180 practitioners from *Who's who in the UK information world*.[24] The selection was not random and two criteria guided our choice: the need for wide-ranging representation and the need for input from the cutting edge. We sent our draft course outline to practitioners in libraries and information centres in universities, colleges, schools, business, commerce, industry, the voluntary sector, government and the media, as well as to public librarians, print and electronic publishers, suppliers and hosts. The draft outline of just two A4 pages consisted of a summary of the context of development, the planned course structure and a broad indication of content. This structure and content is reviewed at the beginning of the next section of this chapter.[7] We posed no particular questions, but simply asked them to give us their views on our proposals. The number of responses was very satisfying (62 or 34%) but their quality even more so.

The general area of management was a subject of great interest to many of our respondents, with regard to both the topics covered in our modules and the kinds of skills graduates would need in order to cope with radically changing organizational structures. The following are representative comments:

> Management skills are increasingly of importance at all levels, especially self-management at a time of dwindling resources. Libraries will be expected to be more entrepreneurial and imaginative, capable of promoting and marketing services to exploit resources to the utmost. (public library)

> The divisions between different aspects of information management and delivery are dissolving and new organisational structures will emerge. You need to equip students for an uncertain future. (academic library)

Many respondents stressed the increasing importance of the financial aspects of management, costing and valuing services, and a client-centred approach:

> Hopefully the Management modules include all aspects of finance – budgeting, costing, accounts and financial monitoring and control. Finance is coming under particular scrutiny in our own organisation, and other libraries in the region report similar emphasis – on costing of services, value for money, benchmarking and budget justifications. Future generations of specialists need the skills and understanding to talk accountants' language. (special library)

In the course outline we had said: 'The degree will also require the student to complete a major piece of research which is rooted in work experience during the course. This is an aspect of our earlier programmes which has always enhanced the employability of our graduates.' This drew considerable positive comment:

> I am pleased to note that research methodology and a major piece of research rooted in practice are essential components. Research in our field is mostly applied research, essential to inform good management practice and, by carrying out and writing up a practice-based piece of research work, students will also gain valuable experience of report writing for management. (academic library)

Since a high proportion of the innovations in our course outline were associated with new technology, it was not surprising that this received much attention from our respondents:

> And then there is the Internet – a whole new area where if it is robust enough to hold up, Information Specialists may well be required as 'Systems Navigators'. (special library)

> If the anarchy of the Internet is an example of the information future then it is crying out for the organisational and retrieval skills of information specialists to impose order on the anarchy. (academic library)

> I am always disappointed at the response from interview candidates when they are asked about their knowledge of IT issues. The standard response is that they can use computerised catalogues and online or CD-ROM databases as a user but the knowledge rarely goes beyond this. (special library)

A number of respondents sketched a profile of the kind of ILS graduates they would seek to employ or of the 'basket' of concepts and skills we should be seeking to equip them with. This example struck a particular chord:

> I have always been in favour of using undergraduate education to give students an intellectual map of a particular area, and an understanding of its relationship to the maps of other areas. I am also in favour of giving students some clear generic competences – I wonder if you are giving this enough attention? I want to employ people who are confident, personable, able to work collaboratively, imaginative, lively, good at presenting and good in meetings. On top of that I want them to have an understanding of the major issues in information transfer in the late 20th/early 21st centuries. (academic library)

The keener requirement for managerial and financial skills is traceable to changes in the information environment. Life cycle costing skills are needed in order to establish the 'real' costs of existing provision of, say, print journal collections[25] compared with the proliferating alternatives. Comparative cost/benefit analysis skills are needed to assess these options and the 'benefit' aspect of this process requires considerable research skills to be applied in the workplace. Moreover, the increasing competitiveness and globalization of the information industry demand skills of financial negotiation with providers at the local level, and of political lobbying at the national level, if information professionals are to secure the optimum deal for their institutions and individual users. Sheila Corrall[26] encapsulates this group of related skills well:

> Purchase decisions may involve cost/benefit analysis of the relative cost-effectiveness of print versus electronic resources, standalone versus networked, locally mounted versus nationally or regionally networked. The information professional will need to use techniques of investment appraisal and life cycle costing, as well as negotiating and influencing skills for striking the best deal with suppliers.

Finally there is the extremely important training and advisory role identified by Follett and Fielden and being actively pursued by FIGIT in a number of elements of the eLib programme.

The response of schools of information and library studies

SILS have been steadily evolving their means of meeting the changing needs of the profession through innovation and adaptation in first-degree and postgraduate course teaching, through research into developing areas, through the encouragement of the active involvement in research by all students, and through providing rewarding opportunities for research to practitioners.

First professional degrees in information studies have changed to meet the changed information environment through regular course reviews and revalidation. For example, at the University of Central England (UCE) the new BA (Hons) Information Studies Programme has been developed in a way intended to balance practical realities and theoretical idealism. The review team felt that it was important to provide a programme which would:

- include a strong core
- allow choice and flexibility
- integrate IT throughout the curriculum
- develop management skills
- acknowledge convergence with other academic subjects
- emphasize research skills and techniques through work-based projects
- develop personal transferable skills
- emphasize a student centred learning environment.

The new programme offers students a coherent route to one of three named degrees: Information and Library Studies, Business Information, and Information and Media. It consists of:

- shared core modules
- distinctive modules developed for each degree
- optional modules, which can be chosen from three sources:
  distinctive modules of the other degrees;
  free-standing modules;
  modules available elsewhere in the faculty.

Changes in the professional environment are reflected in all of these features. For example, areas which were optional in the previous programme (such as advanced electronic information sources and information networks) have been moved decisively into the core. The distinctive modules reflect strong new markets for information professionals in business, information technology, multimedia and publishing. The optional modules, particularly those from other schools in the faculty such as Computing, and Media and Communications, acknowledge the reality of convergence in these subject areas in the most practical way possible by encouraging students to blend in appropriate and approved modules from other disciplines.

The British Association for Information and Library Education and Research (BAILER) encourages exchange of experience between SILS and the spread of best practice. The CTI (Computers in Teaching Initiative) Centre for Library and Information Studies (CTILIS)[27] is also very active in the specific field of information technology. It is currently conducting a detailed survey of teaching methods in IT in SILS in the UK to establish and disseminate best practice. In the pilot stage at the moment of writing, it will involve observation of classes, questionnaires and interviews with students.

Europe and beyond

The theme of convergence, not only of technologies, but also of professional skills, and the resulting implications for LIS education, has been explored in a number of papers recently,[23, 28] and was a recurring topic at the 1995 Euclid/FID/ET Conference held in Copenhagen. Paradoxically, convergence of technologies, skills and knowledge results in curriculum expansion. Throughout Europe, 'traditional' models of ILS education have been found wanting and contemporary pedagogical models encompass aspects of media studies, communication, publishing, business and IT, and telematics as well as information, and sometimes library management.

Herring,[28] discussing the BA (Hons) Information Management course at Queen Margaret College, explains:

> The rationale for the course is based on convergence – of knowledge, skills and technologies – within information management. . . . It is the convergence of this range of knowledge and skills – indeed the convergence of professions – that the course seeks to encourage and exploit, and graduates of the course who become, for example, information analysts or librarians for a part or all of their career, will be well equipped to demonstrate how their recognition of the importance of convergence can provide added value to their role as information professionals.

The Euclid/FID/ET Conference, entitled 'Improved Practice and Integrated Skills in the ILS Field', provided an opportunity for European SILS (broadly interpreted to include speakers from South Africa and Canada) to exchange ideas and debate curriculum design for the millennium. Gilles Deschamps[29] captured the spirit of the conference and articulated the opportunities available in the new age information world:

Side by side with a stable little market, essentially based on the management of institutions (libraries, documentation centres, archival services) and documents, another potentially enormous market is developing, based on the management of information and knowledge without much, if any, reference to institutions or even to documents. This market is and will more and more be based on the management of information resources, products, services or functions (corporate information policies and services, the information-related industry, information superhighways, virtual resources, and so on).

In this new age, 'quick fix' information is available to those with appropriate resources, and some commentators argue that it is becoming increasingly difficult for librarians and information professionals to argue any monopoly of knowledge in relation to information. In a competitive environment, in which it has been predicted that the traditional presence and significance of paper, books and libraries 'seems poised to fade',[30] it is essential that SILS offer courses which ensure that information professionals stay in the information race.

Michel Bauwens[31] optimistically looks forward to a cyberspace peopled by 'cybrarians' or knowledge officers who will inject formal knowledge into informal knowledge processes, building virtual reference centres and filtering information from the outside world through electronic newsletters. It could be argued that this vision is simply extending the role that information workers have always played, but the challenge for the curriculum is to frame these skills in relevant and contemporary language, technologies and culture.

For Deschamps,[29] staying ahead in the information race means building a curriculum which is

> . . . more polyvalent, more flexible, and more solidly based on the management of information and knowledge than on the management of institutions and documents. It means to build a curriculum to educate and train information professionals, in the broadest possible way. Librarians and archivists, of course, but also infonauts, information or technology watchers, information entrepreneurs, knowledge engineers, information resource managers and decision-makers.

Sirjec Virkus[32] recognizes that one of the problems facing educators is the need first to update their own knowledge before being able to offer courses to students. The need to educate educators is being addressed in Europe by initiatives such as the Nordic–Baltic project 'Training of Trainees' which started in 1993. Other Eastern European SILS emphasize the value to them of cooperation with SILS based in western Europe. Gudauskas and Glosiene[33] comment:

> The co-operation of Western partners would help teachers of the Faculty of Communication to get acquainted with the experience and expertise of their colleagues and would facilitate the exchange of ideas.

SILS, research and technologies

Increasingly, educators at SILS are not only teaching about developing technologies and the professional skills needed to operate successfully within them, but are also using the technologies to deliver course content. A recent project undertaken at the Department of Communication and Information Studies at Queen Margaret College[34] concerns the development of a module which aims to produce professionals trained to undertake and sustain teleworking beyond the initial training period. The project group has identified several types of tasks which would be suitable for teleworkers working as information specialists. They include: 'standard' rule-based ILS tasks such as indexing, abstracting and searching; management and planning tasks such as policy formulation and resource allocation; and brainstorming and creative tasks such as designing a research project or specifying a new product or service. The research group hopes that the module will prepare students for teleworking and give them the opportunity to market themselves as teleworkers to organizations.

Levy and Fowell[35] report on the delivery of a new module entitled Elements of information management: effective communication in the networked organization to selected level-one undergraduate students at the University of Sheffield. The module focuses on the exploitation of new communication technologies to support effective teamwork and project management. Students, working in small teams, pilot and evaluate the use of a range of information/communication technologies and resources, and are offered online tutor support, access to Internet and the opportunity to set up their own newsgroups. Levy and Fowell comment that:

> Networked learner support is emerging as a new professional practice, in response to the challenge to provide effective support for all users of networked resources. . . . For instance, much current activity exploits WWW facilities and email for delivering user education and information skills training across campus and beyond.

Experiential learning and action research informed the teaching/learning practice during the course. In turn, the action research undertaken by tutors during the module will feed into the wider NetLinks eLib research project (see below).

SILS are active in research in a wide range of developing areas in the information environment. The Department of Information Studies, University of Sheffield is embarking on an eLib research project centred on the new role of the information professional in 'networked learner support' (NLS). The project is a response to the need identified by the Follett Report for training and awareness-raising initiatives for library staff in networked information resources and retrieval, and in the skills and strategies needed for effective end-user training in this area. The core of the work will be a national survey to establish the spectrum of readiness of HE institutions for facilitating NLS, on the basis of which an attempt will be made to identify examples of good practice, and ultimately to create a framework for professional development and training.

The School of Information Studies at UCE, through its Centre for Information Research and Training (CIRT), is in the pilot phase of another eLib project, Training and Awareness Programme in Networks (TAPin), which seeks to improve the quality of teaching and research staff output by identifying staff information needs and developing their information skills. It aims to emphasize to end-user academics, and thus ultimately to students, the benefits which can be gained by an understanding and awareness of networked information resources appropriate to specific disciplines. It is a collaborative project based on a consortium of six West Midlands universities and involving systems and subject librarians. TAPin will be conducted in three stages:

- a skills and awareness audit, which will involve an investigation of the IT resources, strategies and cultures of academic departments;
- developing network awareness and skills, training librarians first, then academic staff;
- an impact study: a repeat investigation to review the impact on IT resourcing, strategies and culture.

In the important area of document delivery, the Department of Information and Library Studies at Loughborough University of Technology is beginning a three-year research project called Focused Investigation of Document Delivery Options (FIDDO). It will investigate the technical, managerial and economic factors in various document delivery options in academic libraries.

The Department of Information and Library Management at the University of Northumbria at Newcastle (UNN), in conjunction with the Information Services Department at UNN, has been involved in the IMPEL project[36] which focused on the social, organizational and cultural impacts of electronic services on library and information staff working in the Higher Education sector. In 1995, the original project was further developed as an eLib project. The current research project, Monitoring Organizational and Cultural Change,[37] will consist of four linked projects:

- IMPEL Stage 2: Impact of the Electronic Library on Library and Related Support Staff;
- Impact of the Electronic Library on Academic Staff and Students;
- Impact of Resource-based Learning on Library and Information Services;
- Monitoring the Impact of the eLib Staff Training Programme for Educational Development for Higher Education Library Staff.

The scope and purpose of the linked projects is to further validate and take forward the understanding of organizational change in academic libraries already gained in IMPEL 1. Through the monitoring of social, organizational and cultural change in institutions, the UNN team hope to identify the key factors in successful management of change.

Smaller scale individual research, much of it undertaken informally by undergraduate and postgraduate students either as part of their course or as a research degree, also makes an important contribution, not always well disseminated, to new areas in the changing landscape. For example, UCE students have been involved informally in the evaluation of ADONIS at Aston University, working both on the quality of the user interface and on levels of user satisfaction (see Chapter 7). Work like this provides valuable insights and experience for the students and additional external researchers for the library managers. Undergraduate students at UCE must write a 10,000-word project report as part of their nine-month work placement, and many of these reports have focused on innovations in the information environment. Areas investigated have included: an evaluation of user satisfaction and staff satisfaction with a merged library and computing service in an HE institution; a study of Ariel[12] in use in HE; and several cost/benefit analyses of available CAS/IAS for particular library and information services. Currently several placement students are working on audits of Internet resources aimed at identifying those areas relevant to the users in their host organizations: these include consideration of repackaging for current awareness purposes and preparation of user documentation for awareness-raising and promotion.

At Masters level students have undertaken a critical evaluation of the implementation of BIDS on a particular campus[38] and a systematic comparative evaluation of personal bibliographic software packages.[39] At the University of Sheffield a Masters student has evaluated a specialist CAS/IAS based on Uncover.[40] At UCE the introduction of work-based projects[41] into our part-time degree has been keenly appreciated by employers, who have sought to build them into their strategic planning process. In addition the new research entry part-time Masters degree encourages the acquisition of research skills in parallel with the solution of a practical work-related problem, and in this programme students are currently tackling subjects such as a management system for an academic library, the implementation of information audit techniques, and the development of a World Wide Web page for a small organization.

Throughout the information world, ILS educators recognize that professional roles are changing constantly and that the courses they design, at undergraduate, postgraduate and continuing professional development levels, must reflect, and anticipate, these changes. The challenge and excitement of being an ILS educator comes from taking part in the creation and development of new paradigms to suit new times.

References

1   *Convergence: the journal of research into new media technologies*, 1 (1), May 1995.

2   'Library and computing services: converge, merge or diverge?', *Relay: the journal of the University, College and Research Group*, (42), 1995.

3   Macartney, W., 'Convergence planning', *Library Association record technology supplement*, 97 (8), 1995, 3.

4   Royan, B., 'Are you being merged? A survey of convergence in Information Service Provision', *COPOL newsletter*, Summer, 1993, 17–30.

5   Williams, A. G., 'Where are we going? The development of convergence between

university libraries and computing services'. In Harris, C. (ed.), *The new university library: issues for the 90s and beyond (essays in honour of Ian Rogerson)*, London, Taylor Graham, 1994, 55–72

6 Biddiscombe, R., 'Networking CD ROM in an academic library environment', *British journal of academic librarianship*, **6** (3), 1991, 175–83.

7 Stern, B. T. and Compier, H. C. J., 'ADONIS – document delivery in the CD ROM age', *Interlending and document supply*, **18** (3), 1990, 79–87.

8 Craft, E. 'Distributed ADONIS indexing – the Aston University LIS solution', *ADONIS news*, **4** (1), 1993, 1–3.

9 Matthews, S., *CD-ROMs in school libraries*, Hatfield Advisory Unit for Microtechnology in Education, 1990.

10 *School library 2000*, **1**, 1994, Oxford, Learned Information.

11 Hanson, T. (ed.), *Bibliographic software and the electronic library*, Hatfield, University of Hertfordshire Press, 1995.

12 Rowley, J., 'Coming alive to bibliographic current awareness services', *Library Association record technology supplement*, **96** (2), 1994, 19–20.

13 Coleman, J., 'Creating document delivery tools for the Internet: RLG's Ariel software', *Internet world and document delivery world international 94: Proceedings of the 2nd annual conference (London, May 1994)*, Westport, CT and London, Mecklermedia, 1994, 62–4.

14 'KR in buying mode', *Information world review*, **106**, September 1995, 2.

15 'NetFirst to improve end-user access to Internet resources', *OCLC reference news*, **27**, Summer 1995, 1.

16 'Microsoft moves on monopoly complaints', *Information world review*, **106**, September 1995, 3.

17 Joint Funding Councils' Libraries Review Group, *Report* (Follett Report), Bristol, Higher Education Funding Council for England, 1993.

18 'Follett special', *Relay: the journal of the University, College and Research Group*, **40**, 1994.

19 Ramsden, A., Wu, Z. and Zhao, D., *The pilot phase of the ELINOR electronic library project* (British Library R & D Report), 1994.

20 Zhao, D., 'The ELINOR electronic library system', *Electronic library*, **12** (5), 1994, 1–6.

21 John Fielden Consultancy, *Supporting expansion* (Fielden Report), Bristol, Higher Education Funding Council for England, 1993.

22 Batt, C., 'CLIP up-date', *Vine*, **98**, March 1995, 24–7.

23 Reid, B. and Brown, P., 'Asking practitioners', *Library Association record*, **97** (9), September 1995, 488–9.

24 *Who's who in the UK information world*, 4th edn, TFPL Publishing, 1993.

25 Stephens, A., 'The application of life cycle costing in libraries', *British journal of academic librarianship*, **3** (2), 1988, 82–8.

26 Corrall, Sheila. 'Middle managers – a defunct species', *Library manager*, (1), November 1994, 25.

27 *CTI Centre for Library and Information Studies newsletter*, **1** (1), Loughborough, Loughborough University of Technology, 1989.

28 Herring, J., 'Seeking convergence: educating the information manager', *Managing information*, **1** (9), September 1994, 30–2.

29 Deschalets, G., *Reengineering LIS education at the University of Montreal: should we really get rid of the L-word?* (Paper presented at Euclid-FID/ET Conference),

Copenhagen, 21–22 November 1995,

30 Verity, J.W. 'The Information revolution', *Business week*, 1994 (special 1994 bonus issue), 10–18.

31 Bauwens, M., *The role of cybrarians in the cyberspace-oriented corporation* (Paper presented at the Euclid-FID/ET Conference), Copenhagen, 21–22 November 1995.

32 Virkus, S., *Education and training in information technology for the new generation of librarians in Estonia* (Paper presented at the Euclid-FID/ET Conference), Copenhagen, 21–22 November 1995

33 Gudauskas, R. and Glosiene, A., *Education for information specialists at the University of Vilnius: an integrated approach* (Paper presented at the Euclid-FID/ET Conference), Copenhagen, 21–22 November 1995.

34 Davenport, E., Gillham, M. and Cano, V., *Training for telework: a draft specification* (Paper presented at the Euclid-FID/ET Conference), Copenhagen, 21–22 November 1995.

35 Levy, P. and Fowell, S., *Networked learning in LIS education and training* (Paper presented at the Euclid-FID/ET Conference), Copenhagen, 21–22 November 1995.

36 Edwards, C., Day, J. M. and Walton, G., *IMPEL project: the impact on people of electronic libraries* (Proceedings of the 2nd International ELVIRA Conference 1995), Aslib (in press).

37 *Monitoring organizational and cultural change: a proposal to the Follett Implementation Group on Information Technology*. Department of Information and Library Management and Information Services Department, University of Northumbria at Newcastle, July 1995.

38 Mulvaney, T. K., *A critical evaluation of the BIDS ISI Data Service* (MA thesis), School of Information Studies, University of Central England, 1993.

39 McHale, G., *A critical evaluation of three personal bibliographic software packages* (MA thesis), School of Information Studies, University of Central England, 1995.

40 Nicholls, E. J., *BIODOC: an interim evaluation of a rapid document delivery and electronic current awareness service* (MA thesis), University of Sheffield, 1995.

41 Reid, B. and Shoolbred, M., 'Library and information research: new opportunities at UCE', *Assistant librarian*, 88 (10), November /December 1995, 154–5.

11

The continuing end-user revolution

Ray Lester

Introduction

One way that we might paraphrase the 'continuing end-user revolution' is
thus:

> Increasingly, in the future, people who at present use libraries and their librarians
> to help them get the published data and documents they need or want, will find that
> they can get along quite nicely without using the facilities and services provided by
> the libraries, or by the librarians, or by both these types of entity. Instead, the peo-
> ple will directly themselves use the world's rapidly developing public and private
> information technology infrastructures to acquire copies of needed or desired pub-
> lished information. And this will bring (yet further) into question society's needs in
> the future for such libraries and their librarians.

I shall try in this chapter to throw some light on to this question of whether –
at last? – we should be planning for the end of (at least a proportion of) our
current libraries, or of their librarians, or of both the libraries and the librarians. Even though we shall restrict ourselves here to consideration of the role
libraries/librarians currently play in the handling of publicly available (as
against privately available) information, the question is rather difficult to
answer at any level of generality. Certainly, focusing on published information
removes many of the individual and organizational variations we would by
definition find if we were tackling future modes of handling of unpublished,
private information by those who need or wish to use such information. But
that reduction in complexity is more than made up for by the greatly increased
political, economic and, particularly, legal complications which arise when we
deal with information in the public domain, and which affect different
libraries and librarians to a very diverse extent. Indeed, I would suggest that
how national and supra-national intellectual property laws are framed, and
especially how they are adhered to in practice in the future, is likely to be far
more decisive in determining the direction and speed of the 'continuing end-
user revolution', than what happens with the technologies which seem currently to be driving that revolution.

Distinguishing libraries from librarians

In our paraphrase we have implied that we should distinguish the future for librarians from the future for libraries. We will use the word *librarian* here to denote an individual (usually professionally qualified), who personally helps match a user to a publicly available information resource. Such a person might, for instance, be a reference librarian or an information specialist or an information broker. An *end-user* might then be defined as a person who uses such a resource without the assistance of such a librarian. Librarians of the type specified are usually – but not always – employed by *libraries*. The term *libraries* refers to the organizational entities specifically set up to intermediate between the totality of information which is currently publicly available and the library (end-)user who might use a portion of that totality via interaction with one or a combination of the library's designated facilities and services. If all of the users of a particular library became end-users, as defined, then the library would have no more need to employ (professional) librarians, as defined. This does not necessarily mean that the library would not need in the future to employ people who have professional-level skills and expertise: simply that it would not need further to employ those sorts of professional who directly intermediate at the point of information use by the information user.

Actually, the predominant use of all types of traditional paper-based library by all types of user has at least for a century been end-user use. People have usually gone to a library and found the published data or documents they need, themselves, without the assistance of a (professional) librarian. It was only when computer-assisted techniques of acquiring data and documents developed that the question arose as to whether one needed a librarian to help one use the resulting computer-based facilities and services. When people in the last few years have talked about the continuing end-user revolution – or at least the continuing end-user trend – they have more often than not been referring to the fact that users these days seem less and less to need the services of librarians in order to hunt out successfully, and pick out, electronically encoded data or documents. So users are becoming end-users as regards electronic data and documents, just as they have mostly been for their print equivalents.

The electronic imperative

It would be easy then to conclude that as 'real' libraries become 'virtual' libraries and disappear, so too will the professional, intermediating librarians disappear. However, before considering the fallacies in this projected chain of events, let us consider the arguments that remind us of the force of the electronic imperative itself:

1 Publicly available data and documents are, for almost all actual or prospective end-users, a small or very small subset of the totality of data/documents which those users need, or are required, or choose to handle in their daily lives. Thus it is possible to map out a generic technological environment

which will be used in the future for the handling of private information collections, and then to ask how the availability of that environment will affect
the modes of creation, storage, transmission, processing and display of public
information collections.

2 When anticipating future technological developments, it is helpful to
consider conduit separately from content: *conduit* is the computing and networking hardware and software used to create, store, transmit etc. information; *content* is the actual information which is handled via that conduit.

3 The costs of storing, transmitting and processing chunks of electronically
encoded information will continue to shrink dramatically. Increasingly, there
will be no technological limitation to society's ability to use electronic rather
than paper-based means to handle the publicly available information it needs
to generate and display.

4 The technological convergence of the means of handling different media
will also continue apace, so that one conduit will allow us to work with
data/text, image, moving image and voice in a seamless multimedia environment.

5 It seems likely, even in a domestic environment, that the personal computer (whether desktop or portable), rather than the television or telephone,
will expand its capabilities so as to be able to handle, at an acceptable cost and
performance level, all of these types of media within a single operating environment. Which of the presently competing telecommunication systems will
prove paramount – broadcast, cable, wireless or telephone – is less clear (and
will be crucially dependent on the future regulatory environment). But however tremendously important the current battles may be commercially between
the major players in these areas, this does not seem to matter for our purposes
here. All that we need to agree is that end-users will increasingly have the technological ability – depending on their range of choice and financial means –
electronically to retrieve, via one or a combination of routes, any piece of data
or any document which has been generated anywhere else in the world. And
the continuing competitive pressures will ensure that, as time goes on, the
transaction costs of doing this will become less and less (assuming that the
antitrust/monopoly laws continue to be effective spurs to competition).

6 Similarly, we do not need to be concerned here with the future software
environments within which all this worldwide movement of data and documents will take place. Currently Microsoft seems to have the upper edge. But
as we saw with IBM in the 1980s, even the apparently most secure of market
leaders can lose their grip on the market. However, at this stage all we need
to recognize is that Windows 95, or some other forthcoming dominant personal computer workstation environment, will allow the end-user to handle
any type of electronically encoded information he or she chooses to retrieve
from elsewhere: assuming, again, that the user is able to decide that he or she
can afford and justify the capital and other costs of doing so.

7 CD-ROM – and other portable electronic vehicles such as diskette or

magnetic tape – must then compete in such a future technological environment. CD-ROM itself is distinguished from other portable media by being once-only writable and having currently a relatively high cost of data impregnation. Thus end-users cannot normally at the moment write data to (a read/write version of) this medium in the way that they can back-up to diskette or record to audio or videotape. On the other hand, given current domestic, educational and leisure imperatives, it is now usual for personal computer workstations to have present, or to have the potential of having present, drives capable of reading CD-ROMs.

8 Further – as has been discussed earlier in this book – within organizations the local-area networking of CD-ROMs is increasingly common, whether as an alternative to, or in addition to, standalone attachment to the personal workstation. However, in comparison to other mass storage systems, CD-ROM continues to have relatively slow data access times – which means that performance degrades which more than a relatively small number of local-area network users are competing to access the same CD-ROM stored data. And this has led to its use in some situations just as a transport mechanism, rather than as a combined transport and local data storage/access system.

9 Irrespective of whether the information transported from A to B by means of CD-ROM is delivered to the end-user via access locally to the same medium or to another medium (such as magnetic disk) to which it has been transferred, there will inevitably be a time delay, between the creation (or mastering) of the information on the CD-ROM by its original individual/organizational generator, and availability of that information for perusal by the recipient of the CD-ROM. Portable electronic information artefacts take time to get from A to B. In direct contrast, the transfer of information via a telecommunications link can occur at speeds up to real-time. Whether any delay in the transport of CD-ROM stored data and documents matters to its eventual end-user will depend firstly on the volatility of the underlying phenomena to which the published literature relates, and secondly on how important it is for the user to have up-to-date information.

The inevitable chain of events?

Given the rapidly developing technological environment of our (prospective) end-user, is it not then clear that the following chain of events will too rapidly proceed to an inevitable conclusion?

1 Published data and documents which were formerly (unless purchased) only available for perusal as print-on-paper artefacts within libraries are becoming available also (or instead) as electronic artefacts stored within databases.

2 Initially, use of such databases was – or at least seemed to be – complicated for users; and so we needed professional librarians to intermediate (as well as to handle any marginal cost of use and copyright considerations).

3 But gradually, users have started to be able to use the databases them-

selves – for instance, as CD-ROM compilations. In parallel to this, driven by private information imperatives, network connections are being installed in the users' workplaces and homes. The users are then demanding end-user access to the databases, not from within their local library building, but instead directly from their office or home desk.

4 As this process of networking access to the databases proceeds apace, so eventually, once all the data and documents formerly stocked in print format within the library are available electronically, the library closes down, the intermediating librarians having long before been made redundant. With reference to Figure 11.1, publicly available information would be accessed directly by the (end-)users, rather than with the assistance of libraries and librarians.

Plausible as this scenario seems – at least to many of those who currently fund libraries and librarians – I submit that, for the vast majority of current libraries and their librarians, the earliest it will happen to any degree of significance is 10 to 15 years hence. Much of the conventional wisdom (as implied by the title of this chapter and the analysis so far) is that it is the professional intermediating librarians who will disappear first (the users who once needed the librarians' services having all become end-users), and the libraries themselves second. However, in many situations it could well be the other way around. Intermediating libraries may no longer be needed by users – or at least may no longer be funded by their funders – with regard to much of the published data and documents their (former) users needed and desired. But there may well not be a parallel removal of the need for intermediating librarians to help the users to obtain cost-effective and cost-efficient (electronic) access to the data and documents.

The prime reason for the latter contention is a recognition of the highly complex legal/economic/political environments within which the technology must make its impact. A secondary reason is the nature of many of the organizational contexts within which libraries and librarians exist. (We shall consider both these reasons in a moment.) Yet a third reason is simply the breadth and depth of the vast cornucopia of data and document content which will become directly available to the end-user from his or her personal computer, once the electronic imperative makes its full impact on patterns of publication.[1] This cornucopia will be too rich for most user information needs and desires and also too disorganized to be successfully navigated by the user without help. Librarians will therefore still be needed to facilitate the interaction between user and electronic resource. Such librarians may provide such help at the time of interaction, or (probably to a greater extent than in present libraries) they may have more of an up-front role, both training the user, and better organizing access to the cornucopia.

In this chapter I have interchangeably used the terms 'publicly available' and 'published' as well as 'information' and 'data and documents'. That seems adequate in this relatively short space. But there are of course an immense range of forms, formats and media which hide under those umbrella terms, and via which information becomes publicly available, or data and documents are published. Further, to add yet more complication to the present situation (let alone what is to come), a particularly interesting question is the extent to which the electronic imperative will change the means by which people and organizations communicate public knowledge to each other. To take but one example, will the journal, as a periodically published collection of articles on different subjects, survive (whether its content is ultimately made available to the potential user as a print-on-paper, or as an electronic, artefact)? Or will we see individual articles becoming the unit of communication, because the technology can now support that?

Considerations of budget and scale ensure that all current libraries – apart, perhaps in the UK, for the British Library (and even that is becoming doubtful) – are in practice only able to offer to their users direct or indirect access to a relatively small proportion of the world's present stock of electronically encoded published data and documents. The corollary of that of course is that in practice the libraries, with their librarians, necessarily act as filters of the growing electronic cornucopia: they cannot afford, or are not allowed by their parent organizations, to do any other. This means that, when the user moves outside of the controlled environment provided by his or her library, it is very easy for him or her to become lost and confused. Think of the current Internet! There is a world of difference between the end-user 'surfing the waves' within the library' where skilled professional assistance is often close by, as against surfing alone in the office or at home.

One distinct possibility then is that we will downsize, or close completely, many of our libraries, it being cost-effective in the future for the copies of their former holdings to be accessed and retrieved remotely by means of electronic

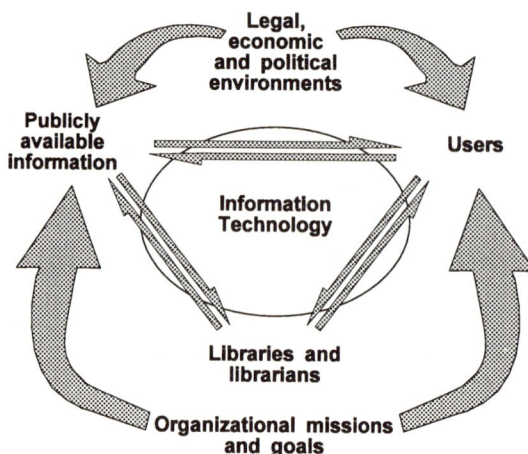

Fig. 11.1 *A model for information access*

techniques. But meanwhile we will retain at least some of the librarians who will provide professional assistance to users in making cost-beneficial use of these remote stores. Maybe such helping librarians will be remotely linked to the user via a personal video-conference link, so that what is happening on the user's PC screen will at the same time be visible to the librarian, and so that the librarian can 'take charge' of the user's PC as and when necessary. (This sort of system is already available.)

One should note in passing that the use of all this electronic wizardry will not necessarily mean that users who in the future access and retrieve data and documents from remote stores via local- and wide-area networks will cease to use print-on-paper as a convenient means of *private* perusal of the data and documents. Nor will it mean that the transport of publicly available information from store to user will necessarily be a wholly electronic process. Substantial documents, especially those whose subject matter benefits from a sophisticated physical appearance, will still naturally be produced and bound as print-on-paper artefacts. Printed newspapers, newsletters and magazines will be purchased by individuals and groups, and browsed through as now in order to keep broadly up-to-date about what is going on. But on what are for most users relatively rare occasions, when specific archival data or documents are needed or desired and are not already available in the user's personal or workgroup library, they will be identified and requested online. Then, when online delivery of a digital version is not possible or acceptable, they may be speedily delivered to the office or home by post or courier.

Organizational missions and goals

Note the above use of the phrase 'personal or workgroup library'. Clearly, if many such collections of physical information artefacts came to exist within specific organizations, and their content overlapped, no doubt some wag would come along and ask whether it would not be more cost-beneficial over-all for the organization if the individual libraries were combined into a single library accessible to all the users.

Libraries, and the librarians who work within them, need to be funded. Broadly, two types of funding mechanism are used. By far the most common still is subvention: libraries are thought to be a 'good thing' and their parent organization gives them a 'budget'. Alternatively, or more usually in addition, the library levies some sort of charge from its users, or from an organizational entity which is representative of the users (whether or not that entity then chooses to pass the charge on – in whole or in part – to its users). Charges may be nominal (to try to defray abuse), cost-recovery, or aimed to make a profit. A key distinction in practice is whether the library charges out the time of its librarians. The latter is especially rare in the public sector – unless the library promotes a fee-based information service.

How (or indeed whether) to try to secure the continued funding of their library or libraries – and of the associated librarians – is perhaps the most acute of the questions framed by the organizations that house such entities. Clearly, the type of answer given will be critically dependent on the sector within which the organization lies: public or private; open access or closed access; work or leisure; and so on. It is not sensible to try to generalize on how such differences will or should affect the speed and direction of the 'end-user revolution'. However, as can be inferred from Figure 11.1, it is essential that those directly concerned with the future of libraries and librarians in specific organizational settings should constantly try to relate what those entities do (and as the IT imperative develops, what they might do in the future) to the overall organizational mission and goals.

This is much more easily said than done. Those in charge of organizations frequently have not applied an 'information lens' to the organization; they equate 'information strategy' with 'information technology strategy'. With all of the hype of the information superhighway, they imagine that on Friday afternoon you close down the organizational library, and on Monday morning you start using the Internet to get the data and documents you used to get via the local library – and so on. One just has to keep plugging away at the facts, unpalatable as they may seem to the senior management.

Legal, economic and political environments

The facts which are especially problematic to those who would turn all real libraries into virtual libraries relate to the realities of the legal, economic and political environments within which libraries exist to handle published data and documents. The complexities of this whole arena are such that I strongly recommend you to read, mark, inwardly digest, and then apply to your own situation, the raft of elements which are relevant to this subject. Such issues might include:

- whether within your setting there is the **political** will to maintain a viable library service for your users – whatever mix of 'real' and 'virtual' it might in future comprise;
- whether your parent organization is willing to grapple with peculiar **economic nature** of information: – recognizing, for instance, that it just does not make economic sense to charge your users simply to peruse the information already existing in the stock of your library, simply because if the users are charged they will make less use of the information (and presumably benefit less) than if they were not charged, even though it would have cost the organization nothing extra to allow them to peruse in the first place;
- and (perhaps the most critical of all) whether there is a recognition of the **legal minefield** which is presently threatening to drown the notion of the virtual library – with, for example, many publishers seemingly intent on blowing fair dealing out of the water, and requiring a royalty charge to be paid each time a copy of a published artefact is retrieved by a user.

Conclusion

The continued good health of almost all our present print libraries – whose stocks are fortunately still almost always accessible by their registered users without any direct charge being levied – rests on two pillars: firstly the notion that libraries are a 'good thing' and should (primarily) be supported via a budget subvention; and secondly the legal doctrine of fair dealing, allowing copies of materials in their stocks to be taken freely by users who wish to use the materials for research or private study. Libraries of this type are an essential and beneficial part of the infrastructure of society.

However, such libraries can nowadays be perceived by the user as being difficult and time-consuming to use, and as the world's stock of publications continues to expand, they can be increasingly costly to maintain – hence the attraction of the concept of the virtual library for many types of user needing or desiring many types of published information (though not of course for 'books'). But to move from our present phase one, with its relatively low concentration of virtuality, to phase three, where virtuality will be dominant, will require us to go through a very difficult and tempestuous phase two. I have suggested above that phase two might take as long as 10 to 15 years to run its full course. And during that phase two, the end-user of publicly available information will constantly need the help of professional librarians, as he or she makes the transformation from using real libraries to using virtual libraries. Handling the technology, navigating the organization, organizing the economics, negotiating the law, will all require the help of skilled professionals. And who better to provide those 'virtual' services to the end-user than the former 'real' librarians. That, truly, would ensure the continuation of the 'end-user revolution'.

Reference

1   For a detailed analysis of one especially complex subject area in this regard, which has also already travelled far down the road to virtuality, see the author's recent study: Lester, R., *Information sources in finance and banking*, Bowker-Saur, 1995.

Index

ABI/INFORM 127–31 *passim*
academic information services 160–1
academic libraries 35–42, 64–78,
    96–108, 162
networks 14, 41–2, 67–72, 76–7, 96,
    102, 130, 131, 138, 139, 157,
    158–9, 162, 164, 174–5; survey
    165–71
access 16, 43–4, 49, 59, 66, 69, 71, 75,
    144, 155, 158, 192–4
accreditation 30–31
acquisition 41, 46
Adobe 152, 158
ADONIS 119, 120–7, 128–30, 131, 174
    cf. BPO 128–31
    currency of 124–5, 129
    inclusion policy 123, 129
    revisions 127
    user interface 122–3, 124–7
    user reactions 121–3, 184
Apple Macintosh 68–9, 73
Architecture on Disc 148
assessment of assignments 103
Assessment of Quality of Education
    (AQE) 38–9
Aston University 119, 120–32

BAILER 180
BIDS 17, 72, 96, 104, 105, 125, 127,
    161, 164, 165, 175, 184
Birmingham University 35–42
    budgetary control 37–8
    CD–ROM resources 36, 40–1
    Electronic Information Sources Group
        36, 39–40
    Information Services division 36
block subscriptions 127, 128
books
    CD–ROM impact on buying 57

multiple copies of 14
vs. CD–ROMs 14–15
BPO *see* Business Periodicals Ondisc
British Association for Information and
    Library Education and Research
    (BAILER) 180
British Library 120, 121, 122, 123, 160,
    161, 175, 176, 192
BUBL 85, 160
budgetary control 37–8
Bulletin Board for Libraries (BUBL) 85,
    160
bulletin boards 40, 85, 160
Business Periodicals Ondisc (BPO) 36,
    76, 121, 126, 127–31, 174
    cf. ADONIS 128–31
    charging 127, 128
    currency of 129
    inclusion policy 129–30
    user interface 129

campus–wide networks *see* wide area
    networks
cataloguing 130
CD–CINC 9
CD–Recorder (CD–R) systems 146
CD–ROM
    charging for 11–17, 60–1, 120–1,
        122, 126, 127, 128
    future of 61, 76–8, 116, 145–6, 190
    introduction of 174
    public library provision 110–17
    user response to provision of 46–7,
        143–4
    vs. books 14–15
    vs. online 46, 54, 158–9
    see also databases; document delivery;
        licensing; software
CD–ROM Consistent INterface

Committee (CD–CINC) 9
CD–ROM Standards and Practices
    Action Group (CD–ROM SPAG)
    6–13
  formation 6–7
  help desk 8
  meetings 11
  objectives and structure 7, 19
  projects and reports 8–11, 12–13
  seminars 7, 11, 12, 13
Census on CD–ROM 67
Centre for Information Quality
    Management (CIQM) 25, 27, 30,
    32, 33
Chadwyck–Healey 14, 49, 67
change
  and information 20, 156, 173–6, 181,
    188–91
  publishing 17–19
charging
  for CD–ROM 11–17, 60–1, 120–1,
    122, 126, 127, 128
  for library use 193, 194
chemical information 97
CIQM 25, 27, 30, 32, 33
client software 72, 73, 74
client–server systems 9, 58, 61, 62, 72–6
codes of practice, help desk 8
communication of technical information
    97–8, 99
Computers in Teaching Initiative Centre
    for Library and Information Studies
    (CTILIS) 180
concurrent access charging 16
convergence 173, 180, 189
copyright 142–3, 149–50, 187, 190,
    194, 195
Croydon Libraries 43–52, 176
CTILIS 180
current awareness services
  CAS/IAS 161, 175, 184
  RAM 135–46
customer support 18

databases
  architectural 148–54
  bibliographic 14, 39, 120, 132, 174,
    175
  broader–based 131–3

business 36, 45, 46–7, 47–8, 51–2
  choice of 45–6, 67
  directory 40
  image 148–54
  in–house CD–ROM 91, 135–46,
    148–54
  installation standards 9–10
  labelling 27–30; problem areas 31–2
  manufacturing 135–46
  medical 53, 54, 55–7, 59, 65, 87,
    125, 129
  poetry 14, 67, 76
  quality 11, 24–6, 32, 83, 89–90
  user selection of 84–5, 88–9, 115,
    143–4, 145
  see also CD–ROM; RAM database;
    software
Datastream 24
delivery
  CD–ROM for 71–6, 190
  ease of 22
  see also document delivery
demonstration disks 40, 46
diagnostic diskettes 8
DIALOG 53, 54, 55, 57, 157
discounts 38, 41
document delivery 119–33, 161, 174,
    175
documentation 26, 31–2, 104, 114, 117,
    144
drop–in training 105

e–mail 105
EDINA 17, 72, 161
Edinburgh Engineering Virtual Library
    (EEVL) 138–9
Edinburgh University Data Library 161
educating and training users see training,
    users
EEVL 138–9
electronic imperative 188–90
electronic journals 119–20, 126, 128,
    131–3
Electronic Libraries Programme (eLib)
    107, 138, 145, 176, 182, 183
Electronic Library Information Online
    Retrieval (ELINOR) 176
Electronic Reference Library (ERL) 72–8
    passim, 132, 159

Electronic Resources/Information Skills (ERiS) 103
ELINOR 176
Embase 30, 127, 161
end–users *see* users
enquiry services, impact of CD–ROM on 55–6
ERiS 103
ERL 72–8 *passim*, 132, 159
ethics, publishers' 15
Europe, LIS education in 180–1
European Communities (EC) 12, 99, 163
EUSIDIC 25
evaluation by librarians 23, 40–1
expenditure, impact of CD–ROM on 54, 55

Fashion Information Service (FIS) 139–40, 141–2
Fenwood Systems 44, 45, 48, 49, 71–72
FIDDO 183
Fielden Report 176
FIGIT *see* Follett Report
file servers 70, 72, 74, 75, 77
file transfer protocol (ftp) 74–5
financial skills 177, 178–9
floppy disks 74
Follett Report 161, 176, 179, 182
foreign student access 48
formal training 101, 113, 168–9
full–text via OVID 73
funding of libraries 37–8, 193–4
future of CD–ROM 190
   academic libraries 76–8, 145–6
   public libraries 116
   special libraries 61

gap analysis 25
Glasgow on Disc 148–54
   concept and development 148–9
   content 149, 150
   copyright 149–50
   design and production 150–3
   Internet site 154
   marketing 153–4
Glaxo Wellcome 53–62
group training 113–14
guides 91, 104, 169–70

hardware 18, 36, 38, 43–5
HEFC 159
help for users 8, 71, 83, 85, 88, 91, 92, 103–5, 167, 168, 169
   see also training, users
Higher Education Funding Council (HEFC) 159
higher education 'three cycle' model 98–9
home PCs 23
housekeeping 130, 131
HTML 9, 158

Idealist 137, 141, 142, 144, 145
image quality 125, 148, 152
IMPEL 183
induction 100
INFO2000 programme 163
information
   change and 20, 156, 173–6, 181, 188–91
   control 24
   providers 21, 22
   skills training *see* training, users
   society 21
information professionals
   changing role of 1–2, 3, 79–94
   education for 176–84
   impact of CD–ROM on 58
   and Internet 178
   see also librarians
installation standards for software 9–10
interfaces
   consistent 8–9, 65, 67, 69, 75, 77, 104, 122–3, 132, 170, 174
   reference librarian as developer 91
   see also search software
interlibrary loan, impact of CD–ROM on 56–7
intermediaries 22, 23, 53, 55, 58, 79–94, 143, 168, 191–4
see also information professionals; librarians
Internet
   access to 155
   at Sheffield Hallam University 102, 104
   browsers 17, 75, 158
   and database labels 31–2

delivery by 73–4
Glasgow on Disc site 154
public library use of 163, 176
quantity vs. quality 17
RADAR tools 175
RAM database 138, 139, 146
role for information professionals 178
searching by users 85–6, 158
start of 157–8
see also World Wide Web
ISI 37, 96, 125, 161
IT skills 177, 178, 179, 180

JANET 14, 102, 130, 138, 157, 159,
    162, 164, 174–5
JASPER 160
Joint Academic Network (JANET) 14,
    102, 130, 138, 157, 159, 162, 164,
    174–5
Joint Information Services Committee
    (JISC) 155, 159–62, 164
jukeboxes 76, 130

Kodak Photo CD 148, 149, 151–2

learning outcomes of training 101–2
liaison librarians 38–9, 40, 41, 176
librarians
    changing role of 1–2, 3, 38, 143, 171,
        176, 188, 191–5; reference librari-
        ans 79–94, 188
    see also information professionals;
        intermediaries
libraries, future of 187–95
Library 2000 project 163–4
Library Association 7, 11, 13, 83, 89, 164
Library Information Technology Centre
    12
licensing 11, 12, 41–2, 49–50, 60, 71,
    72, 76
local area networks 60, 68–70, 190

Macafee 71
Macromedia Director 152
Mailbase 160
management skills 177–9
marriage and sexuality, digital library on
    162
MEDLINE 53, 54, 55–7, 59, 65, 125,

129
METTNET 14
Microsoft 176, 189
multimedia 22, 67, 76, 90–1, 103, 140,
    146, 148–54
multiple–disk sets 65, 66, 69, 70–1, 75,
    76, 77

NCVQ 99
networked learner support 182
networks
    academic libraries 14, 41–2, 67–72,
        76–7, 96, 102, 130, 131, 138, 139,
        157, 158–9, 162, 164, 174–5; sur-
        vey 165–71
    ADONIS indexes on 131
    for CD–ROM 11–17, 41–5, 48–52,
        59–61, 67–72, 76–7, 84–5, 96, 137,
        139, 158–9, 162, 190
    control systems 12, 13, 16, 70, 71,
        72, 76
    demand for 158, 159, 191
    help for users 84–5, 106–7
    justification for charging 13–15
    local level services 162–4
    network node charging 16
    pricing policies 11–17, 41–2, 49–50,
        60–1
    problem areas 48–50, 68–9
    public libraries 43–5, 48–52, 162–4
    RAM project 139
    special libraries 59–61
    upgrades 44–5
    user benefits 14, 15, 96
    user views of 164–5
    see also local area networks; wide area
        networks
NISS 160
Nottingham Trent University 135–46

OCLC Firstsearch 161, 176
online searching 46, 54, 58, 61, 62, 82,
    83, 89–90, 121, 138, 156–7, 161,
    174
    vs. CD–ROM 46, 54, 158–9
    see also Internet
OPACS 81–2, 86, 100, 175
organizational missions & goals 192,
    193–4

OVID Technologies 41, 72–8 *passim*

periodicals 119, 122, 125
   see also document delivery
personal bibliographic software 175, 184
pre–disk caching 42, 71–2
pressure groups 83
pricing *see* charging
printed publications 119, 122, 125, 188,
   190, 192, 193, 195
printing 44, 126, 128
processing 41
product description standards 10–11
product evaluation 23, 40–41
Project Quartet 119, 123
public libraries 43–52, 110–17, 162–4
   CD–ROM training survey 112–17
   constraints on CD–ROM services 117
   networks 43–5, 48–52, 162–4
   user survey 111–12
publishers
   hardware provision 18
   structural changes for 17–19

quality
   database 11, 24–6, 32, 83, 89–90
   Internet 17
   needs of users 32

RAM database 135–46
   CD–ROM production 139–40, 141–2
   choice of CD–ROM for 137–9
   nature of 136–7
   project costs 140–1
reference librarians
   changing role 79, 81–94, 188
   client relationships 80–1
   enquiry desks 83, 84, 88, 91–2
   personal qualities 80
   and technology 81–6, 87, 91
   traditional role 79–80, 88
research 171, 178, 182–4
Research Libraries Group (RLG) 162,
   171
restrictions on use 130–1
royalties 120, 121, 122, 126, 128, 130

Saber 71, 85
sales literature standards 10–11

sales staff 18–19
schools of information & library studies
   173, 176, 179–84
SCOUG 26, 83, 89
search software
   problems with 65–6, 67, 132, 145
   user–friendly 47, 48, 67, 72, 75, 128,
      131–2, 150–1, 152, 174
   see also Idealist; interfaces
security 50, 66, 69–70, 76, 83–4
services, impact of CD–ROM on 54–7
SGML 9
shared resources 77
Sheffield Hallam University 96–108
SIGCAT 9
Silverplatter ERL 72–8 *passim*, 132, 159
SITCom 99, 100, 101, 103, 105, 107
site–based charging 16
software
   client software 72, 73, 74
   installation standards 9–10
   search *see* search software
   see also databases
South Bank University 12
Southern California Online User Group
   (SCOUG) 26, 83, 89
Special Interest Group on CD–ROM
   Applications Technology (SIGCAT)
   9
special libraries 53–63
specifications 25–6
   see also database labelling
standalone access 41, 42, 44, 46, 54,
   65–6, 76
standards
   consistent interfacing 8–9
   licence agreements 12
   local 30
   product description and sales 10–11
   software installation 9–10
Studies in Scarlet project 162
SuperJANET 157

TAPin 183
technical support 45, 59, 68, 74–5, 115
telecommunications growth 156
telephone support 105
teleworking 182, 191
TFPL 13, 40

training
  academic libraries 81, 85, 97–108,
    144–5, 168–9, 170
  educators 181
  information professionals 176–84
  public libraries 47–8, 110–17
  special libraries 53, 58
  users 81, 85, 87, 90, 100–8, 144–5
Training and Awareness Programme in
    Networks (TAPin) 183
tutorials 104–5, 107

UK Office for Library and Information
    Networking (UKOLN) 160–1, 164
UK Online Coordinating Committee 83
UKERNA 159
UKMARC 10
UKOLN 160–1, 164
Ultranet 44–5, 48–9
UMI 36, 37, 67, 127, 128, 130
UNIX servers 72–6
usage statistics 42, 76
user–friendly software 47, 48, 67, 72,
    75, 128, 131–2, 150–1, 152, 174

users
  education and training 81, 85, 87, 90,
    100–8, 144–5
  empowerment of 173–4
  Internet home pages for 158
  needs of 32, 58, 87
  reactions to ADONIS 121–3, 184
  response to CD-ROM provision
    46–7, 59, 143–4
  searching by 22–3, 32, 53–9 passim,
    82, 85–6, 88–9, 158, 166–70; qual-
    ity of 86–7
  user population charging 16
  views of networks 164–5, 166–71
  vulnerability of 23–4, 89

wide area networks 51–2, 60, 70–71,
    156, 159–62, 174
Wirral Metropolitan College 14
workshops, training 102–3, 144–5
World Wide Web 17, 75, 102, 158,
    162, 163, 182, 184

Z39.50 9, 72, 77, 78